*Monograph Supplements to the*
*Scottish Journal of Theology*

General Editors

T. F. TORRANCE and J. K. S. REID

# DAVID FRIEDRICH STRAUSS
# AND HIS THEOLOGY

David Friedrich Strauss in 1837

# DAVID
# FRIEDRICH
# STRAUSS

## AND HIS THEOLOGY

HORTON HARRIS

CAMBRIDGE
AT THE UNIVERSITY PRESS 1973

Published by the Syndics of the Cambridge University Press
Bentley House, 200 Euston Road, London NW1 2DB
American Branch: 32 East 57th Street, New York, N.Y.10022

© Cambridge University Press 1973

Library of Congress Catalogue Card Number: 72 93137

ISBN: 0 521 20139 X

Printed in Great Britain
by R. and R. Clark Ltd, Edinburgh

To
my Parents

To
my Parents

# CONTENTS

|  |  | *page* |
|---|---|---|
| | Acknowledgments | viii |
| | Preface | ix |
| | List of abbreviations | xv |
| 1 | Parentage | 1 |
| 2 | Blaubeuren School-days | 5 |
| 3 | At Tübingen University | 9 |
| 4 | Strauss as a Curate | 21 |
| 5 | Strauss in Berlin | 27 |
| 6 | Tutor in the Tübingen Seminary | 36 |
| 7 | The *Life of Jesus* | 41 |
| 8 | Dismissal from the Seminary | 58 |
| 9 | The Reaction and Counter-Reaction | 66 |
| 10 | Strauss and Baur | 85 |
| 11 | The Third Edition of the *Life of Jesus* | 117 |
| 12 | The Calling to Zürich | 123 |
| 13 | *The Doctrine of the Christian Faith* | 134 |
| 14 | Romance and Marriage | 142 |
| 15 | The Politician | 161 |
| 16 | The Literary Wanderer | 178 |
| 17 | The Return to Theology | 191 |
| 18 | The *Life of Jesus* for the German People | 200 |
| 19 | The Clash with Schenkel | 213 |
| 20 | The War Years | 230 |
| 21 | *The Old Faith and the New* | 238 |
| 22 | The End | 250 |
| 23 | The Origin of Strauss' Mythical Interpretation | 259 |
| 24 | Strauss' Influence upon Theology | 274 |

CONTENTS

| | *page* |
|---|---|
| Bibliography | 285 |
| Index of names | 299 |

## ACKNOWLEDGMENTS

| | |
|---|---|
| Plates 1, 7 and 8 | From the Strauss-Nachlass in Dillenburg |
| Plate 2 | By courtesy of the Schiller National-Museum, Marbach |
| Plates 3, 4, 9–11 | From the Universitätsbibliothek, Tübingen |
| Plate 5 | From Professor Adolf Rapp, Tübingen |
| Plate 6 | From the Württembergische Landes-bibliothek, Stuttgart |

# PREFACE

Of all the nineteenth-century theologians, Strauss was the most notorious. No single theological work ever created such consternation in the theological world as Strauss' *Life of Jesus*. It split the century into two theological eras – before and after 1835.

But Strauss was not merely the most notorious theologian of the century; he was also unquestionably the most consequent. Other theologians might go only half-way; he could not. For him it was all or nothing and no half-and-half solution for the theological problems of the time could satisfy him. He ruthlessly and relentlessly exposed the often inadequate solutions which the orthodox theology had provided to the biblical problems; he mercilessly flayed the answers of the rationalists; but his hardest strictures were reserved for those who stood half-way, for those who hobbled between the old faith and the new – between the old obsolete orthodoxy and the new scientific criticism.

It may also be argued that Strauss was the most important theologian of the century. The rise of historical criticism owes more to Strauss than to any other theologian, for it was as a result of his book that the critical path was opened up in a way which had not been previously possible. True, others before him had made a beginning in biblical criticism, but their investigations were isolated, confined mainly to the Old Testament, or to the less important books in the New, and above all, had never been emancipated from the traditional theological framework of the age. Strauss was the first to break out of the procrustean bed of religious orthodoxy: he dared the ecclesiastical powers-that-be – and paid the price.

He was not the greatest theologian – that crown must go to Schleiermacher – if greatness be measured by the ability to create a theological system. Nor was he, in the long run, the most influential – that prize is won by Baur. But Schleiermacher never made an open break with the old traditional faith in which he had been reared, and, to a large degree, was

ix

by-passed after his death. The greatness of his system was universally acknowledged, but his solution did not generally
commend itself. Baur's influence, on the other hand, was much
more durable, but it was only long after his death – and, in fact,
only in this century – that its full import was able to be perceived. In his own day, he was snubbed in theological circles
and confined as much as possible to his theological backwater
in Tübingen. Moreover, without Strauss' book, Baur's work
would never have attained the heights it did. It was Strauss
who made Baur's critical investigations largely possible, and
in this respect Strauss' influence and importance can hardly be
overestimated. For almost 40 years Strauss was renowned
throughout the length and breadth of the land, and his influence extended to cleric and lay alike. His last book in 1872
went through six large editions in six months – a success which
had never before attended any theological or philosophical
work in Germany.

But not only was Strauss the most important theological
personality during the middle half of the century, he was also
the most interesting. No theologian ever lived such an adven-
turous and exciting life as he. And yet we have no biography in
English except the small and grossly inadequate sketch which
Eduard Zeller composed a few months after Strauss' death in
1874. That was almost a hundred years ago. Moreover, apart
from a few poems, Zeller's book contains practically nothing of
Strauss' own writings and simply recounts the main events of
his life in a very general way. It is the tribute of a friend, an
undocumented and uncritical sketch which makes no preten-
sion to be a full-length biography, and does not aim to deal
with Strauss' theology or theological development in any detail.

As regards biographical material, however, Germans are in
a much more fortunate position than the English, and since
1874, two long biographies, each of 800–900 pages, have
appeared. The first of these was Adolf Hausrath's two-volume
work which was published in 1876–8. The book had two draw-
backs: Hausrath was not completely in sympathy with Strauss'
theological point of view, and he did not have access to the
hundreds of letters which Strauss had written to his friends.
Therefore the later biography by Theobald Ziegler, which
appeared in 1908, offers more source material in the form of

extracts from the letters which Strauss wrote to Rapp, Märklin and other friends. Ziegler also was able to make use of the large and varied selection of Strauss' letters, which Zeller had edited and published in the *Ausgewählte Briefe* (1895). Moreover, Ziegler, as an avowed pantheist, was far more in accord with his hero's viewpoint than Hausrath, and portrayed the theological aspects more accurately, although in some respects, Hausrath has a truer picture of the man.

Neither biography was ever translated into English: nor is this now practicable, for so much belongs to the last century which is no longer relevant for us today. Names and events which were meaningful a century ago are now so obscure that there would be little value in resurrecting them. But the essentials of Strauss' life – the man himself, the important events in his life, his intimate friends, his writings, the controversies, the theological questions which he raised and attempted to answer – all these can and must be salvaged from the past, and restored to life.

Since Ziegler's biography, other Strauss-material has come to light: the correspondence between Strauss and Vischer, and Strauss and Baur has been published; also Strauss' letters to Binder, Georgii, Mörike and Schwegler; the letters to Kuno Fischer are found in the university library at Heidelberg, and the 655 letters to Ernst Rapp are in the Schiller Museum at Marbach, along with many others to and from Strauss. In the last two decades a number of books and articles on various aspects of Strauss' life and thought have also appeared; thus a new biography of Strauss which will take account of this more recent material is almost a necessity for the study of nineteenth-century theology.

This book is entitled 'David Friedrich Strauss *and* his Theology'. It is not intended as a full-scale biography which takes account of every event in his life and every book which he wrote. That would make the book impossibly long and would be quite senseless. But neither is it a plain historical and non-theological account of Strauss' life, for it is impossible to understand the man without a knowledge of his theology. The man and the theologian are inseparable. Therefore, it may be described as a theological biography, with three main aims.

    1. To present a picture of Strauss' life – a true picture of the

man as he actually was – and especially as seen from his own words in his published writings and letters.

2. To trace the development of Strauss' thought, without a knowledge of which a true understanding of his theology is impossible.

3. To clarify the theological problems with which Strauss was confronted, to present the solutions he evolved and to show the challenge which he issued to theology, both then and now.

Strauss was one of the greatest German prose writers and I have wanted him to speak for himself as much as possible. Most of the extracts from his writings – especially from the letters – have never appeared in English before and apart from George Eliot's excellent translation of the *Life of Jesus*, the other translations of Strauss' writings are in out-dated and wooden English, often difficult to come-by. All passages have been newly translated although where an older translation exists, references to it have generally been provided.

Certain German words always pose translation difficulties. *Wissenschaft* and its cognate adjective *wissenschaftlich* have been rendered as 'science' and 'scientific' respectively although these words refer in the broadest sense to intellectual and academic research in all fields of learning. *Geist* has been translated 'Spirit' and capitalised where it refers to the Infinite or Absolute Spirit of speculative philosophy, or to the Holy Spirit of traditional theology; when used in the former sense it is treated as a neuter noun, since the Spirit in speculative philosophy is impersonal; where therefore the word is used as a synonym for God, a disparity of masculine and neuter pronouns will occasionally occur. However, it is better to allow this minor discrepancy to remain than to confuse the philosophical categories. *Pfarrer* has been translated 'pastor' although the term is more equivalent to the Anglican 'vicar'. *Vicar*, on the other hand, has been rendered 'curate'. *Evangelisch* has generally been translated 'evangelical' although it means rather 'Protestant' or 'Lutheran'. The translation of other philosophical terms is explained at the appropriate places.

It only remains to thank those who have helped along the way: Professor Adolf Rapp for most interesting conversations; Professor T. F. Torrance who read through the manuscript and made many helpful suggestions; Uli, for invaluable help with translation problems; Barry, for checking translation; Anne, for typing the manuscript; Frida, Anneliese and Peter for typing the bibliography; and Frau Irma Heusler, who guided me through the family albums of the Strauss-*Nachlass* in Dillenburg, and supplied some of the photographs.

HORTON HARRIS

*Marbach am Neckar*
*1972*

# ABBREVIATIONS

| | |
|---|---|
| *AB* | Strauss' *Ausgewählte Briefe* (ed. Zeller; 1895) |
| *ADB* | *Allgemeine Deutsche Bibliographie* |
| *AKZ* | *Allgemeine Kirchliche Zeitschrift* |
| Benecke | Heinrich Benecke, *Wilhelm Vatke* (1883) |
| *BWKG* | *Blätter für Württembergische Kirchengeschichte* |
| *EKZ* | *Evangelische Kirchenzeitung* |
| ET | English Translation |
| *GS* | Strauss' *Gesammelte Schriften* (ed. Zeller; 1876–8) |
| *HZ* | *Historische Zeitschrift* |
| Hausrath | Adolf Hausrath, *David Friedrich Strauss und die Theologie seiner Zeit* (1876, 78) |
| *JWK* | *Journal für wissenschaftliche Kritik* |
| *KG* | Friedrich Theodor Vischer, *Kritische Gänge* (Tübingen, 1844) |
| *LJ* | Strauss' *Das Leben Jesu* (1835) |
| *Märklin* | *Christian Märklin. Ein Charakterbild aus der Gegenwart* (Mannheim, 1851) |
| *PJ* | *Preussische Jahrbücher* |
| *SVBr* | *Briefwechsel zwischen Strauss und Vischer* (ed. Rapp; 1952) |
| *TSK* | *Theologische Studien und Kritiken* |
| *TZT* | *Tübinger Zeitschrift für Theologie* |
| UBT | Universitätsbibliothek Tübingen |
| Ziegler | Theobald Ziegler, *David Friedrich Strauss* (1908) |
| *ZKG* | *Zeitschrift für Kirchengeschichte* |
| *ZWLG* | *Zeitschrift für Württembergische Landesgeschichte* |

# 1

## PARENTAGE

In the heart of the Swabian countryside, only six miles north of Stuttgart, lies the town of Ludwigsburg, once the summer residence of the king, now a predominantly industrial district. Here during the years 1704–33, the stately and imposing palace in the elegant rococo style was built in imitation of the great palace at Versailles, and until the death of King Friedrich in 1816, Ludwigsburg was a centre of high society during the summer months. It was in this town, with its broad straight streets, its great military barracks and little houses, that four famous literary and theological personalities of the nineteenth-century were born – Justinus Kerner (1786–1862) the Romanticist, Edward Mörike (1804–75) the great lyric poet of Swabia and one of the greatest German lyric poets, Friedrich Vischer (1807–87), famous for his works on Aesthetics and on Faust, and David Friedrich Strauss (1808–74), destined to shake the theological world as it had never before been shaken.

Strauss' grandfather (also named David Friedrich) came from the Hohenloh land in Württemberg and was a merchant. In 1764 he married the daughter of a merchant in Marbach and from this marriage came Johann Friedrich Strauss (b. 1768), the father of the subject of our biography. After the early death of her husband, the mother of Johann Friedrich married the merchant and town councillor Ruoff of Ludwigsburg, and thus it happened that Strauss' father grew up and became a citizen of that town.

The grandparents on Strauss' mother's side were both from Swabia. The grandfather, a pastor in Neckarweihingen, died three months before the birth of his daughter Christiane, who came already as half-orphan into the world. A few years afterwards the mother married again, only to die in childbirth, and the young Christiane, now bereft of both parents, was brought

1

up and educated by her grandfather, a shopkeeper in Bietig-
heim. Her schooldays were very happy, but the grandfather
was growing old, and soon it was time for the maiden to learn,
in other homes, the various practical matters essential for the
smooth running of a household. So alone in the world, she
must have longed for a home of her own, and a proposal
of marriage from Johann Friedrich Strauss was all the more
gladly accepted, the ceremony taking place in Ludwigsburg on
20 October 1796.

At school the young Christiane had learnt to read and write,
and was so well instructed in matters of religion that Strauss
could write that it required many years of study before he had
an equal knowledge of the Bible, and never did he attain her
knowledge of the hymnbook. Besides these humble academic
attainments she learnt to cook, sew and spin and to do all the
other tasks which it befitted a maiden to learn. In matters of
religion she was somewhat rationalistically inclined; she could
not believe many of the miracles in the Bible and was more
concerned with good works than with a string of dogmas. For
her, Jesus was a wise, God-given teacher, a virtuous man,
whose death, however, could in no way help us if we ourselves
were not prepared to follow his teaching and example. She had
little time for a regular reading of the Bible, nor for a mechanical church attendance, although she had nothing against attending church – even the Catholic church – if the preacher were a
practical man whose ideas were in harmony with her own.
Her pleasures were found in the simple things of life – in walking through the surrounding countryside and admiring the
beauties of nature, in tending a small garden lent to her by a
relative, and in doing things for others. In the years immediately following the publication of Strauss' *Life of Jesus* she stood
beside her son, even though she felt that she could not go so far
as he, and she accepted both the honour and the disapproba-
tion which came to her, with serenity and self-composure.

Strauss' father was of a quite different character. His Latin,
which he had learnt in the school at Ludwigsburg, was so good,
that even in his old age he used to carry Virgil, Ovid and
Horace with him on his journeys. He also possessed a distinct
poetical gift and was, as Strauss writes, 'a man of the finest
natural talent', so that relatives and friends often used to turn

to him for advice. He might well have followed an academic career, but as it was the custom for the son to take over the father's business, he accepted his duty, and after two years' apprenticeship in Le Havre, where he learnt to speak French fluently, he settled down to the business of buying and selling, although he appears to have spent more time engaged in his favourite hobbies of bee-keeping and tending his fruit trees.

He was much more religiously inclined than his wife and while in his early years he seems to have hovered between mysticism and orthodoxy, in his later years – and especially after the publication of the *Life of Jesus* – he turned more and more to pietism, which resulted in an unhappy division between father and son.

He so burdened himself with conscientious activity that he had to have something outside himself upon which he could rely. That was the atoning death of Christ, in whose redeeming power he put his trust. It was easier for him to believe once for all with a rock-like faith than to begin the struggle with his desires and passions every day anew.[1]

These, then, were the parents to whom a boy was born on the 27 January 1808. He was baptised by Pastor Vischer (the father of his friend Fritz Vischer) and received the names 'David Friedrich', both of which he used as a writer, although the name by which he was called in the family was Fritz. Two children born previously had both died in early years; a younger brother born in 1810, Friedrich Wilhelm, became a merchant and part owner of a sugar refinery in Cologne.

Those who have been educated in the more liberal system of our day and age will have difficulty conceiving that in the nineteenth century the most important subject was Latin. All scholastic hopes were dependent upon one's ability at translating into Latin, to which were added Greek and Hebrew in the higher classes. Fortunately David Friedrich was here in his element and rose to the top of the class at the Ludwigsburg school.

In Württemberg at that time, academic study was all but closed to those who did not belong to wealthy families, and the only feasible way of gaining entrance to the university was by

[1] *GS*, I, p. 99.

entering one of the four lower seminaries for a theological training in preparation for the ministry. Thus it was foreseen that
Strauss should become a pastor. In nineteenth-century Württemberg this was the usual career for gifted and intelligent boys
and Strauss' father, wishing his son to have the benefit of a
university education which he himself had not had, wisely
forwarded this end. Since the students in the seminary received their lodging, food and tuition free of charge, there was
great competition for a place, and all candidates had to travel
to Stuttgart each autumn, in their twelfth, thirteenth and
fourteenth years, to sit the exams which would determine their
admission to the seminary. The exam was a *cause célèbre* throughout the land and the results were eagerly awaited not only by
boys and parents, but also by pastors, teachers and villagers
alike. The Latin and Greek held no terrors for Strauss. He
passed with high marks, and in the company of his friend Fritz
Vischer, travelled to Blaubeuren in the autumn of 1821 to begin
his four years of study at the lower seminary.

# 2

## BLAUBEUREN SCHOOL-DAYS

At the foot of the Swabian Alb, a few miles north-west of Ulm, where the placid waters of the Blau river – a leisurely flowing stream – wind their way down toward the Danube, the gently sloping Blau valley begins to rise to a small plateau at its head. Here nestles the sleepy little town of Blaubeuren, surrounded by a semicircle of steep, thickly-wooded hillsides. It was not surprising that the Cistercian monks chose this delightful site on which to found their new monastery, for apart from the idyllic setting, there lies behind the monastery a subterranean spring which issues into a pool of fresh, clear water possessing a deep-blue colour from which the pool derives its name of 'Blautopf', or 'Blue-pot'. The monastery was founded at the end of the eleventh century and the unpretentious stone-walled chapel, constructed in the simple Gothic style, contains one of the finest altars in Germany – its paintings and wood carvings the work of the German Master Gregor Erhart. The town with its old houses – some dating back even to the fifteenth century – grew up alongside the monastery and the quiet and restful atmosphere which quickly casts its charm over the casual visitor, spreads its peace over the whole vicinity.

During the Reformation the monastery was taken over by the Lutherans and established as a preparatory school for future pastors. At the beginning of the nineteenth century it was reorganised to form one of the four lower seminaries in Württemberg, along with those at Maulbronn, Urach and Schöntal, and to these seminaries, every four years in rotation, came a group of 30–40 boys, such a group being known as a *Promotion*. The head of the seminary was called the *Ephorus* and he was assisted by two professors, and two tutors – young graduates from the Tübingen seminary whose responsibility it was to help the boys with their lessons, and generally to keep watch over discipline.

As regards the all-round quality of the staff in general, the Blaubeuren *Promotion* was particularly fortunate. Reuss, the *Ephorus*, was a man with understanding for young students, liberal in his approach to discipline, good humoured and friendly. He attempted to mitigate some of the more stringent rules and permitted the boys to visit the village at certain times. His lectures, however, apart from those on his pet subjects – the French Revolution and Württemberg history – were generally considered dull.

The main burden of teaching was borne by the two professors Kern and Baur, and probably, wrote Strauss, no seminary was ever blessed with two such excellent teachers. Kern was the more versatile of the two, friendly and approachable, whereas Baur was taciturn, gruff and distant – not one to whom boys could come with their problems. However, as a teacher, Baur was certainly the more outstanding. Kern did not have Baur's sharpness of judgment and also lacked a certain strength of character. The ancient literature was divided between them: Kern read the poets – Homer, Sophocles and Virgil – and Baur led them through the prose writers – Herodotus, Thucydides, Plato, Livy and Tacitus – to mention only a few of the authors. In addition there were lessons in Hebrew, logic, psychology, ancient history and mythology.

The day began at 5 a.m. (5.30 a.m. in winter) with prayer, and then time for private study until breakfast at 7. The morning was taken up with lectures broken by periods of music and physical education until a lunch-break from 12 to 2 when it was possible to walk outside the monastery. Then came another two hours of lectures and a further period of private study until the evening meal. From 7 until 9 in the evening was a free time of recreation, and bedtime was at 9, although it was permitted to study until 10 if one so desired. Visits to the local tavern were forbidden and disobedience to the rules was punished by a period of solitary confinement. Sunday was apparently the dullest day of the week with a church service and periods of religious instructions. Yet all the disadvantages of such a life were clearly outweighed by the benefits, and if we may judge by the description of Vischer – who was the biggest grumbler and malcontent about the rules and regulations – life was at times highly enjoyable.

An extremely cheerful world developed within our monastery walls:
we put on plays, held masquerades with splendid costumes, comical
processions and the like. The families in the little town accepted us
extremely well. Gradually we became more grown up and learnt
to treasure the feminine graces; pretty girls were not lacking and
the sentimentalism of our first infatuations found an unlimited field:
we played, danced; the school children of the town were pushed into
the background with arrogant victorious power, and the evenings
which I spent with Strauss in the intimate family circle were un-
forgettable through the bubbling fulness of humour and spirit which
he here developed.[1]

The first place in the class was held by Wilhelm Zimmermann, the gifted son of poor parents. His schooling had begun
rather later than that of the other boys in the group, but he had
made such outstanding progress that he outstripped everyone
else, and during the time at Blaubeuren he always remained at
the top of the scholastic list. Especially gifted in languages and
poetry, he had also a great interest in the history and culture of
ancient civilisations, which made him a favourite with Baur.
This early promise, however, was only partially fulfilled in his
later life and he always remained something of a dilettante.
Gustav Pfizer, who was usually second in the class, also possessed a talent for languages and poetry, but was of a more
deeper-thinking and solid nature than Zimmermann. Then
there was Christian Märklin, whose open and happy disposition
won the hearts of all the students; Gustav Binder, whose special
interest was history; and Fritz Vischer, who, as Strauss reports,
was the life and soul of the group with his humour and jokes.
These five students, together with Strauss, composing the inner
circle of the so-called 'genius *Promotion*', passed all their examinations with the mark 1a.

Strauss himself, at that time, was a tall, gangling youth with
fair-brown hair, and although he usually took fifth place in the
class, in front of Vischer, he was hindered only by a lack of
talent for mathematics and French, and in other subjects was
in no way inferior to his friends. His final report read:

Gifts: very good powers of comprehension and judgement with a
certain easiness. Conduct: very good, sociable, polite. Diligence:
very persevering, thorough and interested. Latin and Greek: very

[1] *KG*, p. 88.

good, good style. Hebrew: very good. French: fair. Poetry: outstanding. History: outstanding. Mathematics: average. Logic
and Psychology: good. German style: outstanding. Recitation:
good. Religion: outstanding.[2]

[2] Ziegler, pp. 32–3.

# 3

# AT TÜBINGEN UNIVERSITY

Lying between Stuttgart and the Swabian Alb, Tübingen on the Neckar, with its old castle overlooking the town, the picturesque houses along the river bank, and its enchanting market place, is one of the most charming university towns in Germany. It was first mentioned in historical annals in 1078 when it was described as a strong fortress. In 1342 it was purchased by the count of Württemberg whose descendants afterwards acquired the title of duke. During the seventeenth-century wars it was twice captured by the French – in 1647, and again in 1688, when the walls were destroyed, but from this time forth it enjoyed peace and tranquillity. The University was founded by Duke Eberhard in 1477 and when Württemberg went over to the Reformation in 1536, the Lutheran seminary was established in the old Augustinian monastery. A number of students who were destined to leave their mark in world history had studied here – Kepler (1589–93), Hölderlin (1788–93), Hegel (1788–91), Schelling (1790–5), Mörike (1822–6) – and in the autumn of 1825 the doors of the seminary again opened to receive what was probably the most talented group of students who ever resided within the walls.

At last, the Blaubeuren students had attained their freedom. They could now visit the tavern and smoke; they were able to sleep in later in the morning and to visit in the evenings, with the result that life took on an added interest. The *Ephorus* (Jäger) was little respected among the students and described as a despicable fellow. In the seminary itself the tutors – young graduates with the highest grades – were responsible for discipline, for helping the students to choose which lectures they should attend, for leading the regular discussion groups and for marking the two essays which had to be completed every semester. The five-year course was divided into two parts.

9

During the first two years the students studied the ancient languages and philosophy, and only in the third, fourth and fifth years was a beginning made with theology.

The philological and philosophical professors at the University were at that time distinguished only by their lack of academic talent and especially by their inability to teach. Tafel, who held lectures on Pindar, was held to be 'somewhat of a fool and too much given to the bottle'. The philosophy lectures were apparently little better: Schott was described as petrified; Sigwart as dull; Haug as dry; and Eschenmayer, who had become fascinated by Schelling and had drifted further into mysticism, was regarded as a dilettante. Certainly these descriptions may be somewhat exaggerated and they take little account of the undoubted learning which the professors possessed, but they do characterise the dry and arid teaching which the students were forced to endure week after week.

The Blaubeuren group were therefore left somewhat to their own resources, and during the first two years, Strauss, Märklin, Vischer and the other friends devoted themselves to an assiduous study of the Romantics and especially to the nature-philosophy of Schelling. Kant was found to be too involved, and difficult to understand; his ponderous logic and moral philosophy did not speak to the hearts of the young students with their lust for life, and it was the Romantics whom they enthusiastically embraced. Uhland, then at the height of his fame, was professor of German literature in Tübingen; Tieck was idolised; and Mörike, who also studied at the seminary during Strauss' first two years, was able to further the romantic impetus of the group. But the philosopher of romanticism at that time was Schelling.

We read Kant and pulled a face over the sour apple into which we had bitten; we read Jacobi, he certainly tasted better and we thought that if that was philosophy, then we could surely participate; we read Schelling and whoever knows how to captivate youth, especially those who had been educated like ourselves, he has them in his power. And Schelling now captivated us.[1]

Schelling, with his pantheistic philosophy of nature, has never ceased to attract and to fascinate the human mind. God

---

[1] Strauss, *Christian Märklin, Ein Charakterbild aus der Gegenwart* (Mannheim, 1851) (henceforth cited as *Märklin*) p. 33; *GS*, x, p. 205.

is the soul of the world and nature is the unconscious part of God – God's body. Outside of and apart from God there is no nature, and outside of and apart from nature, no God. How far such ideas were eagerly grasped by the students is shown by a letter which Märklin wrote to his father in 1828 in which he defended his new religious beliefs against the objections levelled by his more orthodox father. Since Strauss and Märklin were always so united as regards their fundamental religious views, the ideas which Märklin expresses may be taken as a fairly accurate picture of Strauss' own views at this time.

I have still not been able to convince myself of the personality of God, as it is found in Theism. In that teaching God is a personal self-conscious God; the consciousness, however, is nothing other than the expression of a particular life of the Spirit which develops *in time*; and in that we conceive God as conscious, just so do we transcribe to him the concept of time, which is precisely the most important thing and which must be denied to him as far as possible. Generally, however, we find after more careful consideration that no individual attribute of God originates except through our presupposition of time in God. The providence of God, for example, which is so lauded, rests solely on this concept; one accepts that God's working is especially prominent in particular events, like the prevention of accidents and so forth; in such a way one introduces God's working into time, and thus when one removes this attribute of time from God, which must be done if a purified conception of God is to be obtained, then that providence for particular cases simply falls away, and nothing remains for us except the general working of God in nature, which in a certain sense at any rate can also be called providence.

We must certainly consider whether we have not made our conception of God too greatly dependent upon the consciousness of our own weaknesses and finitude, so that we conceive a God who is, as it were, a supplement of this finitude. Thus we speak of the needs of the heart which are unsatisfied by pantheism; and it is true that when we require consolation, for example, in misfortune, we necessarily conceive of a personal God, because this conception comforts us. And just here the question arises whether we do not accommodate the conception of God to fit our individual situation, instead of accomodating our individualities to the idea of God. It seems to me that God, as most of the people conceive him, is a man raised to the highest degree, a Being from whom one cannot take away the finite forms, but to whom one ascribes the *highest* power

(the omni- among those attributes) on account of more or less
sensuous needs. Indeed, it appears necessary for men to indi-
vidualize God, because they can only comprehend everything
under the finite forms of reason; but whether the objective truth lies
in the process by which man, in order to conceive the super-
sensory sphere, transcribes to it a consciousness and a personality,
whether the objective comprehension agrees with the subjective,
and whether perhaps those who do not accept the personal element
in the idea of God as a necessary element do not have right – that
is another question.

I cannot believe that in the idea of an infinite All – or however
else one wants to designate the God of the pantheistic viewpoint –
every individual disappears and merges with all the rest (a reproach
of the Fathers, so it appears). For likewise, if every individual is
only a manifestation of the infinite Spirit, he only becomes thereby
the determined individual; he is separated from all the rest and finds
himself (which concerns man personally) in his self-consciousness
as a personal identical essence; but the self-consciousness is just that
principle of the individual-personal life which separates and holds
separate each (human) individuality distinct from all the rest. On
the other hand, however, it is just as certain that each individual
lives with all the rest in the closest relationship; for he finds, whatever theism must accept, that the same power which is the motivat-
ing force in himself, also lives in others, that the divine Spirit has
also revealed itself in others as well as in himself. Thus each life
will have a double relationship; for it is a life for itself in one's feeling
and self-consciousness and a life in the whole and in the unity with
the infinite.

Therefore the Godhead is not to be thought of as an aggregate
of infinitely many finite beings and I do not so think; one could
only make this reproach of me, if, proceeding from the view of the
finite divided world, I wanted to construct the Godhead out of this
dividedness, whereby I should have invented a merely logical concept and not a real, living unity.

However, I set the Absolute, as it were, as the prius (if the form of
time is permissible here); or rather, the Absolute is simultaneously
with its manifestation, the world. Once assume the concept of a
power generally, which expresses itself in definite manifestations,
then this power cannot be thought of except as being simultaneously accompanied by a working, a manifestation. For in the
concept of power lies a priori the concept of activity. Therefore I
distinguish the eternal manifestation from the power itself which
determines the manifestation, and I must assume the power to be
the original unity from which the multiplicity of workings and

manifestations first becomes possible. Thus it seems to me that I could well call a finite being a part of the infinite, so long as this is not understood in a material sense; i.e. the finite is a manifestation, it is brought into being and determined by the infinite; thus in this view the dependence upon God is in no way done away with, but the finite appears absolutely dependent upon God, in whom alone we live and move (Acts 17, 28).[2]

During his first two and a half years at the seminary Strauss immersed himself more and more in the mysticism of Jacob Böhme and experienced a strong conviction of the reality of the supernatural, although this should not be understood in any theistic sense, but rather as a belief in the pantheistic unity of the world.

It was at the beginning of my university years: without any affirmative leading from my philosophical bent I had moved from the Steppes of Kant and his interpreters across to the more succulent pastures of nature-philosophy, and from there I lost my way in the mysterious woods of the old Jacob Böhme. Having only just emerged from the gloom and the shadowy dreams of the period between boyhood and adolescence to a more assured self-consciousness, I believed that it was just in this directness of feeling that I possessed the truth, and I could not perceive the reason for all the fuss and mistrustful precautions with which Kant approached the knowledge of things. Far from understanding the questions and problems with which this thinker was concerned, I certainly did not understand why these questions had even been formulated. In such a situation how must Schelling's intellectual view, Jacob Böhme's direct gaze into the depths of the divine and the natural worlds speak to and enthuse me!... Brought up with simple religious training, I had up till this time believed in a childlike way in the Bible as God's Word; now, from the utterances of Jacob Böhme, I received as strong a belief in the supernatural as anyone who ever believed in prophets and apostles: indeed, his knowledge appeared to me, in some ways, to descend to deeper depths, in other ways, to bear the stamp of direct revelation more definitely than the Bible itself.[3]

The influence of Böhme, and also Tauler, extended at least to the year 1828. In August 1827 Strauss wrote to Mörike:

[2] *Ibid.* pp. 43–5; *GS*, x, pp. 214–16.
[3] *GS*, I, p. 125.

'Read Jacob Böhme if your pastor has something by him; I still derive the most satisfaction from his book.'[4] and the comment of one of his tutors on an essay runs as follows: 'He himself wants his view of revelation to be known as mysticism, not supernaturalism.'[5]

At the beginning of 1828 this rapturous mysticism found expression in a poem entitled 'Thanks for the Awakening', of which the final verse runs:

> Yes, be thou sun, and I a tree
> That hopeful gazes up to thee;
> Be thou in meadows as a spring,
> Let me to thee as green grass cling;
> Yes, let me ne'er be rich and mine,
> But, O Lord Jesus, poor and thine![6]

The year 1827 brought a new interest in spiritism, clairvoyance and spiritual healing. In his essay on Justinus Kerner,[7] Strauss gives us an account of how he and two other friends made an expedition to a neighbouring village in order to visit a certain fortune-teller, and how on the way they experienced a most remarkable demonstration of unseen powers.

The month of February was already almost over yet deep snow covered the roads and it was terribly cold. We had travelled in the early morning for perhaps an hour when one of our party, who had not clothed himself sufficiently, and from the beginning had not taken sufficient care, suddenly found that his hands had become so frozen that all feeling had departed from them. Immediate rubbing with snow was of no avail, but drove the cold even more into the more inner parts so that he was near to fainting and cold sweat lay on his forehead. Luckily we were near a village; we brought our friend into the inn and laid him on a table in the warm room, covering him with a blanket under which he lay with his eyes closed and decidedly weak. We asked if there was a doctor, but were told that there was none in the neighbourhood; however there was a shepherd who knew what to do in cases of bleeding,

---

[4] To Mörike, 10.8.27; *Deutsche Rundschau*, 115 (1903) p. 100.

[5] Gotthold Müller, *Identität und Immanenz* (Zürich, 1968) p. 137.

[6] 'Dank für die Erweckung', *GS*, XII, pp. 9–10.

[7] *GS*, I, pp. 119–73. Justinus Kerner (1786–1862) studied medicine in Tübingen and from 1818 was the senior medical doctor in Weinsberg. His leisure hours were devoted to literature and from his pen flowed a host of poems, as well as novels, medical treatises and numerous other works.

burns and even of frost. A shepherd with mysterious powers of healing – that certainly rang a bell in our thoughts and wishes. The shepherd appeared: a middle-aged man of medium height, intelligent, with an honest face. Asked if he hoped to be able to restore our friend to sufficient health that would enable him to continue with us on the journey, he smiled, and answered that our friend would soon be the freshest and healthiest of us all. Then he took the hands of our sick comrade from under the blanket and murmuring some words, stroked them repeatedly with his fingers and then laid them back under the blanket. Now one may think what one will about the whole affair, but one thing is certain – that after at most five minutes our friend sat up, looked around bright and cheerful, and assured us that during the treatment by the shepherd he had had the feeling that the shepherd with his stroking had drawn the pain out of his hands, so that the pain in the inner parts had then also quickly disappeared. Filled with amazement we sat down with our quickly-recovered friend to a glass of wine, the shepherd, who by his gritty words and sound views completely won us over to himself, in our midst. And when we came to say farewell, I, with a half-superstitious reverence, presented to him a silk scarf which I had been wearing around my neck, and which I could well have used on a journey in such cold weather. We all felt strange as we continued the journey. We had awaited the miraculous at the end of a six hour journey, and now we had experienced it through the necessity of the most curious chance after only one hour. We felt that that day we could not encounter anything higher, and yet we were lucky enough afterwards to learn so many remarkable, and to some degree pertinent, things from the fortune-teller about the past present and future, that our joy and rapture found sufficient nourishment for the period of the whole day.[8]

In the summer of that same year he had another experience of the spirit world when he visited a woman possessing remarkable psychic powers. The young lady, a certain Friederike Hauffe (1801–29), spent the final years of her short life in Kerner's house and was the subject of his famous book *The Seeress of Prevorst*.

Kerner received me with father-like kindness and soon introduced me to the seeress, who lay awake in bed in a lower room of his house. In a short while she fell into the mesmeric trance and for the first time I had a view of this remarkable condition, and, to

[8] *GS*, I, p. 127.

be sure, in its purest and best form. Her face was full of suffering, but noble, with tender features over which was poured a heavenly transfiguration; her speech was the purest German; the delivery soft, slow, solemn, musical – almost like recitation; the content was rapturous feelings like clouds over the soul – sometimes bright clouds at other times dark – and then floating away, or like a breeze – sometimes stronger sometimes more gentle – passing through the strings of an aeolian harp; and conversations with and about good or evil spirits, conducted with a truthfulness which made it impossible for us to doubt that we had here, before us, a real seeress, who was in communication with a higher world. Soon Kerner made ready to set me in mesmeric contact with her: I cannot in my whole life remember such a comparable moment. I was absolutely convinced that as soon as I laid my hand in hers my whole thinking and being would lie open before her; no support, no excuse any more if there was something in my life that I might have had grounds for hiding; as I gave her my hand it was as if someone pulled the ground away from under my feet and I were sinking into a bottomless abyss. Incidentally I passed the test with flying colours: she praised my faith, and in answer to Kerner's question whether there was anything special about my belief, the seeress replied that I would never fall into unbelief. Later I often teased Kerner with this answer; for either, I would say to him, I am not yet unbelieving, or if so, then your seeress was a false prophetess.[9]

Strauss was utterly convinced of the reality of these unseen powers, a fact which Vischer also confirmed.

I met Strauss at his parents' home just after he had returned from his first visit to Kerner. It was as if he was electrified; a deep yearning for the Elysian Fields possessed him; where he thought that he noticed the slightest trace of rationalism in the discussion which was not distinguished from the vulgar rationalism of the Enlightenment, he was up in arms, and everything which did not follow him into his moonlit magic gardens was called heathen and turkish.[10]

In the winter semester of 1827–8 Strauss began the three-year theological part of his study. The older Tübingen School of Storr,[11] which advocated a kind of rational supernaturalism,

⁹ *GS*, I, p. 129.

¹⁰ *KG*, p. 94.

¹¹ Gottlob Christian Storr (1746–1805) was professor of theology at Tübingen from 1777, and concerned to show that revelation was in no way contrary to reason.

had declined, and after the death of the younger Bengel[12] in 1826, Baur and Kern were called to Tübingen as professors, and Steudel[13] became the leader of the School. Steudel, 'whom God in his wrath had allowed to become a university professor', was a man with little talent for teaching and after four weeks Strauss no longer bothered to attend his lectures, declaring that if Christ himself could hear Christianity expounded in such a tedious, paltry and petty manner, he too would have given the whole thing up.[14]

Kern lectured on Dogmatics, but although his lectures were learned and well presented, he lacked a certain soundness and sharpness of judgment, and as time progressed he ceased less and less to satisfy Strauss and his companions. His lectures on the Synoptic Gospels were certainly instructive and it was apparently during these lectures that Strauss' eyes were more and more opened to the inconsistencies in the Synoptic narratives and for the necessity of the critical knife.

The most influential professor at this time was Baur, yet even he had hardly begun the critical research into the New Testament, which characterised his later years, and at this period he exercised no exceptional influence on Strauss' development toward the radical criticism which he employed in his *Life of Jesus*. A lecture on symbolism which Baur held in the winter semester of 1828–9 made no impression on Strauss, and only in the summer semester did Baur turn his attention to one of the New Testament books – The Acts of the Apostles. In the following year he lectured on the Epistles to the Corinthians, but as Strauss remarked long afterwards, Baur showed that he had no intention of stepping outside the limits of critical propriety.

In the meantime lectures had started again and we now heard Baur lecturing on Acts and the Corinthian letters. It was here that Baur showed us through isolated observations, e.g. regarding the miracles at Pentecost, the parties in Corinth etc., the light of Criticism – but even then, only in the distance. For he was far away from the

---

[12] Ernst Gottlieb Bengel (1769–1826), grandson of the famous Johann Albrecht Bengel.

[13] J. C. F. Steudel (1779–1837), professor of theology in Tübingen from 1815, is usually regarded as the last representative of the Old Tübingen School.

[14] *Märklin*, p. 39; *GS*, x, p. 210.

audacity which the author of the *Life of Jesus*, and of this biographical sketch, showed in undertaking to storm the walls of Zion
with a handful of picked troops; he had scarcely begun to construct
the first lines up to the orderly siege-works which he was planning.[15]

Baur himself at this period was particularly influenced by
Schleiermacher and did not hesitate to point his pupils to the
greatness of the Berlin theologian. During 1827, and especially
in the following year, Strauss and his friends concentrated
particularly on the *Speeches* and *The Christian Faith*, and it was
Schleiermacher who led them out of the clutches of Schelling's
nature-philosophy and their curiosity for the occult. But
Schleiermacher was not able to satisfy them, for they perceived
that he too stood on pantheistic ground and was unable, with
his half-rationalistic and half-pantheistic explanations, to avoid
the contradictions contained in the historical Christian faith.

Far from satisfying our scientific minds, the study of Schleiermacher's *Christian Faith* provided us rather with twice as much
impulse to press forward further into regions where the Master,
rather at random, as it appeared to us, had pegged out boundaries;
the everlasting peace-treaty which he prided himself in having
concluded between philosophy and theology seemed to us only a
precarious armistice, and we found ourselves advised to look ahead
to the war.[16]

Schleiermacher, however, was little more for Strauss and his
friends than a transition to Hegel, who in Tübingen at that
time was either unknown, or regarded as a fool, mystic and
fanatic. The stimulus to study Hegel appears to have first
come from Zimmermann, who in 1827 had busied himself with
Hegel's *Encyclopaedia* and had advocated the Hegelian dialectic
in an essay, for which he had been accused of plagiarism. The
only lecturer who appears to have been interested in Hegel's
philosophy was Schneckenburger, and it was he who forwarded
the interest of a small group of students, thirsty for knowledge
of the new dialectic. In 1828 Strauss, Binder, Märklin and
others began to meet twice a week in Binder's room to read and
study Hegel's *Phenomenology* and at the end of two years Strauss
could claim that they had a better basic understanding of the

---

[15] *Märklin*, p. 51; *GS*, x, p. 221.
[16] *Ibid.* pp. 52–3; *GS*, x, p. 223.

Master than Marheineke, the Berlin theologian who had attempted to combine Hegel's philosophy with traditional theology.

A more demanding reading material than the *Phenomenology* was, for young students at the point of our education, not to be found. While the understanding was gripped by the sharpest dialectical school, the deepest presentiments offered themselves to the spirit, the most surprising prospects to the imagination. The whole of world history passed before us in a new light; art and religion in their various forms emerged in their proper place, and this whole wealth of forms proceeded from the one self-consciousness into which it again returned, having thereby come to know itself as the power of all things.[17]

One other interesting biographical event from the year 1828 must be recorded. Strauss entered for a 'prize essay' – not in the Protestant faculty of theology, but in the Catholic – the subject being 'The Resurrection of the Dead'. The biblical exegesis was excellently handled, but the second part betrayed Strauss' philosophical views more than was desirable and he thus tied for first place with a student from the Catholic seminary whose biblical exegesis was of a lower standard than Strauss', but whose second dogmatic part was much more orthodox. The faculty was unable to decide to whom the prize should be awarded, and it was therefore resolved to be decided by lot. How this was accomplished is not related, but apparently the names of the two prize-takers were first revealed and after it was learnt that one of the two was a member of the Protestant faculty, the Catholic student received the prize; Strauss nothing!

Apparently this essay marked an important stage in the development of Strauss' thinking on questions of biblical criticism, as we see from a letter which Strauss wrote to Vischer some years later.

A Catholic prize essay which I worked upon in 1828 was perhaps the first turning point in a critical direction. I proved the resurrection of the dead with full conviction, both exegetically and also from a natural-philosophical point of view, and as I made the last full stop, it was clear to me that there was nothing in the whole idea of the resurrection.[18]

---

[17] *Ibid.* p. 54; *GS*, x, p. 224.      [18] *KG*, p. 98.

The four years at Blaubeuren and the five years at Tübingen had provided Strauss with all the tools he required for the further study of theology – a knowledge of the ancient languages, of philosophy and theology – and he graduated from the University in 1830 as the *primus* among the students. By this time, however, any active faith which he might have had in the traditional Christian beliefs had been completely destroyed, although five years were still to elapse before he gave public testimony to this fact in his *Life of Jesus* – a work which was to cleave nineteenth century theology into two eras – before and after 1835.

# 4

## STRAUSS AS A CURATE

Strauss would have liked to have returned to Blaubeuren as a tutor, but his request to be considered for the vacant position was turned down and instead he was appointed curate in the little village of Klein-Ingersheim. This at least had the advantage of being only a short distance from Ludwigsburg, so that he was often able to return home and visit his parents, especially his mother. The vicar in the village, pastor Zahn, was at that time in rather indifferent health and Strauss had to perform almost all the pastoral duties – baptising, marrying, burying, conducting Sunday worship, catechising and holding religious instruction in the school. However, the congregation was not large and much time remained to him after his responsibilities had been fulfilled, so that he was able to reread the whole of Hegel's *Phenomenology* and make a start with the *Logic*. In addition he studied Schleiermacher's *Christian Faith* which, however, made little impression upon him.

As a curate, Strauss was a great success and there could have been few complaints about the manner in which he carried out his pastoral duties. He was helped in this regard by the fact that there were no pietists or sectarians within the congregation, and in this respect he was more fortunate than his friend Märklin at Brackenheim, near Heilbronn, who laboured under constant difficulties and was continually beset by doubts regarding the ethics of preaching and teaching what he himself personally did not believe. For Märklin had rejected the fundamentals of the orthodox and traditional Christian belief, and now hovered between Schelling and Hegel, uncertain of what he believed. It would thus appear that while some of the congregation thought him a mystic, others suspected him of being a heretic, and Märklin's attempt to introduce the new philosophical principles and ideas received a cold reception.

21

On the other hand he felt ill at ease in his conscience about conforming to the traditional teaching, which he had long abandoned, while preaching the commonly-held errors as if he himself accepted their truth, seemed to him somewhat hypocritical.

There followed a lengthy correspondence with Strauss in which the common Hegelian distinction between the philosophical concept (*Begriff*) – the truth expressed in scientific thought – and the theological representation, or conception (*Vorstellung*)[1] – the popularised and erroneous form of the concept – was discussed; yet, as we see from these letters, even this distinction did not solve the underlying moral problem of whether it was right to teach and preach what one did not believe.

Now when a questioning parishioner – and these are not just merely the so-called educated, but there are also thinkers among the people – comes to me and asks: What do you hold as regards the devil? or, as regards particular (fantastic) miracles in the New Testament? then however I may answer him, there arises a question of conscience for me. If I play the role of the believer then I behave in the highest way dishonestly against myself and must be ashamed of myself; and then he and the whole party are repelled by me, in that they themselves now, and rightly, hold themselves more spiritually mature than I. But if I tell him my real opinion, then either he says: Sir, why then do you teach otherwise in the church? (and at this point I would not want to demand that such a person should be able, like ourselves, to comprehend the identity of concept and representation; that would presuppose a methodical philosophical training) and where is the borderline if I once disbelieve something or other in the Scriptures? Or he exposes me to the danger of being looked upon as a hypocrite or unbeliever, when he spreads my statements – and I cannot forbid him, since just this would be certain to appear highly suspicious to him – among the rest of the people, who do not distinguish between content and form and just

---

[1] The German word *Vorstellung* has both an objective and a subjective meaning. In the objective sense it means a pictorial representation of an abstract concept; but in so far as this representation exists subjectively in the mind of the individual it is a conception. There are certain representations of God, but in our minds we have a conception of what he is like. I have sought to retain these two meanings but the dividing line is sometimes difficult to determine and both senses are often inherent.

accept the form of the representation in religion as the essential, and to the danger of losing the one thing, on account of which I engage in this play with representations – the possibility of planting a religious life among the people. For this cannot happen without that trust which has now been lost. How will you now refute this truly Steudelian statement for me? You will easily see that for my own self, for me as Christian Märklin, religion and philosophy do not devour one another; but for me as curate, as pastor, they do not rightly harmonize.[2]

Strauss saw four possible ways out of the dilemma: first, to return to the old orthodox beliefs – that, for him, was impossible; secondly, to rationalise the traditional representations away – that was destructive and incompatible with his position as a clergyman; thirdly, to resign from the ministry – too radical a step; and fourthly, to preach the philosophical concepts in the traditional language, since the congregation could not understand the modern and scientific ways of thinking. If the people were comforted by the old ideas, then it was the responsibility of the preacher not to disturb their faith before they had been educated to the higher level of knowledge which could assimilate the new concepts. Rather, the preacher was to move slowly and to raise the congregation gradually to the new scientific ideas.

Up until now we have merely asked: What relationship has the preacher who thinks in terms of concepts, to his public, which stands on the level of the representation? Whereby it remained undecided whether it would ever remain standing on the level of the representation or whether it is itself destined to proceed onto the level of the concept. But now you give cause to distinguish clearly the two presuppositions and to answer the question with reference to each presupposition separately. Accepting that the preacher's public, the people generally, will be held fast for ever on the level of the representation, then the comparison would be completely pertinent, that this level is only the people's own particular language, into which the preacher would have to translate his thoughts if he wanted to be understood by his listeners. The preacher who thinks in terms of concepts, therefore, may just so little seek to introduce his public to the concept, as a German missionary may seek to introduce the natives to the German language, and he may just as little make it a matter of conscience

[2] *Märklin*, pp. 61–2; *GS*, x, pp. 231–2.

that he speaks with the public in representations, as the missionary who speaks in the language of the natives. And now you say that that is not simply so in reality, but is a natural and reasonable consequence, that a part of the public has already been influenced by the concept. Certainly you understand this not from a real attainment to the sphere of the concept, but only from an approach to it through reflective, abstract reasoning and thinking. But granted this, in this sense, the influence through the concept may in fact be applied not merely to a part of the public, but to all, in that there will certainly be no one among the people who has not in fact pushed conceptions such as the devil, angels, the atoning death of Jesus, into the background, however many there may be who are of a different opinion and who oppose this corruption when it comes to them from outside. Since then all the people find themselves moving in a process of transition out of the pure form of the representation towards the concept – although one will be unable to bring forth any example of an actual attainment – we would be not just compelled to hold that the goal of this movement was the attainment of the concept, but we could think that the people find themselves only in the fluctuating movement, that at one time they pass out of the representation to reason and to a certain unbelief, out of the sensuous element to the abstractly intelligible and negatively rational, but instead of now attaining the positively rational, they only limp back again from unbelief to the simple belief in the representation. The end of the last century and the beginning of the present provides an example of such a movement for the educated classes of the people. If that were the case, then the preacher, correspondingly, would not have to concern himself with the concept – which would be a futile undertaking anyway – but since he is supposed to preserve the religion which would otherwise disappear in the movement through the intelligible to the negatively rational, he must take care to hold the people fast in the pious representation, and if they should overstep the mark, to lead them back to it. Nevertheless, the preacher may not simply restrict himself merely to representations, but since he wanted to call the people out of the reasoning and back to the representations, he must also enter into this reasoning and refute it. This refutation now would either be a mere tirade or it would be a restoration of the representation through negation of its negation (i.e. of reasoning), i.e. restoration of the representation in a higher form, in the form of knowing and approaching that of the concept. With certain individuals (Zacharias Werner, Eschenmeyer), such a falling back out of reasoning into the representation often, in fact, so shows itself in reality, that afterwards the representation is often held in a more unreasonable and crasser way than previously; with the mass of the people, however, even after such a falling back, something of the thought always lingers on. Accordingly, we see undeniably that the people, considered as a whole, are enveloped in a movement from the mere representation towards the concept, and it is now of no consequence whether we view this movement as an unending approach or as a movement which really ends with the transition into the sphere of the concept. At any rate, this is for us irrelevant, because it follows that in both cases the clergyman has to promote this movement of the people's religion according to the elements of the concept. And just as, on the one hand, he may not remain in the representation, he may not, on the other hand, hasten too quickly to the pure concept, because the development of the people's religion would be interrupted by both these methods. The right way is for him to let the concept shine through the representation as far as possible and to transpose conceptions into the form of thoughts which the people are mature enough to comprehend, such as the conception of the devil into the thought of evil. In the pulpit, teaching the children, dear friend, let us only proceed – and we will do it justice then best of all – when we go to work completely unprejudiced. If a scrupulous fellow comes to us with the question about the devil, then the whole matter completely hinges upon what sort of fellow he is. If he has been influenced by the concept, then he will be able to tolerate it when I pour out the clear wine for him and say that the devil is a picture for evil in general. But if it is an abomination to him that I do not mention the devil in the pulpit; if he is one of those who has bitten his way into the conception, then I would point out to him his struggles against the devil in his inner self and show him, as with a mirror, the devil there. But in general, I must admit to you that I do not think much of such casuistry, for we only plague ourselves with silhouettes and the actual cases do not arise in this way: but if one did so arise, I would look upon the behaviour involved as less directly ethical and much more as indirectly ethical, in that I would view it as a matter of (pastoral) prudence, which certainly also belongs to the ethical sphere.[3]

Strauss himself preached to the congregation in the orthodox scriptural language of the times, and a sermon delivered in the church after a hailstorm had destroyed the fruit crop in the district is so excellently composed, that anyone not suspecting the identity of the author would never have thought it not to

[3] To Märklin, 19.2.31; quoted Ziegler, pp. 75–8.

be from a man of the most orthodox and evangelical persuasion.

Yes my friends, better to perish from lack of earthly bread than suffer from a lack of heavenly manna, the Word of God! Better to go without the fruit of our vineyards than the spiritual drink from the rock, which is Christ! And so has it happened to you: The Lord has struck your fields, but not so that you must hunger; and he has preserved for you his word and his Church: therefore with quickened thankfulness let us celebrate this Church festival and close the old Church year! Amen.[4]

Strauss remained only nine months in his curacy before he was called to the Maulbronn seminary as tutor. There he was responsible for teaching Hebrew, Latin and history to the final year students and according to Zeller, who was the *primus* of the Maulbronn *Promotion*, Strauss fulfilled this position so well that he gained the respect of all the students.

In the same year (1831), he had planned a journey to Berlin in order to hear Hegel's lectures, and to this end he applied for the degree of doctor of philosophy. At that time, for a student who had passed the theological examinations with the highest grades, the obtaining of the doctorate was so easy as to be almost a formality. It was only necessary to present a work of not too great a length, and for this purpose Strauss proposed to present the essay which he had written for the Catholic faculty on the resurrection of the flesh. Alas, when the Catholic faculty was approached for the return of the essay, it transpired that it had been lost. The archives were searched, but the work had disappeared and has still not been discovered. Fortunately, however, during his curacy in Klein-Ingersheim, he had composed another smaller essay on the ἀποκατάστασις τῶν πάντων;[5] this was accepted by the faculty, and he was finally awarded the doctorate with the mark 'bene'. But even before the faculty had finished their deliberations, Strauss had departed from Tübingen and was on board the coach rumbling along the road towards Berlin.

[4] Ziegler, pp. 68–9.

[5] The summing up of all things (Acts 3, 21). The work has been printed in Müller, *Identität und Immanenz*, pp. 50–82.

# 5

## STRAUSS IN BERLIN

In the 1830s Berlin was a rapidly growing city of some 300,000 inhabitants, the capital of Prussia, and the centre of Prussian culture and learning. The city had been a centre of the Romantic movement at the turn of the century and in the salon of Henriette Herz one could meet the Schlegels, Fichte, Schelling, Schleiermacher and other well-known literary personalities. By 1831 Hegel was recognised as the foremost philosopher in Germany and his fame continued to grow steadily. The theological faculty was no less inferior to the philosophical. For thirty years Schleiermacher had been acclaimed as the theologian of the Romantic movement and the liberator of theology from the arid rationalism of the Enlightenment; Neander, a convert from Judaism, was the most eminent Church historian in Germany; Hengstenberg was professor of Old Testament and editor of the conservative *Evangelische Kirchenzeitung*, and Marheineke was attempting a synthesis of Hegel's philosophy with traditional theology.

Hither, in the twenties and up to the middle of the thirties, streamed the elite of the young theologians in order to receive the last consecration of science, a stimulus for one's whole life. And not just those who wanted to take their final theological examination, not those languishing in examination difficulties and the wretchedness of theological perplexity, but maturer men in large numbers, such as had already been ordained to the ministry: curates from Baden, from Switzerland, from Württemberg, tutors and those with doctorates from Tübingen; men who had laboured in their academic pursuits with zeal and distinction, full of respect before the names of Schleiermacher, Neander, Hegel, Marheineke, made their pilgrimage to Berlin in order to return to their native land with a richer knowledge in the practical matters. It was, at that time, the golden age of our theology![1]

[1] Karl Schwarz, *Zur Geschichte der neuesten Theologie* (4th ed.; Leipzig, 1869) p. 56.

The cholera epidemic, which had hitherto been raging in Berlin, had almost died out when Strauss entered the city in November 1831, and the prospects for the semester appeared to be everything that one could hope for. Hegel was to lecture on the history of philosophy and the philosophy of religion, and a number of interesting lectures in the theological faculty had also been announced. On the day before lectures commenced Strauss made the personal acquaintance of Hegel and reported that he had been extremely favourably received:

I visited him last Thursday. As I told him my name and birthplace he said immediately: Ah, a man from Württemberg! and showed a wonderful joy. He asked me about all kinds of matters concerning Württemberg, for which he still has a live interest and true-hearted affection, e.g. about monasteries, about relations between old and new citizens of Württemberg and the like. Regarding Tübingen, he said he had heard that malevolent and to some degree malicious conceptions about his philosophy reigned there; the saying is also pertinent here, he said smiling, that a prophet has no honour in his own country.[2]

Hegel on his part was delighted to meet such a keen disciple of his philosophy, especially someone from Württemberg who would be able to propagate his views back in Tübingen, and he invited Strauss to visit him frequently. The following day Strauss attended Hegel's first two lectures and was elated by the excellent beginning.

On the morning of the 15th, however, he visited Schleiermacher for the first time, and when Schleiermacher informed him that Hegel had died of cholera on the previous day, Strauss was unable to contain his deep disappointment and unthinkingly blurted out the words: 'But it was for his sake that I came here to Berlin', which Schleiermacher took as a personal diminution of his own prestige; from that moment on Strauss was accorded cool treatment from the great theologian.

He was indeed cordially received by Schleiermacher, but shown to the door in an unfriendly way, for in his dismay on hearing of Hegel's death, he had innocently exclaimed that the reason for which he had come to Berlin was just to hear Hegel, and Schleiermacher perceived in this remark a slight against himself. This went so far that soon afterwards, as Strauss was introduced to his theological

[2] To Märklin, 15.11.31; *AB*, p. 9.

Master at a social gathering in the house of the criminologist Hitzig, Schleiermacher turned away brusquely with the reply: 'I've already met him'.[3]

Ziegler, for some reason (probably to contradict Hausrath), questions the historicity of Strauss' alleged remark and suggests that the story was invented later by Strauss' friends back in Tübingen.[4] There is no real evidence, however, for this suspicion, and the fact that Strauss, in a letter to Grüneisen, declared that Schleiermacher had received him favourably when he had mentioned Grüneisen's name, doubtless refers to the initial conversation which took place before Schleiermacher revealed the fact of Hegel's death. Vatke must have heard the story soon afterwards and it is highly unlikely that Benecke's account of Schleiermacher's open rebuff is untrue or that the cause was anything other than the incident related. Strauss was naturally and understandably reticent about mentioning his *faux pas* and his letter to Märklin contains no reference to the incident, although his mention of the precipitate end to the interview certainly confirms the truth of the whole episode.

I had hoped to be able to write you something cheerful from Berlin! Imagine my experience. I hadn't been able to meet Schleiermacher until this morning. He naturally asked me whether the cholera had not scared me from coming, to which I answered that the reports had become continually more reassuring and that the cholera was now indeed practically at an end. Yes, he said, but it has still claimed a great sacrifice – Professor Hegel died of it yesterday evening. Imagine this impression! The great Schleiermacher, at this moment he was unimportant to me when I measured him against this loss. Our conversation was at an end and I withdrew hastily.[5]

Strauss was now thrown into uncertainty as to whether he should remain in Berlin or return to Tübingen, but as he thought the matter over it became clear to him that 'although Hegel had died in Berlin, he had not died out',[6] and he therefore resolved to remain and attend lectures from the other Hegelians, along with theological lectures from Schleiermacher and Marheineke.

---

[3] Benecke, pp. 71–2.                    [4] Ziegler, p. 94f.
[5] To Märklin, 15.11.31; *AB*, p. 8.     [6] Ziegler, p. 96.

But the greatest personal joy for him was his friendship with Wilhelm Vatke, the lecturer in Old Testament at the University. Vatke, only two years older than Strauss, was a zealous Hegelian, so that not only were they agreed on all fundamental points but they were able to complement one another, since Vatke had applied his Hegelianism to the study of the Old Testament while Strauss had concentrated on the New Testament and Dogmatics. Strauss shifted his lodgings to Vatke's house and there they shared a most intimate friendship with walks during the day and music during the evenings.

Here they both enjoyed wonderful days and when they were tired, late in the evenings, Vatke played piano pieces by Bach, Mozart and Beethoven. In this enjoyment Strauss was insatiable; he was so enraptured by the music that he could listen for hours. In the choice of composers the difference between the inner dispositions of the two men made itself evident: Vatke found his ideal in Bach...for Strauss, no one could surpass the music of Mozart; that was for him immediate enjoyment without any reflection, the most soul-filling satisfaction, costly gratification of human nature which aspired to the highest. And yet both found a common meeting point in the titanic power of Beethoven. 'First play some Bach for yourself, then some Mozart for me and then Beethoven for the two of us.' And when Strauss' programme had been performed, then it had to be begun again right from the beginning; only when friends arrived, who thought it all so much noise, was the piano shut until the following day.[7]

Even Schleiermacher's unfriendliness did not deter Strauss from his resolve to attend his lectures and give him a fair hearing. To begin with he found Schleiermacher's thought difficult to grasp and was not greatly impressed.

It is not easy to write down what Schleiermacher says because he extemporises; up till the present he has not at all – his sermons also included – particularly attracted me; I must first get to know him better personally.[8]

However, as he attended Schleiermacher's lectures and listened to his sermons, he gradually received a much more favourable impression, and a letter to Märklin in February 1832 reveals how much his first opinions of Schleiermacher had changed:

[7] Benecke, p. 73.     [8] To Märklin, 15.11.31; *AB*, p. 10.

Through the loss of Hegel I was, at that time, in a certain state of irritation and unwilling to allow that loss to be in any way compensated for – least of all through a man whose direction was contrary to mine. In addition came the difficulty concerning Schleiermacher's lectures – that one must be used to them in order to get a grasp of him. Here we find the pure method of reasoning, not as in his writings, where everything is held together in a scientific form, but free, running hither and thither through the material, seizing at one moment on this side, at the next moment on the other side. Now this was annoying to me at the beginning and offered me the appearance of confusion, but it soon became clear that Schleiermacher distinguishes with great prudence between a written presentation and an oral presentation for students, the former, to be sure, in a rounded-off, self-contained objectivity (so far as was possible from his standpoint), the latter, however, in a completely subjective manner, so that one could see the process of development and learn to imitate its inner structure. Thus now his lectures have not only attracted me, but I have also learnt something essential from him about the method of presenting academic lectures.[9]

and a month later he could write:

One gets to know this wonderful Schleiermacher better when one hears his lectures, attends his sermons, or, when one is lucky enough to be in the same company with him – which happens rarely. He is regarded by all the professors, also by the public in Berlin, with the highest regard... I have found him clearest in his lectures on the life of Jesus, from which I received a transcript which had been written down word for word and afterwards written out legibly; there, his sharp mind knows how to discover connections or contradictions which would never have occurred to me, yet the result is thoroughly unsatisfying and remains essentially on the standpoint of Paulus;[10] he has raised himself above Christ the individual, but has not yet attained to the Spirit. Thus on the one hand too much is attached to these New Testament reports, on the other hand the reports are distorted in order that they may not emerge as too supernatural.[11]

Strauss' attention was gripped by Schleiermacher's exposition of the life of Jesus. Unfortunately Schleiermacher did not

[9] Ziegler, pp. 100–1.
[10] H. E. G. Paulus, the famous rationalist professor of theology at Heidelberg.
[11] To Georgii, 11.3.32; 'Briefe von D. F. Strauss an L. Georgii'. *Tübinger Universitätsschrift* (ed. H. Maier; Tübingen, 1912) pp. 5–6.

lecture on the subject in the course of the semester, but Strauss managed to obtain the notes of two students who had heard the lectures previously, and from these two copies he completed his own draft which provided him with an adequate outline of the essential subject matter. The subject challenged him and thoughts so flooded into his mind that he determined to lecture on the subject himself as soon as he returned to Tübingen; and, doubtless, behind the thought of the lectures lay the idea of a book for which the lectures would form the initial sketch. The letter to Märklin in which he expresses his ideas for the first time is so important in revealing the embryo of his later *Life of Jesus*, that we quote the entire letter.

As regards my actual intellectual activity, I'm attending, indeed, too many lectures, some more satisfying, others less; along with these I have worked my way through the notebooks of several Hegelian lectures such as Logic, History of Philosophy, Philosophy of World History, and Philosophy of Religion, and taken many notes, since these lectures will not be published immediately; finally I'm very busy with plans for my own future lectures...

What engages me in the most lively way (at present everything is just in my mind and I haven't time to work anything out) is the plan for a course of lectures on the life of Jesus. You will perhaps wonder about this choice, but you will see that this is actually the best preparatory work for the greater dogmatic plan which at present has been completely relegated to the back of my mind. I already have a fairly well-defined outline of these lectures on the life of Jesus: An introduction which must investigate in a religious-philosophical manner how significant it is when the contemplation of the divine as one life enters into a religion; then lives such as those of Adonis, Osiris, Herakles must be compared with the lives of Christians and the essential difference observed. The whole thing would fall reasonably into three parts, a traditional, a critical, and a dogmatic part, or, into a directly positive, a negative, and a part which would recover the true positive. The traditional part would contain the life of Jesus as it lives and continues traditionally in the consciousness of the Church, primarily in objective form, in the Gospels, from which a brief summary emphasizing everything miraculous would be presented; secondly, the life of Jesus as it lives subjectively in individuals, where depending upon disposition and circumstances, one emphasizes this aspect, the other that aspect – here would belong extracts from the writings of pious Christians – Luther, Arndt, etc. Thirdly, the identity which the Church brings out between the objective presentation in the Gospels and the subjective consciousness would have to be considered, in that the Church, in the 2nd article of the Apostles' Creed, emphasizes the essential features of the objective presentation for the subjective consciousness.

But the dance really gets started in the second critical part. The first thing that would have to be settled in a general article dealing with the Gospels is the fact that the external testimonies are not adequate to ensure that the Gospels were written by eye-witnesses, and that their historical value must therefore be validated from the evaluation of the Gospel narratives. This would then be undertaken. The mythical element in the history of Jesus before he appeared publicly, would be shown in the narratives announcing his coming, and those dealing with his birth. In the history of his public ministry, first his teaching would be considered, then the miracles – here the contradictions in many of the stories would then be exhibited and other bits and pieces such as how such stories could have originated without any historical basis (as, for example, the feeding of the five thousand from Christ's utterance: ἐγώ εἰμι ὁ ἄρτος τῆς ζωῆς[12]). Finally the prophecies made by Christ would be illumined, and especially that he did not prophesy his own death. As regards the third part which would deal with the history of his death and resurrection, there would be two possibilities to consider: either that Christ never died or that he was never bodily resurrected; the last is more probable since he only appeared to the rest of the disciples as he appeared to Paul, and in his case it was certainly only an inward experience, and also because the narratives of the appearance of the Resurrected One are completely contradictory: he has σάρκα καὶ ὀστᾶ[13], lets himself be touched; that means a material body which has the attribute of all material, repulsion, impermeability – then he passes again through locked doors, which means that he is permeable. In this way I would partly destroy, partly shake the infinite significance which faith attributes to this life – certainly only in order to restore it again in a higher way.

I could, therefore, as soon as something is destroyed critically – also in the individual details – immediately restore it dogmatically, whereby the whole would lose much of its hardness and offensiveness; but I won't do this, in order that the contradictions may be set forth as sharply and clearly as possible. Thus at the end of this second part would arise the inevitable pain over the loss of this treasure, indeed, indignation over the desolation of the sanctuary.

---

[12] I am the bread of life (John 6, 35).
[13] Flesh and bones.

From this would then arise the endeavour to restore what has been lost, and this would form the transition leading into the third dogmatic part. This restoration would consist of three sections showing first, the crudity of supernaturalism, secondly, the emptiness of rationalism, and thirdly, the truth of science. Now supernaturalism in its crude form opposes every negative work of criticism with the bare assertion: You may say what you will, it all happened as is recorded in the Gospels and not a single jot can be discarded. This crude supernaturalism, however, soon passes into the more elegant supernaturalism of Schleiermacher, who permits criticism in itself, surrenders many individual details to it, but marks out one holy circle in the name of faith over which criticism shall have no power – namely, that this historical individual was the absolutely perfect one. Against these two forms of supernaturalism now appeared, secondly, rationalism, also in two forms. The vulgar rationalism of Paulus maintains that even if all those facts are denied to be miraculous and divine, there would still remain sufficient positive content in the moral worth of Jesus. The discussion now takes place between this crude supernaturalism and that crude rationalism and both the combatants are equally justified, since rationalism in the critical form is right, as is supernaturalism in the dogmatic form to which it holds fast. But now out of this crude rationalism evolves the refined rationalism of de Wette, which is prepared to allow the fact – indeed every fact – to disappear, while at the same time retaining it as the symbol of a dogmatic idea. Its deficiency is just this lax concept of the symbol; the death of Jesus – symbol of resignation – certainly that is a miserably poor interpretation; but he can give no better one because he, like all rationalism, does not have the concept of the Spirit, which belongs only to science. It is science now – and this is the third point of this third part – which sees in the life of Jesus the consciousness which the Church has of the human spirit objectified as divine spirit; this consciousness is now projected into particular features, into miracles which are then allotted their significance; in the history of Jesus' death and resurrection, however, that idea in its whole process sums itself up systematically and shows that the Spirit attains the true positivity, the divine life – indeed the sitting at God's right hand – only through the negation of its negation, which is naturalness.

I think, dear friend, that you will be in agreement with the main points of this presentation; the first part could appear superfluous simply because it repeats what is already known. But one cannot begin from the negative and this first part is the absolutely necessary basis. The second part is the most difficult, but it also offers the most help; it begins with writings from old Celsus and continues through the English and French authors (for which I perceive a true yearning, just as one will play gladly with a wild animal when he knows that it cannot do him any harm) down to Dr. Paulus. The last part offers the least help, but it is the easiest for me. But you ask: Will you give these lectures in Tübingen? and you don't believe that the lecture room will be barred to you? Yes, something of the sort is certainly possible and I am often quite sad that everything I would like to do in theology is just such a perilous task. But I cannot alter it; in some way or another this material must come out of me and be worked into shape, and I want first to lecture and then write. For the present we will commend it to God who will somehow open such a door for us.[14]

Schleiermacher announced that in the forthcoming summer semester he would again lecture on the life of Jesus, but since Strauss already possessed a rough outline of the lectures and was impatient to return to Tübingen to begin work upon his own presentation, he decided not to remain; and having expressed this intention to Vatke as they walked in the Tiergarten:

Schleiermacher has greatly stimulated me and I owe him a lot; but the man has still not satisfied me. He only goes half way; he doesn't pronounce the final word. This word will be spoken by me; I'm returning immediately to Tübingen and listen Vatke, I shall write a Life of Jesus according to *my* idea.[15]

he set off back to Tübingen to begin work in earnest on his own revolutionary portrayal of the life of Jesus.

[14] To Märklin, 6.2.32; *AB*, pp. 12–15 (incomplete); Ziegler, pp. 126–30.
[15] Benecke, p. 75.

# 6

## TUTOR IN THE TÜBINGEN
## SEMINARY

In May 1832 Strauss was recalled to Tübingen as a tutor at the seminary and the three years which he spent there were among the happiest of his life. His friends from the Blaubeuren *Promotion* also returned as tutors – Pfizer in the same year and in the following year Binder, Märklin, Vischer and Haug. Two other close friends at this time were Louis Georgii, two years Strauss' junior, and Eduard Zeller, the *primus* of the Maulbronn *Promotion*.

Not only was Strauss the leader of the intellectual life in the seminary, but he also knew the best taverns in the town and was zealous in promoting the social activities of students and tutors. A cheerful and happy atmosphere generally prevailed – not without its romantic side. Strauss himself courted the daughter of one of the inn-keepers and had thoughts – probably not very serious – of marrying her. And yet life was not without its disagreements and we know that Strauss' relations with Georgii became so difficult, that only after Georgii's departure from the seminary did Strauss once more find a measure of peace.[1] There was also an argument between Strauss on the one side, and Märklin and Vischer on the other, and this also caused a dissension which disrupted the fellowship for a number of years.[2] The break in relations occurred as far back as 1829 when Vischer, having poured out his invective and scorn in some religious dispute, was bluntly told by Strauss that he was babbling like a fool. Vischer became angry and declared that the friendship was at an end; not until 1833 was Strauss' friendship with Märklin (who had taken Vischer's side) completely restored, and although to a lesser degree Strauss and

[1] Ziegler, p. 107.    [2] *Ibid.* pp. 108–9.

Vischer were also reconciled, the relationship between them always remained brittle. A letter which Strauss wrote to Märklin in 1835 does all credit to Strauss' character:

Don't be angry that I...return to things which happened in the past. I offended you through a defect in my nature – and not merely in my nature, but also in my character – which had been pointed out to me some time previously by Vischer. I'm sincerely grateful to Vischer for this and am of the opinion that his lessons will still be of benefit to me, even if they have not yet produced this desired effect. But I believe that he treated the whole affair far too – if I may so express it – judicially, merely from the standpoint of honour, while with people such as ourselves, who stand in such a close relationship with one another, a more educational treatment is possible for which, as I may well say, I have always been receptive. And now it seems to me that you also committed yourself too much merely to that standpoint of honour on which Vischer and I stood, and that you thereby made the wound in our relationship incapable of healing. Nevertheless, I will neither try to justify myself nor even dismiss the hard accusations about me which *you* then made. For the egoism of which you then accused me lies by us all in the background and then breaks out when we feel weak, while yet claiming to be strong, when every strange power which confronts us makes us feel this disparity in a stinging way. I at least have had the definite experience: when I go to pieces, when I am dissatisfied with myself in a more than merely momentary way, then I am also envious, petty-minded, irritable, bad-tempered; but when I have again recovered the feeling of my power, then I can endure and acknowledge the merit of others, even merit that I have to set far above my own. And so, since I have emerged, through a definite employment and directing of my powers, from the unhappy state which burdened me most terribly, just in the middle of our gathering here, certainly no more offences of that kind would have happened: but it seems to me now also possible to make up for the past events. Now no further word about the matter.[3]

In the summer semester of 1832 Strauss was made responsible for the seminary course on metaphysics and it so happened that he thereby came into conflict with Professor Steudel, the Director of the seminary, who was in attendance. During the lecture Strauss expressed the view that the traditional Church doctrine concerning the Person of Christ was more applicable

[3] To Märklin, 13.9.35; *SVBr*, I, pp. 284–5, footnote 12.

to humanity as a whole than to Christ himself, whereupon
Steudel rose to the defence of the orthodox teaching and criticised Strauss for expressing views which were in direct opposition to the doctrines of the Church. The whole affair was
somewhat painful and after the lecture Steudel also rebuked
some of the theological students for not contradicting Strauss'
erroneous teaching, declaring that if they were in sympathy
with these Hegelian ideas, it would be better for them to give
up theological study and their intentions of entering the
ministry. Strauss himself took the whole affair as a warning,
from that time forward exercising greater caution and living
'quietly and without any new revolution'.[4] He felt, however,
that there might be more trouble when he came to deal with
the doctrine of immortality, in which he had ceased to believe,
and which he regarded as the watershed which separated
the people into two camps – those who followed the new scientific thought and those who remained in their outmoded and
antiquated ideas.

My belief is unchanging that the inexorable discarding of the view
of a personal life after death must be the stone on which we shatter
and crucify our own and others' unphilosophical, trivial consciousness, in order to be able to ascend in the concept; and you will
interpret me correctly if I have also here spoken somewhat strongly,
without in a short letter being always able to set forth the necessary
proofs, which I can surely leave to your own insight to amplify.[5]

As a lecturer in the seminary Strauss also had the right to
lecture in the University so long as these lectures were not
detrimental to the lectures given by other members of the
University faculties. He decided therefore to use this privilege
in order to forward the new Hegelian philosophy. In the
summer semester of 1832 he lectured on 'Logic', interpreted in
the Hegelian manner; in the following winter semester on the
history of recent philosophy since Kant, and also, for the first
year students, on Plato's *Symposium*; in the summer semester of
1833 on the history of ethics. All these lectures were a brilliant
success and the lecture room was crowded with over a hundred
listeners – quite an exceptional thing for Tübingen. But such

---

[4] Ziegler, p. 110.
[5] To Binder, Ascension Day 1832; *Deutsche Revue*, 30, II, p. 205.

success could hardly have been expected to be greeted with favour by the other lecturers in the philosophical faculty, for they found their hearers being drawn away by the new ideas which they themselves had resisted. It was hardly surprising, therefore, that there was much displeasure over the young lecturer's triumph. The professors in the philosophical faculty showed their resentment openly by refusing to grant the large auditorium for Strauss to lecture in, while, instead, allowing its use by a lecturer from the medical faculty. Secondly, they protested that lectures from seminary tutors who had not habilitated[6] in one of the faculties should not be counted in the total number of philosophical lectures which at that time every student was obliged to hear. Further – but with probably more right – they alleged that Strauss in one of his lectures had adversely criticised one of the other lecturers in the philosophical faculty in a particularly irresponsible manner. The seminary, however, protected him, demanding that any charges be substantiated and insisting that any reproof should come from the seminary alone. The philosophical faculty was unsatisfied and complained to the Ministry of Education in Stuttgart; the Ministry, however, was unwilling to take action and replied with only a rather ambiguous rescript providing no real settlement of the dispute.

Strauss had considered habilitating in the philosophical faculty, but probably the feeling against him was so great that he decided against the move. Yet to lecture in the theological faculty carried just as many difficulties, and, as he expressed the situation in a letter to Binder:

The theological faculty gives the appearance of being for us and of wanting to mediate in the matter, but in actuality it thinks: *nostra res agitur*[7], sooner or later one could bring the same trouble upon us.[8]

This situation and the desire for the necessary time in which he could write his *Life of Jesus* made him resolve to discontinue lecturing and to concentrate on producing the theological work which would finally bring all speculation about the historical Jesus to an end.

[6] Habilitation is the process by which a candidate qualifies for inauguration as a university lecturer.    [7] It's our affair also.

[8] To Binder, 5.1.33; *Deutsche Revue*, 30, II, p. 344.

How the book originated was often related in the following way by the late General-Superintendent Dr. Hoffmann, who at that time was a tutor with Strauss in the Tübingen seminary. Hoffmann on one occasion entered Strauss' room and found him exceedingly disgruntled. 'What's up?' he asked him. 'There! read that,' replied Strauss and cast a letter at him. It was a letter which accompanied a review which Strauss had written for the Hegelian *Journal für wissenschaftliche Kritik* and which had been sent back to him. He had already written a number of reviews for the journal and had been highly praised for them. This time, however, Marheineke wrote a letter full of compliments which led up to the statement: the review is certainly acceptable, but it cannot be printed; what is good for the intelligent is too strong a meat for the others. 'Now, what do you say to that?' asked Strauss, as Hoffmann handed back the letter. 'It's roguery,' replied Hoffmann. 'That's just what I say too', answered Strauss; 'and now they will have to have as a whole book what they wouldn't suffer as a review; it's time that an end was made of this deceitful concealment of views.' Hoffmann then usually added: Strauss wrote the book well-knowing that in so doing he was casting away the chance of an appointment to Berlin – a great honour which would certainly have come to him at the next opportunity.[9]

[9] *Allgemeine Evangelisch-Lutherische Kirchenzeitung*, 1874, p. 180.

# 7

## THE *LIFE OF JESUS*

'Do you remember, Vatke?' reminisced Strauss, as the two friends sat together in 1860, 'there was a good wine in 1835!' 'Good thoughts too!' replied Vatke.[1]

It is not too much to say that nineteenth century theology was split in two by the publication of the *Life of Jesus* and that the year 1835 was the most important theological milestone of the century. Certainly no other book in the nineteenth century caused so great a stir in the theological world, for it was the first open and public assault on the bastions of the traditional Christian faith, in an age where atheism was treated with abhorrence and attacked with the weapons of academic and social ostracism. The book produced a reaction, unseen since the days of the Reformation. Strauss became a notorious celebrity overnight, and was everywhere regarded as the arch-fiend of the true Christian faith.

What then was so drastically new in the book which could cause such consternation throughout the land? What was it which distinguished Strauss' book from the works of other theologians whose opinions about the traditional beliefs of the Church were not markedly different from his own? Why were the pietists and orthodox so enraged about the views expressed there?

What shocked the orthodox believer most of all was the frank and open repudiation of the historical veracity of the Gospels. What had previously been accepted as irrefutable and invulnerable to all attack, was now set in doubt. The mighty fortress had now been undermined and appeared to be about to collapse in ruins. It was not merely that the Christain faith had been repudiated – Voltaire and the French *Philosophes* had poured out their vitriolic scorn on Christianity without causing

[1] Benecke, p. 489.

41

any great theological commotion. No, the truly alarming feature of Strauss' book lay rather in the *way* in which he had destroyed the whole historical basis of Christianity. Voltaire and his friends had merely denied the traditional doctrines; Strauss had destroyed the foundations on which those doctrines stood. No longer, it appeared, could anyone believe the things written in the New Testament, for Strauss had remorselessly exhibited the discrepancies, contradictions and mistakes in the Gospel narratives and made the supernatural explanations appear weak and untenable. The natural and rationalistic interpretation fared even worse: the attempt to give some credibility to the biblical passages was shown to be forced, unnatural, and often ridiculous. But when these two modes of interpretation had been so thoroughly discredited, then where was one to go? Was there any other alternative apart from throwing oneself straight into the arms of Strauss' solution – the mythical interpretation?

The presupposition on which the whole *Life of Jesus* was written was a denial of the miraculous and supernatural in the world. The traditional supernatural interpretations of the events narrated in the Gospels had no place in Strauss' view of the world, and God's activity was possible only indirectly through the laws of nature.

God works directly in the world as a whole, but only indirectly in each individual object in it, through the mediation of his workings in every other individual object, i.e. through the laws of nature.

When we take this view, then the verdict on the historical worth of the biblical history is no different from that considered above. The miracles which God works for Moses, Jesus, and through them, are in no way secondary products of his direct working in the whole, but presuppose a direct influence in the individual object and, in so far, are in opposition to the usual kind of divine activity in the world. Now the supernatural view presupposed an exception to this kind of activity, valid only for the sphere of biblical history. That is a presupposition which we with our standpoint (this is the critical research which has no presuppositions – a claim which we make for the present investigation...) cannot share. Our standpoint allows the same laws to hold sway in every sphere of being and activity; and therefore where a narrative runs contrary to the laws of nature, it must be regarded as unhistorical.[2]

[2] *LJ* (2nd ed.) I, pp. 86–7.

Strauss meant his investigation to be without presuppositions – i.e. he refused to start with the supernatural presuppositions of orthodox theology, but his investigation was, in
fact, simply based on the diametrically opposite presupposition
– viz. that there was no supernatural activity in the world and
independent of the world, apart from the laws of nature. If
such a being as a personal God actually existed, then he was
not free to break into history. That meant there could be no
incarnation, no supernatural, divine Christ, no miracles, and
no resurrection of the dead. Jesus was human, but not divine!

But now Strauss was forced to explain the Jesus of history.
If Jesus was not the long-awaited Jewish Messiah prophesied
in the Old Testament, if he was not the divine Son of God,
then who was he? Was he simply a great ethical teacher or
religious genius; was he a fraud or was he mentally sick? And
further, if he was only a man, how had the supernatural
picture painted by his followers originated? For the biblical
portrayal of Jesus involves not merely a *quantitative elevation* in
the estimation of Jesus' human personality, but a *qualitative
jump* from the merely human category into the supernatural
and divine. This jump had to be accounted for, and if the
supernatural interpretation was unacceptable, then there were
three other possibilities for explaining how the Gospel writers
had come to portray a supernatural and divine, instead of a
purely human, Christ.

1. Reimarus[3] had maintained that the Gospel stories were
the work of frauds, liars and hypocrites, who had invented
everything for their own personal gain. This judgment, however, was generally considered too harsh; it found few sympa-
thisers and Strauss also wasted little time in setting it aside.

2. The second and most popular alternative was the natural
explanation which had been most fully and consistently employed by Paulus[4] of Heidelberg. Behind the actual stories lay

[3] Hermann Samuel Reimarus (1694–1768) was headmaster of a secondary school in Hamburg. Parts of his most well-known work, *Defence of the
rational worshippers of God* were published by Lessing in his *Wolfenbüttel
Fragments* (1774–8).

[4] Heinrich Eberhard Gottlob Paulus (1761–1851) studied theology in
Tübingen (1779–84) and after some years at Jena and Würzburg was
called in 1811 to Heidelberg. His best-known works were his commentary
on the Gospels (1800–4), and his *Life of Jesus* (1828).

an historical core which had been embellished in a supernatural manner by Jesus' disciples, who, for one reason or another, had either misperceived or misunderstood what had actually happened. Jesus, for example, had not actually walked on the sea, but by the sea-shore; in the mist his disciples had taken him for a ghost, and when Peter threw himself into the water, Jesus drew him ashore just as he was sinking. The healing miracles were explained by a variety of means, among which were special medicines known to Jesus alone. The feeding of the five thousand was interpreted in the following way: When Jesus saw the multitude he said to his disciples: 'We will set a good example to the rich people among them, that they may share their supplies with others', and he began to distribute his own provisions and those of his disciples. This example had its desired effect and there was soon plenty of food for everyone.

The resurrection of Jesus was explained by the theory of apparent death: Jesus had not actually died, but was only in a coma. The spear thrust in his side was, in fact, only a mere surface wound, and in the coolness of the tomb, aided by the aromatic ointments and the noise of a fortuitously occurring storm and earthquake, he recovered consciousness. The earthquake also had the effect of rolling the stone away and Jesus was able to creep out of the tomb unnoticed. However, in consequence of the ill-treatment he had received, he was still very weak and incapable of continuous exertion. He lived quietly, gathering strength for the brief moments in which he appeared to his followers, and finally took his farewell from them on the Mount of Olives. A passing cloud which came between them, hid him from their sight, and he disappeared for ever. Where he died, no one ever knew, and they came to describe his departure as an ascension.

With such explanations Paulus sought to salvage the underlying historical facts of the Gospel story and demonstrate that the biblical narratives were not unreasonable when so interpreted.

3. Neither of these alternatives satisfied Strauss. The first was too extreme and quite against any reasonable interpretation of the biblical narratives; the second was distasteful and sometimes even descended to the level of the absurd. And so

Strauss adopted the third possibility – the mythical interpretation – which provided the best and easiest way out of the
dilemma.

The advantage of Strauss' new theory lay in the fact that the
fictional narratives in the Gospels were henceforth to be
accounted for not by dishonest trickery or gullible stupidity,
but by an unconscious mythologising process in which the
supernatural and historical events recorded in the Gospels were
all deduced from the Old Testament. That was the new principle which Strauss brought to light! In this manner the
dilemma was overcome. Those who had invented the miraculous stories were neither frauds nor fools, but sincere and
intelligent men, deeply immersed, however, in the thought
patterns of their time and culture. If Jesus was the Messiah –
so they would have reasoned – then the messianic prophesies in
the Old Testament must have been fulfilled; and if they had
been fulfilled then it was entirely legitimate to demonstrate
their fulfilment by concrete examples, the actual historicity of
which was neither here nor there. Thus according to Strauss,
the mythical stories in the Gospels arose spontaneously and unconsciously in the minds of certain individuals who were quite
unaware of any dishonesty when they told these stories – which
they themselves had come to believe – to others. The stories
must have been true, since the events had been prophesied in
the Old Testament. These stories soon gained acceptance in the
circles in which they were often related, so that within a very
short period of time they had quickly become established as
historical fact. That, basically, was the new mythical interpretation which Strauss elaborated and refined.

Strauss was not the first to accept the presence of myths
(legends) in the New Testament.[5] In the previous century
Heyne had distinguished between historical myths or saga –
where an actual historical event lies behind the stories – and
philosophical myths, which were invented for an educational
purpose or to explain certain natural events, such as the creation. Eichhorn and Gabler had proceeded further and argued
that angels and miracles were mythical, wherever they might
be found (the Bible included); and G. L. Bauer had gone so

[5] For a more detailed account of the origin of the mythical principle,
see chapter 23.

far as to include the virgin birth and transfiguration of Christ
in the same category. By the 1830s many theologians, including Schleiermacher, held the birth and infancy stories of Jesus
to be fictitious. But all these writers emphasised only the
presence of the mythical (legendary) element in the Gospels;
they did not, however, deal with the problem of how these
stories originated.

When we again consider the sketch of the *Life of Jesus* as
Strauss had envisaged it in 1832, the remarkable thing which
we notice is the complete absence of the mythical interpretation.
Strauss was fully conversant with the mythological ideas of the
time and he expressly states his acceptance of the proclamation
and birth of Jesus as myths: but the mythical interpretation as a
whole is absent and his sketch is anchored, fundamentally, in
the framework of Hegelian speculative philosophy. He recognised only the presence of individual myths in the Gospels, but
had not yet discovered the mythical principle which was to
provide him with the completely new basis for the proposed
book, from that basis contained in the earlier sketch.

It must have been shortly after his return to Tübingen that
Strauss read an anonymous article entitled: 'The different
aspects with which and for which a biographer of Jesus can
work',[6] and it was this article which, more than any other,
revealed to him the possibilities of the new mythical standpoint
which he henceforth adopted. Formerly the presence of isolated myths had been accepted, but had caused no radically new
interpretation of the Gospel history. Strauss now adopted the
principle advocated in the anonymous article, and used it as
the magic formula to solve all the difficulties which the rational
explanation had been unable to surmount. The new principle
provided an explanation of the origin of the myths themselves.
Instead of simply asserting the stories to be mythical or legendary, as had previously been the case, Strauss declared that they
had been written solely in order to prove that Jesus was the
Messiah prophesied in the Old Testament. And so, boldly, in
the first words of the preface to the book, Strauss announces
his intention: the old interpretation is now, at long last, to be
overthrown and replaced by the new and scientific understanding.

[6] See Chapter 23.

It appeared to the author of the work, the first half of which is herewith submitted to the public, that it was time to substitute a new mode of considering the life of Jesus, in place of the antiquated systems of supernaturalism and rationalism...The new point of view which must take their place is mythical.[7]

However, as Strauss pointed out, this did not mean that the whole of the history of Jesus was mythical; only that all the narratives had to be carefully examined to ascertain whether or not there were mythical elements contained within them. The Church had always set out from the double presupposition that the Gospels contained a history, and that this history was a supernatural one. Rationalism had rejected the latter of these presuppositions, but had clung more tenaciously to the former, maintaining that the Gospels present unadulterated, though only natural, history. But science could not rest satisfied with such half-measures and the inquiry had to be extended to the actual historicity of the stories themselves. Yet even if, finally, all had to be declared unhistorical, this – according to Strauss – would be of no great importance for the Christian faith.

The author is aware that the inner core of the Christian faith is completely independent of his critical investigations. The supernatural birth of Christ, his miracles, his resurrection and ascension, remain eternal truths, whatever doubts may be cast on their reality as historical facts.[8]

That was just to console the reader before the great debacle began.

### THE CONTENT OF THE BOOK

'Considered as a literary work', wrote Albert Schweitzer, 'Strauss' first *Life of Jesus* is one of the most perfect in the whole range of scientific literature. In over fourteen hundred pages he has not a superfluous phrase; his analysis descends to the minutest details, but he does not lose his way among them; the style is simple and picturesque, sometimes ironical, but always dignified and distinguished.'[9] The 1550 pages are divided into

[7] *LJ*, I, pp. iii–iv; ET (2nd ed.; 1892) p. xxix.
[8] *Ibid.* I, p. vii; ET, p. xxx.
[9] *Von Reimarus zu Wrede* (Tübingen, 1906), p. 76; ET: *The Quest of the Historical Jesus* (London, 1910) p. 78.

five main parts: an introduction in which Strauss formulates
and explains his mythical principle; a final section which considers the dogmatic importance of Jesus' life; and in between,
the three longest sections, treating the birth and childhood of
Jesus, his public ministry, and finally, his passion, death and
resurrection.

Within this framework the Gospels narratives are examined
singly. First the supernatural interpretation is given and the
errors, contradictions and mistakes so painstakingly pointed
out that the reader can hardly escape the conclusion, such
interpretations are untenable. Then the absurdities of the
rationalistic explanations are brought into full light and shown
to be ridiculous and quite impossible to accept. Finally, as the
*coup de grâce*, Strauss shows how the only feasible explanation
remaining is his own – the mythical interpretation. This three-
fold dialectic is best illustrated by some examples.

The doctrine of the miraculous conception is first stated in its
traditional form and the difficulties – the angel announcing the
birth to Mary, the discrepancies in the genealogies etc. – are
set forth in full detail. Then follow the rationalistic explanations – that the words of the angel in Luke 1, 35 'The Holy
Spirit will come upon you', are to be interpreted subjectively as
meaning that Mary, through a pure and holy delight in God
and through God-pleasing activity (by which the activity of
her husband Joseph is meant) will bear a child; or, another
less acceptable explanation, that Mary had been seduced by
Joseph (or somebody else) masquerading as an angel, and
having been completely deceived, was under the impression
that her conception was the work of the angel. When both
explanations have been shown to be untenable, and uncere-
moniously dispatched, Strauss asserts that the story was invented with no malicious or deceitful motive, but solely to
confirm that Jesus was the Messiah, since it had been prophesied in Is. 7, 14 that a virgin would conceive a son, who would
be the Messiah of Israel. *Ipso facto* – if Jesus was the Messiah,
he must have been born of a virgin, and the story needed no
further evidence to justify its composition.

The same interpretive principle was employed to harmonise
the birthplace of Jesus with the Old Testament. Since it had
been prophesied that the Messiah should be born in Bethlehem,

the story of the census was invented in order to provide a reason for the parents' journey from Nazareth. According to Strauss, however, not only is there no evidence in the New Testament that Jesus was born in Bethlehem, but, in fact, all the indications point to Nazareth as his birthplace.

In similar fashion the appearance of the star which preceded the wise men from the east needed no complicated astronomical explanations, for it was invented in accordance with the prophecy of Num. 24, 17, 'A star shall come out of Jacob'; and the story of the three kings who came to Bethlehem from the east stems from Is. 60, 3: 'And nations shall come to your light, and kings to the brightness of your rising'.

The narratives dealing with the public ministry of Jesus arose from a desire to show that Jesus was a greater prophet than Moses. The forty days' temptation in the wilderness parallels Moses' time on Mount Sinai, and the story was made up in order to fulfil the prophecy in Deut. 18, 15–18, that the Lord will raise up a prophet like unto Moses. Similarly with the story of the transfiguration: Paulus had explained this as the confused testimony of the disciples who, while half-asleep on the mountain-side, mistook the early-morning sun shining upon Jesus' face for a visitation of God. Strauss' explanation was much simpler: since Moses had been transfigured upon the mountain top, Christ must also have a transfiguration experience to show that he was in no way inferior to the first and greatest prophet of Israel.

The healings which Christ performed are likewise attributed to Old Testament prophecies. Thus the stories of cures upon the blind and deaf were written to show the fulfilment of Is. 35, 5: 'Then the eyes of the blind shall be opened, and the ears of the deaf unstopped'; and those narratives relating the healing of paralytics are based on such texts as 'then shall the lame man leap like a hart' (Is. 35, 6).

The section dealing with the raising of the dead follows the usual tripartite structure. The improbabilities of the events are first presented, followed by the rationalistic explanations – the widow's son was not actually dead, but only in a coma, and Jesus, who happened to be passing by, noticed signs of life; the young girl was only in a deep sleep, and Lazarus, too, was either in a coma, or else the whole affair was concocted in order to

C

provide Jesus with the chance to make it appear as if he possessed miraculous powers. Strauss' explanation – ingenious as it
is simple – is that since in the Old Testament Elisha had raised
the dead, then Jesus also could not be portrayed as having any
lesser powers, and thus the conclusion follows:

While Paulus extends to these narratives in the Old Testament the
natural explanation which he has applied to those in the New,
theologians of wider vision have long ago remarked that the
resurrections in the New Testament are nothing other than myths,
which had their origin in the tendency of the early Christian Church
to make her Messiah agree with the type prophesied by the prophets,
and with the messianic ideal.[10]

Next follows a chapter entitled 'Storm, Sea and Fish Stories'[11]
which are obviously – according to Strauss – designed to show
Christ's power over nature. The feeding of the five thousand
is the New Testament parallel to the supernatural feeding of
the Israelites in the wilderness, the power of Elijah to multiply
the widow's oil and meal (1 Kings 17, 8–16), and the feeding
of a multitude by Elisha (2 Kings 5, 42f.). The turning of the
water into wine rests on the story of Moses bringing forth water
from the rock (Ex. 17, 1f.).

In the final section dealing with the passion, death and
resurrection of Jesus, all the historical events are veiled in
obscurity. According to Strauss, Jesus had no precise fore-
knowledge of his death and resurrection, and the prophecies
pertaining to these events – all derived from the Old Testament – were put into his mouth by his disciples. The same
applied to the prophecies of the second coming, although
Strauss here concedes that Jesus may have thought of himself
as returning to earth within a generation. All that can be
known of the final week in Jesus' life is that he was put to death
by crucifixion sometime during the Passover, but the details –
the entry into Jerusalem (derived from Zc. 9, 9), the agony in
the Garden of Gethsemane, the words uttered from the cross,
the spear-thrust and the out-poured blood and water – are all
so untrustworthy that nothing can be accepted as historically
true. Even Joseph of Aramathea's ownership of the grave is
disputed, and the actual place of Jesus' burial remains un-

---

[10] *LJ*, II, p. 173; ET, p. 495.

[11] In the second edition this was changed to the simpler 'Sea Anecdotes'.

known.  The setting of a guard to watch the tomb was a later addition to counter the calumny that the disciples had stolen away the body.

That Jesus actually died is clear – Strauss will have nothing to do with the rationalistic theory of an apparent death – but as regards what happened afterwards, all is shrouded in mist and nothing more can now be ascertained.

What happened to the body is a mystery which Strauss does not attempt to solve.  The appearances of the risen Christ to his disciples are ascribed to mystical visions, behind which lies no objective reality, and which are probably to be accounted for as the result of the stress and strain in the days before and after the crucifixion.  As for the ascension, that was based upon the taking up of Enoch (Gen. 5, 24), and of Elijah in the fiery chariot (2 Kings 2, 11).

Such were the main results of Strauss' investigation.  It was not surprising that the orthodox were enraged, for the bible, which had previously been accepted as a strong and impregnable fortress had now, so it appeared, been almost reduced to a heap of rubble.

Through the results of our investigation, everything that the Christian believes concerning his Jesus now seems to have been annihilated; all encouragement which he draws from this faith has been taken from him; he has been robbed of every consolation. The boundless treasure of truth and life, on which humanity has been nurtured for eighteen centuries, now seems to have been destroyed, the most sublime thrown crashing to the ground, God divested of his grace, man of his dignity, the bond between heaven and earth rent asunder. Piety turns away in horror from such a monstrous act of desecration, and from its impregnable self-assurance of its faith makes the authoritative pronouncement: an insolent criticism may attempt what it will – everything which the Scriptures declare and the Church believes of Christ, will still remain eternally true, and not one iota of it needs to be discarded. Thus at the conclusion of the criticism of the history of Jesus, the task presents itself: to re-establish dogmatically what has been destroyed critically.[12]

The problem which confronted Strauss in the concluding dogmatic section was just how this positive reconstruction was

[12] *LJ*, II, p. 686; ET, p. 757.

to be accomplished. Having already destroyed the historical basis of the Christian faith with the assertion that practically nothing could be known about Jesus, such a reconstruction appeared a difficult, if not hopeless, undertaking, and the only feasible solution appeared to lie in following the route taken by Lessing, who distinguished the accidental truths of history from the necessary truths of reason. And yet, if the historical basis of Jesus' life had been so completely knocked away, how could a Christology be erected? Would not such an undertaking be like that of a man who set out to build his house upon the sand, while cheerfully reassuring his dubious friends that no foundations were necessary? Somehow Strauss' assertion that the virgin birth, miracles, resurrection and ascension of Christ remained eternal truths, although possessing no historical reality, was not terribly convincing and was treated with no small amount of suspicion. Was not Strauss – it was asked – trying to have the best of both theological worlds – the orthodox and the critical? Was he not attempting to cover up the fact that the traditional doctrines of the Christian faith were simply meaningless for him? And was he not trying to build his house with an Hegelian superstructure, thinly disguised by a coating of orthodox paint, and furnished inside with a suite of mythical furniture? That, at least, was how it appeared to the orthodox.

In the preface to his book, Strauss had given the assurance that whatever the outcome of the investigation into the historicity of Jesus' life, the dogmatic significance of his life would remain inviolate. The question was exactly where this dogmatic significance lay; in short, the meaning of Christology. It is here, and only here in the book, that Strauss' Hegelian views make themselves apparent. The problem, in effect, was how to construct a Christology without the traditional view of the historical Jesus as the incarnate Son of God, or, in other words, how to explain the Christian dogma of Jesus as the God-man.

Strauss first of all examined the orthodox Christology, in which the divine and human natures are united in the Person of Jesus Christ. How this unity could subsist, however, was inconceivable to him, and the orthodox view was pronounced untenable. In like manner the Christologies of the rationalists (Jesus viewed as a hero or great teacher), Schleiermacher (Jesus as a man possessing the highest God-consciousness),

Kant (Jesus as the ideal of moral perfection), and de Wette (Jesus as a courageous example of self-sacrifice) were all rejected as inadequate. Finally came the speculative Christology of Hegel, Marheineke and Rosenkranz, and if we are to understand the whole purview of this concluding dogmatic section, it is essential to comprehend what Strauss understands by the unity of God and man; for Strauss viewed God, not as the personal transcendent Creator of the universe, but as the (impersonal) infinite Spirit which manifests itself in the finite forms of the natural world and the human spirit.

When it is said of God that he is spirit, then it follows, since man also is spirit, that the two are not essentially distinct. To speak more particularly, it is the essential property of the Spirit, in separating itself from itself, to remain identical with itself and possess itself in another than itself. Hence the recognition of God as spirit implies that God does not remain an inflexible and immutable Infinite outside of and above the finite, but that he enters into it, dirempts[13] himself and thereby produces the finite, nature, and the human spirit, from which he likewise eternally returns into unity with himself. So little as man, considered as a merely finite spirit clinging to its finite nature, has truth, just so little has God, considered as a merely infinite Spirit shut up in his infinitude, reality. The infinite Spirit is real only when it discloses itself in finite spirits, just as the finite spirit is true only when it merges itself in the infinite. The true and real existence of the Spirit, therefore, is neither God by himself, nor man by himself, but the God-man; neither the infinite alone, nor the finite alone, but the interchange of sacrificial diremption and subsumption between the two, which on the part of God is revelation, on the part of man religion.[14]

But now came the question: If God and man are really one, then how is this unity manifested? The speculative philosophy

[13] The technical term for this philosophical process is 'diremption'. The Spirit dirempts itself when it separates itself from its original state, proceeds out of itself, and enters into a lower state. The complementary process in which the dirempted Spirit now sheds its finite clothing and returns to unity with the infinite Spirit is designated by the German word *Aufhebung*. This carries the sense of raising, or taking up into something higher, while the original state of that raised or taken up is abolished in the process. The German words *aufheben* and *Aufhebung* are best rendered by the English verb 'subsume' and its correlate noun 'subsumption'. These words are used here with the meaning we have defined.

[14] *LJ*, II, pp. 729–30; ET, p. 777.

answered that it had to be manifested in a human individual who would be recognised as the visible God.

It may be said of this God-man, who unites in a single being the other-worldly divine essence and the this-worldly human personality, that he had the divine Spirit for a father and a woman for a mother. In so far as his personality reflects itself not in himself, but in the absolute substance, in so far as it wills to exist only for God and not for itself, he is sinless and perfect. As a man of divine essence he is the power that subdues nature, a worker of miracles; but as God in a human manifestation, he is dependent on nature, subject to its necessities and sufferings, is in a state of abasement. Must he even pay the last tribute to nature? Does not the fact that the human nature is subject to death preclude the idea that nature is one with the divine? No; the God-man dies, and thus proves that the incarnation of God is real, that the infinite Spirit does not scorn to descend into the lowest depths of the finite, because it knows how to find the way of return into itself and is able to retain its identity in the most entire diremption of itself. Further, the God-man, in so far as he is the Spirit reflected in its infinity, stands contrasted with men, is so far as they are limited to their finiteness: hence opposition and contest result, and the death of the God-man becomes a violent one, inflicted by the hands of sinners; so that to physical degradation is added a moral degradation of ignominy and accusation of crime. If God then finds a passage from heaven to the grave, so must a way be discoverable for man from the grave to heaven: the death of the prince of life is the life of mortals. By his entrance into the world as God-man, God showed himself reconciled to man; by his dying, in which act he casts off the limitations of mortality, he showed the way in which he perpetually effects that reconciliation: namely, by dirempting himself into natural existence, which he again subsumes, while ever remaining identical with himself. Inasmuch as the death of the God-man is merely the subsumption of his diremption, it is in fact an exaltation and return to God, and thus the death is necessarily followed by the resurrection and ascension.[15]

It was at just this point that Strauss parted from Rosenkranz, Marheineke and even the Master himself, who wanted to deduce from the philosophical argument of a real unity between the divine and the human, that this unity had been manifested in the person of one individual in history. Strauss

[15] *LJ*, II, p. 731–2; ET, p. 778.

did not dispute that this unity had actually been manifested; only that it was manifest, not in one individual, but in the whole of humanity.

If reality is ascribed to the idea of the unity of the divine and human natures, is this equivalent to the admission that this unity must actually have been once manifested, as it never had been, and never more will be, in one individual? That, indeed, is certainly not the way in which the idea realises itself; it does not pour out its fulness into one exemplar while being niggardly towards all others, but loves to distribute its riches among a multiplicity of exemplars which reciprocally complement each other in the process of life, where individuals continually come into and pass out of existence. And is this no true realisation of the idea? Is not the idea of the unity of the divine and human natures much more a real one in an infinitely higher sense, when I conceive the whole of humanity as its realization, than when I single out one individual as such a realization? Is not an incarnation of God from eternity, a truer one than an incarnation limited to a particular point in time?[16]

Instead of an individual at the centre of Christology, Strauss placed an idea. It is in humanity that the divine Spirit manifests itself, and it is humanity which is to be regarded as the true Christ. The work of the Spirit is to negate the material and sensual life of man, to free the human spirit from its earthly shackles, so that it may rise to the higher spiritual life, which is the true goal of every finite spirit.

Humanity is the union of the two natures – God become man, the infinite dirempting itself into the finite, and the finite spirit remembering its infinitude. Humanity is the child of the visible mother and the invisible father: of nature and spirit. It is the worker of miracles in so far as in the course of human history the spirit more and more completely subjugates nature, both within and around man, until nature lies before it as the inert material on which it exercises its active power; humanity is the sinless existence, for the course of its development is a blameless one; pollution cleaves only to the individual, but is subsumed in the race and its history. It is humanity that dies, rises and ascends to heaven, for from the negation of its finite, natural life there ever proceeds a higher spiritual life; from the subsumption of its finitude as a personal, national and terrestrial spirit, proceeds its unity with the infinite Spirit of the heavens. By faith in this Christ, especially in his death and resurrection, man

---

[16] *Ibid.* ii, p. 734; ET, pp. 779–80.

is justified before God; that is, by the kindling within him of the idea of humanity, the individual man participates in the divine-human life of the species. Now the main element of that idea is that the negation of the merely natural and sensuous life, which is itself the negation of the Spirit (the negation of the negation, therefore) is the sole way for men to attain true spiritual life.[17]

This alone, according to Strauss, is the absolute sense of Christology, and when one considers the great universal process in which the Spirit moves inexorably toward its final goal – the final absorption of the finite into the infinite – there is little significance to be found in an isolated historical event, which is but a small moment in the great process.

Thus when we know the incarnation, death and resurrection, the *duplex negatio affirmat*,[18] as the eternal circulation, the infinitely repeated pulsation of the divine life, what special importance can attach to a single fact, which merely represents this process in a perceptible way. Our age demands to be led in Christology to the idea in the fact, to the race in the individual: a dogmatics which, in its doctrines of Christ, stops short at him as an individual, is no dogmatics, but a devotional talk.[19]

The final half-dozen pages deal with the position of a clergyman holding such views as had been expressed in the book, and these lines were obviously written after Strauss' own dismissal from his position as tutor in the seminary. As Strauss saw the situation there were four ways lying open to such a clergyman: (i) he could seek to change the views of the Church itself; such an attempt, however, was bound to fail. (ii) he could accommodate himself to the traditional teaching; that rendered him liable to the charge of hypocrisy. (iii) he could resign from the Church; but if everyone took this course theology would simply fall into the hands of the unscientific-minded laity. (iv) he could adhere in form to the traditional views, but preach on the moral and spiritual significance of the New Testament events, without reference to their unhistorical character. One might proceed from the story of the resurrection of Christ, but dwell on the being buried and rising again with Christ. And just at this point, we catch a glimpse of Strauss the existentialist.

---

[17] *LJ*, II, pp. 735–6; ET, p. 780.
[18] The double negation which affirms.
[19] *LJ*, II, p. 738; ET, p. 780.

The history is not enough; it is not the whole truth; it must be trans-muted from a past fact into a present one; from an event external to you, it must become your own intimate experience![20]

The existentialist motif is never prominent in Strauss' writ-ings – indeed scarcely ever apparent: it lay deep below the surface of his life. But in these few words, we do catch just a glimpse of the path which theology was later to tread in the twentieth century.

Such was the book and the ideas expressed within its pages. The dark storm-clouds of reaction slowly gathered over the head of the author who dared to set himself in opposition to the holy doctrines of the Church; then they burst with a mighty torrent of criticism, the like of which had not been heard or seen in the theological world since the time of the Reformation.

[20] *Ibid.* ii, p. 743; ET, p. 784.

# 8

## DISMISSAL FROM THE SEMINARY

The first volume of 730 pages appeared on 1 June. On the 11th of the same month a rescript went out from Flatt,[1] the Director of Studies at the seminary, addressed to the Inspectorate, asking whether Strauss' views were compatible with his status as a lecturer. Both Hausrath[2] and Ziegler[3] complain that the length of time – at most ten days – was insufficient for a scholarly reading of the book, but in fact it would have required only a few hours to perceive that Strauss' views were utterly at variance with the traditional teaching of the Church. And so an answer was demanded as to whether a tutor who held the greatest part of the Gospel records to be spurious and mythical could be retained in his position.

The Inspectorate, which consisted of various professors from different faculties, divided, as could be foreseen, into pro- and anti-Strauss factions. Steudel, two other supernaturally inclined theologians and Sigwart – Strauss' enemy in the philosophical faculty – were determined that he should be dismissed. Only Baur defended him, with the protest that Strauss' book was simply the logical development of a certain theological viewpoint in protestant theology. The two remaining members of the board, Kern and Schmid, attempted a half-hearted mediation, but realised that they had no hope of succeeding. And so the report of the Inspectorate, while calling attention to Strauss' scholarly talent, condemned his religious views as clearly being in opposition to the traditional orthodoxy of the Church, and viewed the effect of his ideas upon the students at the seminary with great misgiving.

[1] Karl Christian Flatt (1772–1843), younger brother of the theologian Johann Friedrich Flatt. Although Flatt belonged to the supernaturalist party, he was described by Ziegler as an intelligent and reasonable man.

[2] Hausrath, I, p. 175.          [3] Ziegler, p. 179.

The Director of Studies therewith, in a rescript of 2 July, demanded from Strauss a personal declaration to the question:

How the views concerning the narratives of the words and acts of Jesus expressed in the first volume of your *Life of Jesus* can be harmonized with the position of a teacher of religion within the Protestant Church, who, in sermons to the people as well as in religious instruction for the young, is to build upon the historical foundation of the Gospel, and accordingly, how your official relationship with candidates for the ministry is compatible with such views?[4]

Strauss was thus placed in a difficult position. Not only was he required to justify his views, but he had also to show how such views were compatible with the traditional doctrines of the Church. The long letter in which he replied on 12 July is of so much interest that we reproduce it in full.

The royal, highly-esteemed Director of Studies has bestowed upon me the careful consideration, which I acknowledge with grateful respect, of wishing to receive from me an explanation regarding the question submitted to its decision, namely, how far my position in an educational establishment for future teachers of religion is compatible with the views expressed in my book on the life of Jesus. In that I devote myself deferentially to this privilege, I must begin by claiming the kind indulgence of a highly-esteemed Director of Studies for a comment, without which I would scarcely have enough courage to embark upon the responsibility of answering the question submitted to me. When a young man comes before the public with a work whose basic views depart from – indeed oppose – those generally accepted, this so easily provokes the appearance of a youthful arrogance which flatters itself with paradoxical assertions deviating from the faith of the majority. I well understand how little the highly-esteemed Director could be served by such assurances that this is not the case with me; therefore I content myself by referring to the fact that in this present time, views such as those expressed in my book are not merely the notions of one individual, but conclusions of a whole direction of theological science. Since the end of the last century, as a higher Church authority will well know, philosophy, which has continually entered into a closer alliance with theology, has unceasingly aimed – according to the one view – to spiritualize the positive, factual element in Christianity, according to the other view, to sublimate it; this is especially the case in the most recent important publication in this field – Hegel's philosophy of religion – where this process is carried out in all the main doctrines of the Christian Faith. On the other hand, New Testament criticism has recently made unexpectedly bold progress and questioned the authenticity of several of the main New Testament writings, earlier John's Gospel and now Matthew's, and has generally pronounced the first three Gospels to be post-apostolic works of tradition. Now if these two designated directions in the present-day theology – the philosophical and the critical – worked in this manner, hand in hand with each other, then whoever has become intimate with both, as I have, must find himself challenged to bring these two directions into association, and, supported by the philosophical conviction of the intrinsically true content of the New Testament history, to allow its historical form to be ruthlessly investigated by criticism. Thus during all the years of study, I have been extremely conscious that I was working not merely for myself, but in the service of an essential direction of the theology of our time, and however much error in my book may be due to my personal ineptitude, I cannot believe that this consciousness has deceived me so far as the general content is concerned.

In answer to the question submitted to me as regards my position in the theological seminary, I would emphasize just this: If the basic view expressed in my book belongs to an essential theological direction of the present day, then it does not seem unfitting if this direction is represented in a theological seminary through one of its staff, just as other directions are represented by others. If the book in its essential content contains nothing other than an openly expressed and connected account of that which one could read isolated, dark, and hidden in other books, then it seems to me that just as openness lessens danger, so now here the view in question can no longer deceive through false illusions, but brought into the light in its true form, will scare away many from this time forth, who would previously have been led astray by it. But he who has laid his views before the larger public in a book will seek to obtrude his views as little as possible on the smaller circle of those to whom he must give oral instruction, since the incentive for the more specific oral obtrusion becomes extinguished in the more general written communication. I can testify that since the time when I began to express my theological views in writing, I have kept more silent about them before the students, and have confined myself more to guiding the discussion and to the historical aspect. If the book in question which has now appeared is also being read by the seminary students on account of its relationship to the theological development of the time, then it cannot be more harmful that its author is on the staff of the theological seminary. For if also, according to the wisdom of the younger generation, many students submit themselves to authorities, it has never yet been observed that this created a distinction as to whether or not the originator of a view belonged to the governing body whose personal and disciplinary contacts with the students are more suited to call forth a certain opposition against their views.

But how can one who has adopted, or who may adopt, such views as those presented in my book, remain fitted for the calling of a teacher of religion within the Church? How, in teaching the people, can he build on the historical foundation of Christianity contained in the Gospels, when this foundation has become doubtful for him? At this point may I first be allowed to remark that in my book by no means everything in the gospel history is set in doubt. There is a great distinction made between the acts and events related about Jesus, and his actual words, and in regard to the latter, which in religious instruction for the people and the youth are the most important and efficacious, the content of these words contained in the first three Gospels is not at all impugned, but only here and there with reference to their context; and then again, everything of the deeds and fate of Jesus which is essential for the acknowledgement of his exalted character – his exemplary conduct, his noble, unselfish work and his final sacrifice – remains unshaken. And in particular, impartial judges of my book will not overlook the service I have rendered – even if it is small – through my interpretations, in strongly rebutting even the slightest suspicion which springs out of many of the rationalistic interpretations of Jesus' character.

But – one can object – according to the basic principles of the questionable book there is nothing supernatural remaining in the life of Jesus. But rationalism also allows nothing supernatural to remain, and yet there were, and still are, many rationalists – even those who have expressed their views in books – in the ministry of the Church, in all parts of the country, and not a few whose effectiveness has been acknowledged to be blessed. Yet one can say, rationalism at least allowed the historical details to stand even if it did abolish its supernatural character, while this newest direction destroys the whole historical basis of Christianity. From my own standpoint I must here permit myself the question: What then does religion still possess in the *caput mortuum*[5] of history, which rationalism allowed to remain after extracting everything supernatural, and whether it is not better – and I can only explicate this in the concluding chapter of my work – to find in many parts of the Gospels

---

[5] Dead head.

only an historical clothing of ideas rather than a history bereft of ideas. Indeed, the Christian teacher of religion is supposed to present the content of the Gospel to the people as stories, as true stories: if in this religious instruction he now dissolves their historical character, he undermines the basis of the people's religion; if he allows these stories to remain historical when instructing the people, while he himself regards them as myths, then he becomes dishonest and a liar in the holy place. Here, I believe, that however much of a unity of conviction between the preacher and the congregation must be demanded in essentials, there must always be a certain space left for differences in less essential matters. And these differences will be especially based on the fact that much of what the people still accept as history will be understood by the clergyman only as idea. If we start at the beginning, there is nothing more certain than that the Mosaic account of the creation is accepted by the people as real history; yet how many theologians are there who still conceive the six-day work historically, since indeed for many, an act of creation in time has already become generally unthinkable? When now these theologians treat those narratives in their addresses as history – and that will be certainly the most advisable course as regards the youth and the country folk – we would certainly not want to accuse them of dishonesty, but let it be to their credit that they are conscious of wanting to communicate the same content – which for themselves is present in the form of the abstract concept of an absolute dependence of everything finite upon God – to the people, only in another form, in the concrete form of a story, which is the only form they are able to understand. Since philosophy has begun to influence Christianity, the teachers of religion have had to hold the consciousness of the essential similarity of content under a different form – more historical on the one hand, more conceptual on the other. In order to remain standing within the more recent period, the theologians influenced by the critical philosophy ascribed a merely symbolic value to the Person of Jesus, his supernatural conception, his miracles, his death, his resurrection and ascension; it was only ideas which they sought, in that, to a lesser or greater degree, they pushed history into the background, and yet those theologians – so far as they re-presented their ideas to the people only in the form of this history – remained unhampered in their positions and activity in the Church.

But – it can be said – the effectiveness of such a clergyman will be even greater when his conviction about form and content is identical with that of his congregation. I doubt whether there are such clergymen and whether, if there should be one, he, along with those who tend to this view, can have taken science seriously, is a question which I must leave undecided. But I cannot hold that a blessed ministry – even with this difference of conviction – is impossible. Certainly I have only had a limited experience in the practical side of the Church; but notwithstanding the fact that my views at that time were the same as they are now, I was still able to notice that I did not leave the consciousness of the congregation disturbed, because I did not presume to leave out or to change anything of the doctrines of their faith; but moving within the Church forms, I strove in each of them to find something for myself by translating them into my own scientific way of thinking. At any rate, the task of a clergyman, in his addresses to the people, will become more difficult, the more he must make a detour and translate his own thoughts from the form which they have in him into the popular form; but this difficulty lies in the process of education of our time and the clergyman is not to be denounced when he does not spare himself this greater trouble. I have myself, already, earlier, seriously considered the question whether a theologian whose conviction deviates is not obliged to resign his position in the ministry; I have however found that the contrary is our obligation. If all those who have accepted the critical and sceptical elements of the time wanted to resign from the ministry, only the unscientific faith would finally remain to it; the critical doubting would devolve onto the educated in the congregation and the Church would have to split into two halves between which, finally, agreement would be no longer possible; but as against this, so long as the sceptical and critical direction remains represented in the ministry, such a mediation, and therewith a continuing progress of religious and theological education, is assured.

I have herewith availed myself of the freedom permitted me by the highly-esteemed Director of Studies to speak on my own behalf, certainly in a manner which makes it necessary for me, finally, to excuse both the detailed way in which it is written by the importance which the matter has for me, and also the candid speech, by the confidence in the goodness and indulgence of the highly-esteemed higher Church authority, into whose hands I commit my concern with the glad confidence that it will not decide otherwise than is necessitated by the inseparable well-being of Church and Science.

I remain most respectfully,
Tutor Strauss.[6]

Flatt found much ambiguity in Strauss' declaration and in his report to the Ministry of Church and School he advised

[6] Ziegler, pp. 183–90.

that Strauss should be removed from the seminary for the sake of maintaining the confidence of the people. For the general public, he urged, would receive the impression that a seminary where Strauss was a teacher and supervisor was incompetently governed; and even if Strauss did not express his views openly to the students, the whole seminary knew all too well what he thought. Thus to pacify these doubts and remove the bad influence which Strauss' views would cause among the students, it was recommended that he be transferred to the secondary school in Ludwigsburg as a teacher having responsibility for classical languages. Moreover, Flatt requested that in the event of Strauss refusing to comply with this decision, it should be made quite clear to him that he had no hope of any other position in the Church.

The Minister, Herr von Schlayer, was somewhat inclined in a liberal direction and not unsympathetic to Strauss' case. However, there was little he could do in the face of the great opposition which Strauss' book had provoked, and after softening the recommendation by describing Strauss' removal (it was in effect a dismissal) as a 'call' to the new position in Ludwigsburg, and informing Director Flatt that it was in no wise his responsibility to pronounce on Strauss' chances of obtaining another position within the Church, he had no option but to accede to the proposed course of action.

Strauss, on his part, had little choice but to accept the new 'call'. Since, however, he was still engaged on the second half of his book, he asked permission to remain a few weeks longer in Tübingen so that he might make the final additions and corrections. This request was granted and the second volume appeared in October 1835.[7] It must have been during this period that the following incident took place which Robert von Mohl related in his memoirs.

My first meeting with Strauss was not occasioned by anything pleasant. The students understandably took Strauss' side; the whole affair fermented mightily amongst them and it was finally resolved to make public demonstrations in his favour – torch-light processions and the like. This was now most disagreeable to the University authorities; they feared disorder, the necessity of intervention and punishment, dissatisfaction of the government. I had just been

[7] Not in 1836, as appears on the title page; Hausrath, 1, p. 182.

appointed Rector and received the commission to hinder things where it was possible. It was clear to me that to forbid the whole thing would only pour oil on the fire; I therefore decided to deal with Strauss personally and attempt to persuade him that he himself should decline the intended ovations. I found the young man very understanding and calm, although at the beginning little inclined to accede to my request. It was certainly asking a lot that he himself, who had been so severely dealt with and whose whole career was threatened, should hinder tokens of sympathy and approval. Yet in the end, through describing the not merely possible, but highly probable consequences, I won his consent. I have always esteemed him highly for this. A hundred others would not have done it, least of all, I believe, his friend Vischer.[8]

[8] *Lebenserinnerungen* (Stuttgart and Leipzig, 1902) I, p. 210.

# 9

---

# THE REACTION AND COUNTER-
REACTION

Thrown like a fire-bomb into the tinder-dry pietistic forest
of Württemberg, it was indeed not surprising that the *Life of
Jesus* ignited a conflagration which quickly spread through
the whole of Germany. What in fact roused the anger of the
orthodox was not the Hegelian conclusion – which was hardly
more than a theological appendix – but the fact that Strauss'
book – if its conclusions were to be accepted – would demolish
the whole historical foundation of the Christian faith. The
bastion on which the Reformation had been built now seemed
to have been completely undermined, and the mighty fortress
about to collapse. Those who had set their faith on the biblical
Christ now learnt that practically nothing could be known
about the historical Jesus. God, Christ, the Bible – all appeared
to have been overthrown by the intensity of the daring frontal
assault, so that like the temple of Jerusalem, not one stone remained upon another.

In the inevitable nature of the treatment which here consummated
itself like a process of nature, in this dispassionate objectivity with
which the author, as it were, steps back from his work and is only
the man who tabulates and counts the individual posts, lay the
imposing, or perhaps more correctly, the alarming feature of the
book. It stood there with the hard indifference of fate; it was the
final account drawn up in the criticism of the Gospel history and
the inventory read: Bankrupt! For this reason the effect of the
work was enormous. An electric shock ripped through the whole
of German theology. Not since the time of the Wolfenbüttel
Fragments and the polemical writings of their famous editor[1] had

---

[1] Gotthold Ephraim Lessing (1729–81). The reference is to Lessing's
publication of excerpts from the writings of Reimarus and the subsequent
dispute with Götze.

the theological world been set in a similar agitation. The sensation which this work provoked, above all in Tübingen and Württemberg, soon spread, like an avalanche gathering momentum, through the whole of Germany and far beyond her borders.[2]

The implications of this attack were only too well understood: no longer could the Bible be trusted, and worse – the Jesus of the Bible was no longer the Son of God, as he had been traditionally understood to be. Strauss had denied the divinity of Christ, and when the orthodox read the words of the apostle: 'Who is the liar but he who denies that Jesus is the Christ. This is the antichrist, he who denies the Father and the Son',[3] it was not difficult to put two and two together and conclude that the antichrist had already appeared on earth in the person of the author of the *Life of Jesus*. Moreover the fact that in the Old Testament jackals and ostriches[4] inhabit the waste-land which God in his wrath has forsaken[5] lent added weight to this view, and when a learned pietist discovered that the numerical equivalents of the Hebrew letters forming Strauss' name added up to 666,[6] then it seemed that the world might really come to its end in 1836, the date calculated by the great biblical exegete Johann Albrecht Bengel.

Basically, however, the pietists viewed the whole affair not as an intellectual problem, but rather as a matter of faith. If Strauss denied the historicity of the bible, that only showed him to be an unbeliever, and the following friendly letter from a pietist pastor expresssed the hope that Strauss would soon realise his error, turn to the Saviour for forgiveness and be speedily converted.

Finally my worthy Herr Doctor, do not expect here the slightest scholarly proof. This letter shall display its power to you by the grace and mercy of God, without any erudition, and I address myself to him who can speak best of all – even to the most learned. My words are these: 'Lord Jesus! Hear me for thy name's sake and may Herr Doctor Strauss perceive in a living way that thy Gospel and the Bible are true; make him to be a living witness of thy Word, and work a miracle in him as thou didst in Paul. Do that Lord and

[2] Karl Schwarz, *Zur Geschichte der neuesten Theologie* (4th ed.; Leipzig, 1869) p. 97.    [3] 1 John 2, 22.

[4] 'Strauss' is the German word for ostrich.

[5] Is. 13, 21; 34, 13; Job 30, 29.

[6] The number of the beast (Rev. 13, 18).

I hope in thee!' See, my worthy Herr Doctor, the matter depends from now on on me and my hope. Live well, and be completely convinced that nothing but love and goodwill have driven me to writing this letter. With these thoughts I have the honour with all due respect to be the most-obedient servant of my highly-honoured Herr Doctor,

———————

Pastor.[7]

The reaction to the book among the orthodox varied considerably between those who saw its author as the servant of Satan and wanted the work banned, and those who adopted a more conciliatory line and set their hopes on refuting it with rational and scientific explanations. On the whole, the majority of the orthodox theologians[8] condemned the book, although not a few attempted to make concessions at various points. Tholuck,[9] for instance, rejected Strauss' conclusions on the ground that they had been dictated in advance by his presupposition that miracles were impossible; yet Tholuck himself allowed that miracles might possibly be explained by unknown natural powers which Christ possessed, and even went as far as acknowledging the presence of mythical elements in the New Testament. Neander[10] also toyed with the scientific explanation and suggested that Christ's miracles might be explained as an influencing of nature. With regard to the miracle at Cana, Christ might – he thought – have communicated to the water a higher power whereby it was enabled to produce the same effect as wine.

[7] Cited Hausrath, I, pp. 233–4. Strauss published the letter (omitting the pastor's name) in a leading Church journal.

[8] The more important works were written by J. C. F. Steudel; C. A. Eschenmayer; Wilhelm Hoffmann; K. H. Sack; Adolf Harless; J. P. Lange; August Neander; F. A. G. Tholuck; Friedrich Kern; Karl Ullmann; Julius Müller.

[9] *Über die Glaubwürdigkeit der evangelischen Geschiche, zugleich eine Kritik des Lebens Jesu von Strauss, für theologische und nicht theologische Leser dargestellt* (Hamburg, 1836), Friedrich August Gotttreu Tholuck (1799–1877) was the most influential theologian among the pietists during the middle years of the eighteenth century. He was professor of theology at Halle from 1826 until his death.

[10] *Das Leben Jesu Christi* (Hamburg, 1837). Neander (1786–1850) was professor of theology in Berlin and the most acclaimed Church historian during the first half of the century.

More important to Strauss was the criticism of his Tübingen student friend Wilhelm Hoffman.[11] Two years older than Strauss, Hoffman had formerly been a convinced Hegelian and was one of the leaders in the group which – much to Steudel's annoyance – used to meet on Sunday morning to study the speculative philosophy, instead of attending Church. Not only had Hoffman encouraged Strauss in his study of Hegel; he had even presented him with a copy of Hegel's *Phenomenology* as a birthday present. However, during his curacy Hoffman renounced his Hegelian ideas and became a fervent pietist who felt it his duty to take up arms against the false teaching of his former friend. Strauss had not expected an attack from this quarter and although in no way convinced by Hoffmann's arguments, he was hurt by the fact that such strong and hard criticism had come from one with whom he had once been so friendly.

The fear that Strauss' views would unsettle the faith of the people was indeed widespread and Ullmann[12] even expressed his regret that the book had not been written in Latin to prevent it becoming known among the laity. An anonymous dialogue written at this period portrays a schoolmaster who has been persuaded into reading Strauss' book, coming in distress to a clergyman, anxious to get rid of the doubts which the book has aroused in him. After he has successfully been cured, the reverend gentleman dismisses him with the following exhortation:

Now I hope that after the experience you have had, you will in future refrain from reading books of this kind; they are not written for you, their subject matter does not fall within your profession and if they require a refutation you are not equipped for the task. You may be quite sure that anything useful or profitable will reach you through the proper channel and in the right way, and, that being so, there is no need for you to jeopardise any part of your peace of mind.[13]

[11] *Das Leben Jesu kritisch bearbeitet von Dr. D. F. Strauss* (Stuttgart, 1836).

[12] Karl Ullmann (1796–1869), professor of theology in Heidelberg and (from 1829–36) in Halle, was co-founder of the *Theologische Studien und Kritiken*. His review of Strauss' book is contained in the 1836 number, pp. 770–816.

[13] *Zwei Gespräche über die Ansicht des Herrn Dr. Strauss von der evangelischen Geschichte* (Jena, 1839). Quoted Schweitzer, *Geschichte der Leben Jesu Forschung*, pp. 98–9; ET, pp. 100–1.

On the whole it was the rationalists[14] who had come off worst, for Strauss had held up their explanations of the miracle stories to ridicule and ruthlessly exposed the ludicrous nature of their arguments. And yet it was the rationalists who were the mildest of all in their replies. It was as if they all knew that their explanations were quite untenable, and only required to see the objections in black and white before admitting – at least to themselves – that Strauss had certainly proposed a better solution. Paulus especially had most cause to be bitter over the way that Strauss had poured out his scorn upon his rationalistic arguments, and yet there was no rancour in the very friendly and respectful review which he contributed. 'It was', wrote Albert Schweitzer, 'as though he felt that the end of rationalism had come, but that, in the person of the enemy who had defeated it, the pure love of truth – even if in another form – which was the only thing that really mattered, would triumph over all the forces of reaction.'[15]

The reaction of the orthodox was, of course, expected, but Strauss had hoped that the rationalists at least might have admitted the absurdities to which their explanations had led. That they failed to acknowledge his mythical interpretation as the key to unlock all mysteries in the Gospel stories was a bitter pill for him.

Nor was it any better with the theologians whose liberal views were akin to his own. For his book had brought down the wrath of the orthodox not merely upon his own head, but upon all those attempting to pursue a mediating and conciliatory line; it dashed any hope of a relaxation of theological freedom and heightened the struggle between the orthodox and liberal lines of thought. It was as a consequence of this fact that the theologians were forced to give at least a token sign of their orthodoxy, and, as Baur later remarked, the best way of obtaining theological promotion was to write a critical refutation of Strauss.

But the real grievance of the liberal theologians and clergy against the book was that Strauss had forced them to examine their consciences. Hase[16] used to say in his lectures that the

---

[14] Notably H. E. G. Paulus; W. M. L. de Wette; J. F. Röhr; K. G. Bretschneider.     [15] *Geschichte der Leben Jesu Forschung*, p. 102; ET, p. 104.
[16] Karl August von Hase (1800–90) was professor of theology in Jena.

book 'was a kind of decision whether one could remain in the ministry', and Baur wrote some years afterwards:

It was as if in this book a mirror had been held up to the inner selves of all the theologians. They had only one choice – either to acknowledge that they also had already taken the path of the critic who was now in such bad odour and that they could scarcely do anything other than continue with him on the same way, or else, to deny their former freer convictions and surrender unconditionally to the ecclesiastical orthodoxy, which, in the face of such new innovations, appeared all the more to offer the best protection for State and Church. The passionate outcry which immediately arose from so many sides, the crude tumultuous polemic with which one could not quickly enough hurry to write a refutation, the excited haste with which almost everyone who ascribed a literary significance to himself – or who hoped to gain it by using such an opportunity – believed himself obliged to present the public with documentary evidence that he was unable to acknowledge such principles and views as his own,[17] that he knew all too well how to assess their dangerous consequences and made it his primary business to set himself against these ideas – such and similar happenings showed clearly how the great majority decided to choose.[18]

Even in the Catholic world Strauss' book aroused quite a sensation and the papal troops, under the leadership of Hug,[19] finally sunk their differences with the heretical protestants and threw themselves into battle against the arch-heretic Strauss. The Germans were the first to take up arms, but the Frenchman Edgar Quinet[20] also sounded a warning trumpet blast and called for a mighty effort to oppose the new danger which confronted not only protestantism, but the sacred city itself.

Barbarians with their strange gods are streaming from every quarter of the horizon and preparing to besiege the holy city of Rome. As Leo once went forth to meet Attila, so now it is time for the Papacy also to put on its purple and come forth and, if it is still possible, to terrify with a mere wave of the hand that devastating horde back into the wilderness of morality which is its native home.[21]

---

[17] Baur himself falls under his own condemnation. See next chapter.
[18] *Kritische Untersuchungen über die kanonischen Evangelien* (Tübingen, 1847), p. 49.
[19] J. L. Hug (1765–1846) was professor of theology in Freiburg.
[20] 'De la vie de Jésus par le docteur Strauss', *Revue des deux mondes* (4th series; 1838) xvi, pp. 585–629.     [21] *Ibid.* 627–8.

There were in the main, three points around which the discussion of Strauss' book revolved:

### 1. The Relationship between Myth and History

Herein lay the very heart of the whole problem – how to ascertain which parts of the Gospel narratives were historical and which parts were mythical. It was clear that there had to be at least some historical basis behind the life of Jesus as portrayed in the Gospels; on the other hand it was possible that a mythical element also existed and the question was whether the evidence adduced in its favour was convincing. Were the Gospel stories which contained a miraculous or supernatural element all explicable by Strauss' mythical theory? Was it really possible to explain the feeding of the five thousand by the feeding of the Israelites with manna in the wilderness or the miraculous feeding of a multitude by Elisha? Here was the dubious part in Strauss' interpretation. 'This story', wrote Albert Schweitzer 'has far too much individuality to be so explained, and stands, moreover, in a much too closely connected historical connection. There must be some or other historical fact which lies behind it. It is not a myth, but it contains myth.'[22]

But this, in effect, was simply throwing the ball back to the rationalists. As soon as it was admitted that the story actually had an historical basis, then one was obliged to speculate what this basis could have been – unless one simply wanted to evade the whole issue by declaring everything a great mystery impenetrable to historical investigation. That an historical core was present in the Gospel could hardly be questioned; but the problem was to extract this core and get behind the sources to the original historical Jesus. Who was this Jesus? This was the question which Strauss set in motion and which has busied theologians ever since. Was Jesus merely a great moral teacher, a religious genius possessing amazing supernatural and parapsychic powers? If so, then the miracles might be capable of being interpreted rationally, as Paulus had done. But such an explanation would have damaged the whole unity of Strauss'

[22] *Geschichte der Leben Jesu Forschung*, p. 82; ET, p. 84.

mythical interpretation and the problem of the relationship between myth and history would have required a broader and more complex solution than that proposed by Strauss in 1835.

## 2. The Relationship between the historical Jesus and the supernatural Christ

The main bone of contention in Strauss' book was the fact that his portrayal of Jesus had been so negative. The Jesus of history was no longer the divine incarnate Son of God, but a merely human figure, who could only be fleetingly glimpsed through the historical mists which swirled about him. Strauss had shown only what Jesus was not, but had not explained what he was.

But how could Strauss say anything definite or positive? He did not accept the traditional doctrine of Christ's divinity and the old Church dogmas were, for him, just empty formulations. And if the historical records were so untrustworthy that practically nothing certain could be known about Jesus, then Strauss' portrait could scarcely have been any different from what it was.

One thing, however, did emerge from all the arguments, namely, that the reality of the biblical conception of the supernatural Christ was ultimately dependent upon the reality of the historical Jesus. If the Jesus portrayed in the Gospels was not the historical Jesus as he really was, then the whole dogma of the supernatural Christ was worthless. That was one of the results which emerged from the whole discussion, and it was ultimately this question which precipitated the historical investigation of the Gospel sources and, more immediately, of the fourth Gospel.

## 3. The Relationship between the Fourth Gospel and the Synoptics

The great debate which arose over the genuineness of the Gospel of John was occasioned by Strauss' denial of its authenticity. At the beginning of the nineteenth century John had been regarded as the most historically accurate of all the

Gospels. It is true that doubts as to its authenticity had been previously expressed, and in 1820 the famous rationalist Bretschneider had collected many of them together in his *Probabilia*.[23] At the time the book had caused some stir, but Schleiermacher had defended the Gospel's apostolic authority, and since it contained fewer miracles than the other Gospels it was the favourite Gospel of the rationalists. Thus the acceptance of its genuineness was never seriously in danger and even Bretschneider declared that he had been brought to a better opinion through the controversy. During the next 15 years, therefore, the historicity of the Gospel remained virtually undisputed until Strauss' assertion that John was in fact inferior to the Synoptics as an historical source once more revived the argument.

The surprising thing, according to Albert Schweitzer, was that of all Strauss' critics only Hengstenberg[24] really perceived what was at stake.[25] He alone understood that those theologians who wanted to compromise on the authority of the Scriptures were slowly being driven back into an indefensible fortress; that having admitted the existence of mythical elements in the Old Testament, and then at the beginning and end of the Gospel history, they were now obliged to abandon the Synoptics in favour of John. But even here they were not safe, and Strauss was at the gate besieging their last stronghold.

They withdrew into the Gospel of John as into a fortress and boasted that they were safe there, although they could not suppress a secret consciousness that they held it only at the enemy's pleasure; now the enemy has appeared before it armed with the same weapons

---

[23] *Probabilia de evangelii et epistolarum Ioannis Apostoli: indole et origine, eruditorum iudiciis modeste subjecit* (Leipzig, 1820). Karl Gottlieb Bretschneider (1776–1848) was Superintendent General of the Church in Gotha.

[24] Ernst Wilhelm Hengstenberg (1802–69) was a brilliant student with rationalistic inclinations. Following his conversion he decided to study theology and at the age of 22 became a lecturer in the theological faculty at the University of Berlin – at that time the leading university in Prussia – where he taught Aramaic, Hebrew and Syriac. In 1828 he was appointed full professor and through the *Evangelische Kirchenzeitung* – the conservative Church newspaper of which he was founder and editor – he exercised a commanding influence in the Church for almost 40 years. A doughty defender of the orthodox faith, he was the tireless foe of all rationalism, pantheism and unbelief.

[25] Schweitzer, *Geschichte der Leben Jesu Forschung*, p. 114; ET, p. 115.

with which he was formerly victorious; the Gospel of John is now in as desperate a plight as the Synoptics had previously been. The time has come to make a bold decision, a decisive choice; either they must surrender everything, or else successively re-occupy the more advanced positions which they had earlier successively abandoned.[26]

The on-going dispute over the relationship between John and the Synoptics does not further concern us here, but what must be noticed is that Strauss' book opened up the whole field of Gospel criticism. There is a very real sense in which the whole flood of writings on the Synoptic and Johannine problem originated with his *Life of Jesus*, which first emancipated these questions from a conservative and orthodox framework and brought them out into the open air for free discussion.

## THE *STREITSCHRIFTEN*[27]

Strauss had taken up his new position at the school in Ludwigsburg in November 1835, but he found little satisfaction in the tedious, time-consuming, and generally disagreeable task of correcting Latin exercises. The books he required were usually unavailable in Ludwigsburg and he was forced to make a journey into Stuttgart to obtain them. Added to these difficulties was the upleasantness at home caused by the constant strife between himself and his father; and so for all these reasons, and especially that he might have the necessary time to spend on his *Streitschriften*, he resigned from his post at the school in December 1836, and took up residence in Stuttgart.

We have seen something of the scope of the reaction which followed the publication of the *Life of Jesus*, although the intensity of this reaction can hardly be gauged today. Not only in the theological seminaries did the book produce a great sensation and continuing controversy over the problems which it raised, but in every church, in every town, in an age when the church formed the central position in the lives of the

[26] *EKZ*, Vorwort (1836) p. 44; cited Schweitzer, *Geschichte der Leben Jesu Forschung*, p. 114; ET, p. 116.

[27] *Streitschriften zur Verteidigung meiner Schrift über das Leben Jesu und zur Charakteristik der gegenwärtigen Theologie* [*Polemical Writings in Defence of my Book on the Life of Jesus and characterizing present-day theology*] (Tübingen, 1837).

majority of the populace, Strauss' views were the focal point of all religious discussion.

And now came the counter-reaction from Strauss. It had been his original intention to write a series of *Streitschriften* – a whole 'gallery' – dealing with each of his opponents individually, but after the first three, in which he settled accounts with his orthodox and Hegelian opponents, he felt he had written enough. He had planned another against the rationalists, but since Paulus had treated him in such a friendly manner and since he had already said all that required to be said about them, he lost his desire to continue the attacks.

The first of the three *Streitschriften* was devoted to Strauss' old professor of theology in Tübingen, the rational-super-naturalist Steudel. Steudel had published a rather long and weary criticism of the *Life of Jesus*[28] and Strauss, in return, gave vent to the anger he had for so long suppressed. Certainly Steudel's book had been mild and courteous in tone and hardly deserved the vituperative scorn which Strauss poured upon it, but on the other hand it was a mixture of traditional belief and compromising rationalistic explanations, and for such com-promises Strauss had no time.

Yes, I hate and despise that pious, meek and fearful talk in scientific investigations, which all the way along threatens the reader with the loss of his salvation, and I know why I hate and despise it. In scientific matters the Spirit is free: it is supposed to lift the head to freedom, not sink it to slavery; for science, there exists directly nothing holy, but only truth: truth however demands no pious clouds of incense, but clarity of thinking and speaking: yet the Spirit, where he is conscious of following the truth, knows one danger: but he is completely at peace about the goal to which the danger will lead him, convinced that it will be the best. But all that pious, oppressive element in matters of science can only serve to make thinking shy and embarrassed, to corrupt it with strange considerations, and instead of leading it to the goal – which is truth – it leads it backwards in the circle where for a long time prejudice stood, and also wishes to remain henceforth.[29]

[28] *Vorläufig zu Beherzigendes bey Würdigung der Frage über die historische oder mythische Grundlage des Lebens Jesu, wie die kanonischen Evangelien dieses vorstellen, vorgehalten aus dem Bewusstsein eines Gläubigen, der den Supranaturalisten beigezählt wird, zur Beruhigung der Gemüther* (Tübingen, 1835).

[29] *Streitschriften*, i, pp. 92–3.

Far more hostile than Steudel's book was the polemic of Eschenmayer, Strauss' bitter opponent in the philosophical faculty. The title of Eschenmayer's book *The Ischariotism of our Days*[30] set the tone of the debate and in this interesting and readable work, Strauss is portrayed as the most recent Judas in the Church, and accused of blaspheming against the Holy Spirit. Strauss' counter polemic in the first part of the second *Streitschrift* described Eschenmayer's work as a product of decadent thinking and intellectual imbecility, a proof of his pious intolerance in condemning everything he could not understand. Eschenmayer was not to be outdone and in a new publication[31] in which he described his observations on the case of a demon-possessed girl, he cited Strauss' book as evidence of the existence of Satan. At the close of the work he portrayed an amusing contest in hell where the devil was to present a prize to the one who had done the most harm to Christianity.

All run thither, but the prize now hovers between two: between a grey-headed, gay old man (Dr. Paulus) and a young controversialist scarcely weaned from the milk of the muses (Dr. Strauss).

The old man cries: 'I deserve the prize. For fifty years all my endeavour has aimed at divesting the Jewish Jesus of his divine Sonship. Thousands of pupils have imbibed my basic principles etc. etc. What has this young puppy to point to in comparison with my service?'

The youth answers: 'Dear Satan, you see the future with certainty, that I will be able to accomplish ten times more for the good cause than this old burnt-out oil-lamp. For what the old man allowed to remain, I have completely wiped out etc. etc.'

And now the youth receives the prize and the old man the 'highly-commended'.[32]

The second part of this second *Streitschrift* was directed against the literary critic Wolfgang Menzel, editor of an influential journal in Stuttgart. Menzel, a strong opponent of the idea that Goethe was the be-all and end-all of German literature, had attacked Goethe as an irreligious egoist and poor

[30] *Der Ischariotismus unserer Tage* (Tübingen, 1835).
[31] *Conflict zwischen Himmel und Hölle, an dem Dämon eines besessenen Mädchens beobachtet von Professor C. A. Eschenmayer. Nebst ein Wort von Dr Strauss* (Tübingen, 1837).    [32] Cited Hausrath, I, p. 258.

patriot, and then turned his guns on the younger writers, Heinrich Heine, Gutzkow[33] and finally, Strauss. Menzel, however, was theologically unimportant and Strauss' critique, which was mainly a discussion of Goethe, recent philosophy, and morality, added nothing of significance to the theological debate.

The third *Streitschrift* was divided into three parts, the first being devoted to Hengstenberg, the second to the Hegelians, and the third to Julius Müller[34] and Ullmann.

Strauss and Hengstenberg had much in common in that both wanted nothing to do with half-way compromise solutions. Both had a certain respect for each other – the whole was always better than the half – and for this reason Hengstenberg greeted Strauss' book as 'one of the most pleasing contributions to the field of recent theological literature',[35] since it was through and through consistent and showed clearly where the Hegelian philosophy would lead when taken to its logical conclusion.

Strauss has done nothing more than bring the Spirit of the age to consciousness of itself and of the necessary consequences which proceed from its essential character; he has taught it to strip away the extraneous elements which still adhere to it because of a lack of thorough development.[36]

In the opinion of Hengstenberg it was a case of all or nothing. If one granted the presence of myths in the Old Testament then the presence of myths in the New had also to be conceded; one either held fast to the whole, or threw everything overboard. Thus Hengstenberg found Strauss' mythical views no worse than those of the rationalists; the honourable thing about Strauss was that he no longer bothered to hide his atheism under a rationalistic veneer, but came out into the open.

Two peoples are in the womb of our time and only two. They will oppose each other ever more unyieldingly and resolutely. Unbelief will more and more cast off elements of belief to which it still clings,

[33] K. F. Gutzkow (1811–78), German novelist and dramatist whose novel *Wally die Zweiflerin* (1835) possessed an anti-religious tendency and advocated extra-marital relations.

[34] Julius Müller (1801–78), professor of theology in Marburg and from 1837 in Halle. His review of Strauss' book is found in *TSK* (1836) pp. 816–90.

[35] *EKZ* (1836) p. 382.          [36] *Ibid.* (1836) p. 434.

and belief will do likewise with elements of unbelief. And from this process inestimable blessing will arise.[37]

Hengstenberg had no intention of entering into details of New Testament criticism and made no scientific attempt as such to refute Strauss' views. The whole question of the mythical interpretation, as he saw it, was fundamentally a matter of the initial premises from which one started. If Strauss was an unbeliever, then all he had written was dominated by his atheistic (or pantheistic) presuppositions; the question was not, essentially, concerned with knowledge, but with faith – by which Hengstenberg did not mean a blind faith without intellect, but an intellectual understanding and trust which was not dominated by unbelief.

Strauss, on his part, greeted Hengstenberg's criticism with a certain pleasure.

I must admit, that I am not unhappy at having to do with the *Evangelische Kirchenzeitung*. One knows where one is with it and what to expect from it. At a time when the intellectual directions run through each other in such a criss-cross way and when in consequence of the most multifarious crossing of the races almost no pure type still exists, it makes a good impression to meet once again an unmixed colour, a decided direction.[38]

For Strauss, however, the question of the mythical element in the Scriptures could not be made a matter of faith, but had to be decided by scientific arguments. For if there were discrepancies and contradictions in the Bible, then it simply proved that the biblical narratives were completely untrustworthy and for the most part unhistorical. And if the Bible could not be trusted, then Hengstenberg's beliefs were void of any scientific or historical foundation. It was at this point that the battle had to be joined.

The second part of the third *Streitschrift* was devoted to the Hegelians, who had tried to shut their eyes to the fact that the black-sheep, Strauss, was also one of the family. For the speculative philosophy had been brought into disrepute by Strauss' book and opponents of the Hegelians were not slow to seize upon the pernicious consequences which Strauss had drawn, with the cry: 'See! That's where the Hegelian philosophy

[37] *Ibid.* Vorwort (1836) p. 44.          [38] *Streitschriften*, III, p. 117.

leads you!' Whereupon the Hegelians naturally hastened to
declare that Strauss did not belong to them. But not only did
the *Life of Jesus* bring odium upon the followers of Hegel; it
also caused consternation in the camp itself, since its conclusions
threatened the Hegelian attempt at a synthesis between philosophy and theology. A month after the publication of the first
volume of the *Life of Jesus*, Vatke was visiting Marheineke.[39]

'Now what do you say about our Strauss?' exclaimed Vatke.

'It's bad for us, we won't overcome this blow!'

'Why not? Now's just the time to get into the fray. Isn't it a joy
to be a theologian?'

'It was, dear Vatke; but you were right by the way about David
Strauss – what has this man made of himself?'[40]

Strauss divided the Hegelians into three groups: the right
wing consisting of Bruno Bauer[41] and Göschel;[42] the centre
represented by Rosenkranz,[43] and the left wing – himself.
Those on the right wing stood solidly for the view that the
unity of divine and human nature was realised in the historical
individual Jesus; they also wanted to retain the Hegelian concept of the reality of miracles – the concept and the terminology,
but not the historical reality. Bauer wrote a highly critical
review of the first volume of Strauss' book,[44] in which he reproached Strauss for rejecting the miraculous element in
Christianity. The whole review was clothed in the most abstruse
and complex Hegelian terminology and Strauss expressed his
disgust with it in a most interesting letter to Vatke.

A more foolish piece of pen-pushing than this review I have not yet
seen: complete ignorance of what criticism is, and its relation to
speculation: phrases with which a definite conception is intimately

[39] Konrad Philip Marheineke (1780–1846) was from 1811 professor of
theology in Berlin. The best known of the early Hegelian theologians, he
occupied an independent position between those belonging to the right
wing and Rosenkranz in the centre.

[40] Benecke, pp. 185–6.

[41] Bruno Bauer (1809–82), from 1834–9 lecturer in the Berlin theological
faculty, slowly drifted into atheism and a total denial of the historical
authenticity of the Gospel records.

[42] Karl Friedrich Göschel (1784–1861), a lawyer, sought to harmonise
philosophy and theology by means of the speculative philosophy.

[43] Karl Rosenkranz (1805–79), professor of philosophy in Königsberg.

[44] *JWK* (1835) II, pp. 879–911.

bound up; and just the aim of my work has been to make an end of the lordship of this conception. Can one read anything more ridiculous than the deduction of the Virgin conception? And this Herr Bauer, in a letter which I received just recently, thinks that I will collaborate in a theological journal which he is going to edit. Heaven protect me from contributing even a stone to the outrage at the tower of Babel which this fellow proposes to build through the most senseless confusion of philosophy and orthodoxy. I would rather contribute essays to Hengstenberg's *Kirchenzeitung* or to Röhr's *kritische Bibliothek*, for these men do not commit the sin of bearing the name of free, speculative thinking in vain. You were also named as a collaborator in the future journal, but you will certainly not willingly let yourself be thrown in a cauldron where Göschel and company form the ingredients and a wolf in sheep's clothing is the cook. Be so good as to give Herr Bauer my refusal in order to spare an unnecessary letter on my part.[45]

Those who held a mediating view, on the other hand, were willing to make every possible concession to Strauss, and the difference between him and Rosenkranz centred upon the concept of the unity of the divine and the human in the person of the God-man Christ. Rosenkranz had maintained that this unity attained its absolute and perfect expression in the life of one individual – Christ – and with this formulation he attempted to retain some semblance of the old traditional belief in the uniqueness of Jesus. Strauss, on the other hand, held that this unity belonged only to humanity as a whole, and that its fullest expression was found in Christ only to the highest quantitative degree. In the end, however, this difference was solely a question of definitions, and the line between centre and left was extremely ill-defined.

Following a debate with Julius Müller, who denied the existence of any mythical element in the New Testament, the third and final *Streitschrift* drew to a calm and courteous conclusion with an 'Open Letter' to Dr. Ullmann. Here Strauss could afford to be generous, since Ullmann had laid himself open to the charge of compromising, by admitting the presence of myths within the New Testament; if Ullmann could charge Strauss with holding that the Church had invented Christ, Strauss was no less able to return the compliment with the rejoinder that Ullmann himself had conceded a mythical element

D                    [45] Benecke, pp. 185–6.

in the Gospels; it was only a question of a 'more or less'.

Such was the array of foes which surrounded Strauss on every side. But did he not have allies who could come to his aid? His friends from Blaubeuren and Tübingen were all placed in difficult situations, for to have expressed their sympathy with him would have rendered them liable to recriminations from the orthodox. Märklin and Binder were pastors, Märklin in Calw – a centre of Württemberg pietism – and Binder in Heidenheim. But already they were both under the suspicion of the orthodox and it would have meant risking a good deal to come out in Strauss' support.

At first, then, they remained silent and Strauss, feeling that he had been somewhat forsaken by them, wrote to Binder:

> I must admit to you honestly that, on the one hand, I have been often vexed with my isolated position and annoyed with my friends that now, when the situation becomes serious, they suddenly leave the cart standing which for so long we all pulled together.

But he was also fair, and recognising the dangers involved, continued:

> On the other hand I would not wish that you, as father of a family, should compromise yourself in any way and prejudice your external position. Märklin wrote to me most honestly: 'How annoying it is for me, that I must keep quiet in the whole affair, that no one may know how and in what way I am concerned about it'. So then, rather, let your hand stay away from the cauldron so that you will not become black on your
> D. F. Strauss[46]

It was probably on account of this letter that Binder composed a small booklet[47] which brought Strauss much joy.

> It is written in a really elegant and cultivated style; you break in among the pietists like a Greek among barbaric Scythians, Goths and Vandals; but whether they will understand it – that is another question. I do not mean that they will not understand the sense – that is clear enough – but whether they will know how to appreciate the finesse. The pietists scarcely... [48]

---

[46] To Binder 12.5.36; *Deutsche Revue*, 30, II, p. 351.
[47] *Der Pietismus und die moderne Bildung* (Stuttgart, 1838).
[48] Quoted Ziegler, p. 214.

And in a letter to his mother he wrote:

> Today I read the booklet by Binder and was unusually gratified;
> he hews the pietists mightily and deals honourably with your son,
> although it seems to me that he says one thing while meaning
> another. According to his utterances he is more believing and
> pious than you; I can tell you that the reading of this booklet has
> given me a right pleasurable day.[49]

In the following year Märklin published his critical assess-
ment of pietism[50] which called forth a hefty counter-attack
from his pietist opponents. From this time on his days in the
Church were numbered and he was extremely happy when a
position as teacher in the secondary school at Heilbronn became
vacant. His application for the post was approved, and in 1840
he resigned from the ministry in which he had for so long felt
dissatisfied.

Only Vischer, now lecturer in Tübingen for German Literature and Aesthetics, was really free to write, and not
until 1838 did his long essay on Strauss appear,[51] which, as
Ziegler remarked,[52] was only likely to pour more oil on the
fire.

Strauss had hoped for a flood of articles and books taking his
side and lending support for his views, but apart from the
writings of these three friends almost no one took his part. He
stood isolated and almost completely alone. But what of his
former professors Kern and Baur – could they not have come
to his aid? Kern came out against Strauss on the side of the
supernaturalists, and although in his article[53] he took a mild
and compromising line, there was clearly no help to be expected
from that quarter. And Baur? The complex theological and
interpersonal relationship between Strauss and Baur has never
been satisfactorily analysed, and although such an analysis will

---

[49] *Ibid.* p. 214.

[50] *Darstellung und Kritik des modernen Pietismus. Ein wissenschaftlicher Versuch*
(Stuttgart, 1839).

[51] 'Dr. Strauss und die Wirtemberger', *Hallische Jahrbücher* (1838).
Reprinted in *KG*, pp. 3–130.

[52] Ziegler, p. 213.

[53] 'Erörterung der Haupttatsachen der evangelischen Geschichte in
Rücksicht auf Strauss' Schrift: Das Leben Jesu', *TZT* (1836) II, pp. 14–160;
III, pp. 3–159.

necessitate a long digression leading us through the next quarter century, it will be most appropriately undertaken at this point, since a true understanding of their relationship is crucial for the understanding of Strauss' further theological development.

# 10

## STRAUSS AND BAUR[1]

The publication of Strauss' *Life of Jesus* placed Baur in a difficult position. On the one hand, he could not simply repudiate
his pupil's work since – as he admitted years later – he had
discussed the forthcoming book with Strauss during its composition, and was clearly in substantial agreement with the
basic principles. On the other hand, however, Baur was already in bad odour with the orthodox party and it would have
been fatal for him to have made any utterance which signified
even a qualified approval of the work. For Baur was now tired
of Tübingen and hoped for a new position in one of the larger
Prussian faculties. In 1834 the Prussian Minister of Education
had considered him favourably for the vacant chair of theology
in Berlin, but a call was blocked by Neander, and the conservative party under the leadership of Hengstenberg.[2] That showed
how the situation lay. Baur's chances of obtaining a chair anywhere else were slender enough, but to have defended Strauss
publicly would have put paid to them once and for all. Thus
Baur was forced to walk a theological tightrope and he adopted
the obvious expedient of saying as little as possible. He wanted

[1] The relationship has been analysed by Wilhelm Lang: 'Ferdinand
Baur und David Friedrich Strauss', *PJ*, 160 (1915) pp. 474–504; 161
(1915) pp. 123–44; and Adolf Rapp: 'Baur und Strauss in ihrer Stellung
zueinander und zum Christentum', *BWKG*, 3. F. (1952) pp. 95–149;
(1953) p. 157; (1954) pp. 182–6. Lang's discussion is more detailed, but
because he considered the relationship essentially in personal terms ('Baur
never said an unkind word about Strauss' etc.) and pushed the theological
issues into the background, he basically misunderstood the whole relationship and had little comprehension of the real issues which caused the
estrangement. Rapp had a much clearer understanding of the true situation, although his analysis is not quite so comprehensive as Lang's.

[2] See my forthcoming article: 'Die Verhandlungen über die Berufung
Ferdinand Christian Baurs nach Berlin und Halle', in *ZKG*.

to be a 'passive spectator' and declared that he was not in a
position to give a judgment on Strauss' book since he had not
yet made a thorough investigation of the Gospels for himself.
Nor did Baur make any defence of Strauss in the report which
he wrote in December 1835.[3]  On the contrary, in the whole
ten and a half closely written pages Strauss was scarcely mentioned and the whole discussion centred on the question of
freedom to teach.  Baur was, in fact, fighting far more for himself than for Strauss, and only in so far as Strauss was also to
be accorded this right, can it be said that Baur was actually
defending him.  Lang's description of the report as 'a brilliant
justification of Strauss'[4] is quite misleading.  It is true that at
the end of the report Baur made a strong attack on Eschenmayer, who had written a hostile criticism of Strauss, but in
doing this Baur was in little danger of becoming involved in
doctrinal issues, and Eschenmayer by his exaggerated language
had laid himself open to such an attack.  Thus Baur did not
express his support for the book and said nothing in favour of
his pupil, who had some months previously been forced to
resign from the seminary.  Certainly, under the circumstances,
Baur did the only rational thing, for Strauss' fate was sealed
from the moment that his book appeared in print and Baur saw
that nothing which he might have said at this juncture could
have had any bearing on the matter.  Had Baur stood alongside
Strauss, he would have gained nothing and only brought about
his own downfall.  There was, as he saw it, little sense in accompanying Strauss to the executioner's block and he had
really no alternative but to remain silent.  In private, however,
he expressed his views in a letter to his friend Heyd.

Many thanks for the two letters in which you informed me of your
view of Strauss' *Life of Jesus*. I was certainly most interested to
hear of the impression it had made upon you and I was all the more
glad that it has been commended – more highly than I expected –
by such an unprejudiced and competent critic, since up to this time
I saw myself with my view of the book standing almost completely
alone. I am far from giving him my unqualified approval and I
know only too well what can be criticized and what is lacking, but
the main question involved is whether the basic principles from which
he proceeds and the consequences which result directly from them,

are or are not correct. One should at this point give him his due, far more than one appears formerly to have been inclined to do, and not continually turn the dispute into a dispute about principles, from which nothing ever emerges, since science in its most recent development has obtained rights which can no longer be contested by any kind of interest in orthodoxy. One saw only too clearly from the panic-stricken terror which the book has spread almost everywhere, especially in North Germany, how weak the judgment of such a great part of the theological public is. In a certain sense, one can rightly say that the work actually contains nothing new; it simply pursues a path long ago struck out and followed to its natural end, draws the conclusions from premises set up long ago and collects together what had hitherto appeared only in an isolated way and lacking most of all the consistency of thinking which is the strength of the book. Therefore the astonishment and outcry when one weaves the threads spun long ago into a fabric.

In addition to the repeatedly offending coldness, especially towards the Person of Jesus, what I most of all object to in the book is the far too negative criticism. I believe also, that starting from this critical standpoint a broader basis may be yet won for the historical element in Jesus' life, and that in comparison with the destructive criticism, the constructive criticism has received far too little emphasis. Even in the history of Jesus' condemnation one misses all too easily a clearer comprehension of the actual course of events. There are some historical data here that seem to me too little positively estimated. Also, the general question whether an historical person who has attained such significance must not, in accordance with his whole objective appearance, have been more than that which is here partly presupposed and partly is supposed to have resulted from the inquiry. This has nowhere been given proper consideration, and that all this first began in the Person of Jesus is viewed far too much as a matter of chance. If one steers the dispute to this side then many points can certainly be debated with success and, on the whole, the result may even turn out somewhat differently. The most dubious point seems to me to be the resurrection, in which everything is brought completely to a climax; and yet even Schleiermacher had already reckoned the resurrection among the secondary matters without anyone being greatly offended. I believe here also, that if the matter is to be explained by the way which Strauss has adopted, then the explanation can only turn out more satisfactorily when the whole on-going investigation sets the impression of Jesus' personality, and his whole significance, higher than as is here the case. If Jesus in his whole appearance was not more than results from this investigation, then it remains all the more puzzling how the conviction of the disciples, that he *must* have risen from the dead, could have developed.

The whole result does not strike me as so revolutionary as it will seem to you. In my view all history can be regarded only as a moment for the development of the Spirit, as the external but necessary impulse to bring to the Spirit's consciousness the eternal truths which lie within it. For this reason the whole history of development ever aims – again and again through a new impulse – to tear the Spirit free from external and given things, from the letter and from tradition. Also, from the time of the Reformation, as you rightly remark, one has set Scripture in too high a place, and such an emancipation therefore lies fully in the natural course of events; how long has this already been sought and how little is this actually anything new? The most difficult thing, certainly, always remains the relationship to the people, yet one surely imagines that the practical difficulty is far greater than it actually is, and difficulties are always first caused by those who believe that they must use such opportunities for their narrow-minded interests. It must, however, be conceded, that only by this way – the critical conception of history – does one ever learn to separate correctly the essential and less essential elements of Christianity and religion, also in regard to the needs of the people.

I quite agree with what you said about the presumptuous tone which here and there is noticeable, especially in the foreword to the second volume, and about a few other things of this kind; only one must also know – which concerns the foreword – how he has been provoked into it, especially by the Director of Studies who at once condemned his book with the most disparaging expressions. Even his removal would, in my view, not have been at all necessary; only the pietists would have been offended by his longer stay at the seminary; but one should not yield so much to them.

His appointment as minister in a church is another question; but that question, in my opinion, should be completely decided by whether a congregation is satisfied with such a clergyman or not, and at this point it must then be decided whether one who holds such views can work in a practical constructive way.[5]

Three points may be noted briefly in passing:

1. Baur clearly recognised that the central issue at stake was the mythical principle, which was coupled here with the right of scientific criticism. Of the right of such criticism there can be no dispute; what is at issue is the extent to which this

[5] To L. F. Heyd, 10.2.36; *PJ*, 160, pp. 483–5.

criticism is governed by philosophical presuppositions, and just here is the point at which the presuppositions of both Strauss and Baur must be subjected to the same criticism as that to which they would subject the historical sources. For both began with the assumption that miracles (in the usually accepted meaning of the word) do not and cannot occur. And both wanted a history which was not based on supernatural presuppositions, i.e. the existence of a transcendent personal God. They wanted a presuppositionless history, but in fact they merely substituted one presupposition for another and replaced a history where the miraculous was possible with a history from which the miraculous was excluded. If there were no God then it was clear that there could be no miracles and, to reverse the argument, the impossibility of miracles was best explained by the fact that there was no God.

On this point both Strauss and Baur were tacitly united[6] and any discussion which fails to grasp the significance of this underlying unity can never truly evaluate the relationship between them. It is the crucial base-mark criterion in the determination of Strauss' negative and Baur's positive criticism. The problem was made more complex, however, in that both went one step further and identified their philosophical principle with the possibility of scientific, critical and historical research. From this time on historical research was to be a presuppositionless investigation whose only allowable presupposition was the exclusion of every miraculous and supernatural event. All historical criticism not sharing this view was henceforth to be labelled unscientific, and this was the false step which dogged the whole programme of critical research for the remainder of the century and even beyond.

2. Baur's main criticism of the work was that it was too negative. By this he meant that the picture of Jesus which remained after Strauss' critical knife had done its work, failed to measure up to the reality of the historical evidence. For how could the disciples have been convinced of the reality of Jesus' resurrection from the dead, asked Baur, if the personality of Jesus was not more imposing than Strauss had portrayed it to be? Baur had certainly no intention of claiming that Jesus was

---

[6] Cf. the statement of Zeller quoted on p. 113.

any supernatural person, a divine being as in the traditional belief of the Church, but he also knew that the origin of the Christian Church could hardly be explained by the pale and enigmatic figure which dimly emerged from Strauss' investigations.

3. In later years, Baur's main criticism of the book was that Strauss had failed to take into account the Gospel sources – that he had written a criticism of the Gospel history without a corresponding criticism of the Gospel records. In 1836, however, there is no mention of this shortcoming, and it is clear that this omission is to be traced back to the fact that at this stage Baur stood substantially behind Strauss' views. If a story contained a supernatural element then it was mythical – whatever the source from which it derived – and on this matter we find no suggestion whatsoever that Baur diverged from the mythical theory in principle. Nor do we find any hint in the letter that Baur wished to ascribe any parts of the Gospels to a *conscious* mythologising process. That came only later. Baur never criticised the mythical principle in itself, nor did he ever provide any better answer to the problem of how Christianity originated; on the contrary he steered clear of the whole question and nowhere in his later writings did he deal with it.

We have seen how Baur wanted to remain quiet and say nothing openly. However, in the May issue of Hengstenberg's *Evangelische Kirchenzeitung* for 1836 appeared an article[7] criticising Baur's latest book on the Pastoral Epistles, and asserting that his views were fundamentally no different from those of his notorious pupil:

As regards Professor Baur, he has already become known as an exceptionally talented and thorough investigator, but also a very sceptical one. A new book from him has just appeared: *The so-called Pastoral Epistles of the Apostle Paul: A New Critical Investigation* (Stuttgart, 1835), in which a sceptical capriciousness appears which can in fact only be compared with that of Strauss. There runs through the whole work a bitter and irritable spirit against all those who oppose the sceptical criticism in a hostile manner, a spirit which one can hardly explain except as proceeding from an intimate acquaintance with the theology of his friend Dr. Strauss.[8]

[7] 'Die Zukunft unserer Theologie', *EKZ*, May 1836.
[8] *Ibid.* p. 290.

and after describing Baur's investigations as arbitrary and impertinent (Baur had dated the Pastorals in the second century and hinted that 1 Peter, Philippians and Mark should be likewise dated), the writer continued:

After this book on the Pastoral Epistles, we must in fact believe that Herr Baur, just like Strauss, has already thrown the historical authority of the Gospel of John overboard.[9]

The article could not have come at a worse time, for at that very moment Baur was under consideration for the vacant theological chair at Halle. The question was whether or not he should reply: if he said nothing it would be taken as a silent admission of his guilt; on the other hand, a reply might stir up the hornet's nest even more. Baur thought the matter over, decided that attack was the best policy and composed his 'Abgenöthigte Erklärung' which appeared in the third issue of the *Tübinger Zeitschrift für Theologie* for 1836.

He began by rejecting the assertion that his criticism of the Pastorals had been influenced by the views of Strauss. He had finished, he declared, the greater part of his research into the Epistles before the *Life of Jesus* had been published, and he resented the insinuation that he owed anything to its author. He then defended himself against the charge that his investigation into the authenticity of the letters had been arbitrary or impertinent. No one, he maintained, had spent so much trouble investigating the origin of the letters as he, and the accusations which had been levelled against him could only come from those who were completely biassed against all scientific criticism.

It is true that Baur had attained his new historical insights independently and that he was not indebted to Strauss. It is also true that Baur never denied the 'spiteful accusation' of friendship with Strauss, which had been levelled against him by the *Evangelische Kirchenzeitung*, although it was well nigh impossible for him to do so; for their association (one hesitates to call the relationship a friendship) was a known fact which Baur could not have denied without incurring the contempt of all his acquaintances. But for Strauss, the most vexing thing was that Baur had tried to make it appear that he stood on a

[9] *Ibid.* p. 291.

completely different basis from that on which he himself stood. For Baur had written:

Not only are the basic principles of criticism of another kind, but also the object of the critical question under discussion is essentially different, as everyone must immediately see. Is the whole objective basis of Christianity called into question through my investigation, in the same way as it was through Strauss'?[10]

And what was Strauss to think of the following passage? Was not Baur attempting to create the impression that he disagreed with Strauss' mythical approach, and that he held fast to the historical reality of the miracles recorded in the Gospels?

As regards my and Strauss' criticism, there will be scarcely anyone generally competent to make a judgment in such things, and who does not – out of a malicious will – have a special interest in denying the truth, who fails to recognise the difference between my method of treatment and that of Strauss. The particular feature of the Straussian criticism, as is known, consists in the mythical explanation of the facts of the Gospel history. This explanation is supposed to result partly from the character of the Gospel narratives, partly from the untenability of the supernatural and rationalistic views. Now I ask: Where in my book – in even just one passage – is my criticism based on the mythical view? Where do I reject even one historical fact that is of importance for the critical judgment of these Epistles, solely for the reason that it is a miracle...?[11]

Strauss was annoyed by the article and wrote to Baur expressing his grievance.

Likewise I have to thank you for your goodness in sending me your defence against Hengstenberg. It is a masterly piece of polemical writing, not merely by virtue of the clarity of the exposition and the compelling evidence, but generally by virtue of the moral value with which you oppose the pious baseness of these people, in a way that I can scarcely remember having found elsewhere. For me, certainly, (since indeed even you yourself make reference to me along with the purely scientific question) it had an unhappy outcome, in that through the unwarranted mixing which Hengstenberg made of our respective works and tendencies, you saw yourself caused, on your side, to emphasize the difference and the not-belonging-togetherness of us both, as strongly as possible, and as a sure guarantee of this, to pass strictures on my work and method.

[10] *TZT* (1836) III, pp. 207–8.　　　[11] *Ibid.* pp. 205–6.

I do not know whether these strictures were necessary for your cause (for mine, which has already received so many strictures, they were certainly not), and whether – through the not-wholly-clear remark inserted subsequently, that to some degree the difference of object makes a comparison of our respective criticism impossible – these strictures were properly limited. I at least believe myself to be conscious of the fact that what you in your letters call my negativity, has, to be sure, half its ground in a personal short-coming, but certainly the other half in the fact that for the time and events of Jesus' life the customary historical control is lacking in a completely different way from that, for example, in the time of the Pastoral Epistles. Or how would you find proof of the unhistorical character of the narrative of a miracle such as the feeding of the five thousand – apart from accepting the incredibility of the story or in any way departing from the reports? And for all that, would you not declare the narrative for unhistorical without further historical data?

Please do not misunderstand my feelings in these remarks. Just because I know myself bound to you through friendship and grati-tude in the most intimate way, I believe that I should not remain silent about these matters nor conceal from you that, in this respect, your article belongs to the most distressing aspects which, in regard to my book, I have experienced. Through experiences such as mine, one, to be sure, becomes hardened to the unfairness of strangers and those who are indifferent – among whom I also reckon Dr. Kern – but towards the wounds caused by friends – may they be ever so slight – all the more sensitive.

Please excuse this sensitivity and do not on this account withdraw your goodwill from

Yours sincerely,<br>D. F. Strauss.[12]

and in a letter to Georgii during the following week, he ex-pressed his anger more openly.

As regards the 'Abgenöthigte Erklärung' I will just remark that through this article Dr. Baur, my hitherto truest friend on the critical field, has treated me in a pretty poor way in that he forswore everything we have in common and even made reproachful remarks against me in order to get out of Hengstenberg's accusation, that

---

[12] To Baur, 19.8.36; Printed in *AB*, pp. 22–3; also in Ernst Barnikol's edition of the Strauss–Baur correspondence, *ZKG*, 73 (1962) pp. 74–125; 88–9.

his book on the Pastoral Epistles has the same tendency as my *Life of Jesus*. Now one who is of the opinion that I deserve reproach can certainly reproach me; I have nothing against this; but when, at the present time, it's a friend who makes it, in order to obtain peace with the *Evangelische Kirchenzeitung*, then the friendship is at an end. I have also more or less said that to him.[13]

In the next few weeks, however, relations were again patched up. Baur replied to Strauss' letter and visited him during the holidays to discuss the matter personally. On 4 November Strauss again wrote to Georgii:

I have settled my differences with Baur, partly in writing, partly orally, since he visited me during the vacation. In his direct presence, especially, I can never withstand the honest man – I mention this however merely historically and, like Treuburg's secretary, am open to correction.[14]

During the following years relations continued on much the same basis as previously, with an exchange of letters and occasional meetings. The main development which interests us here is Baur's criticism of Strauss' mythical principle. Baur was convinced that John's Gospel could not be explained as an unconscious mythical composition; it possessed too much originality and was clearly a carefully composed literary work, largely dependent upon the material contained in the earlier Synoptic Gospels. But this meant that many of the Gospel stories did not require to be explained by – and could not be explained by – Strauss' mythical interpretation. Strauss was also convinced by Baur's explanation and he never disputed Baur's assertion that conscious mythology also had its place in the Gospels. But what Strauss did hold to tenaciously was that the root and core of the whole Gospel history had its origin and foundation in the unconscious mythologising process in the early Church. Secondary myths dependent upon the original stories might be added later by a conscious process of composition, but an unconscious process lay behind these primary myths; and although Baur emphasised the conscious mythologising process – mainly in order to show his independence of Strauss – he never disputed that an unconscious inchoate process

---

[13] To Georgii, 26.8.36; 'Briefe von D. F. Strauss an L. Georgii', p. 16.
[14] *Ibid.* p. 17.

was responsible for the formation of the primary mythical material in the Gospels.

In the summer of 1846 while Strauss was staying at his brother's house in Cologne, he read through Baur's investigation into the Gospel of John, which had appeared in the *Tübinger Zeitschrift für Theologie* for 1844. He regarded the treatise as a masterly piece of work, although he considered that Baur had been unjust to him personally, as we learn from the letter which he wrote to Märklin on the 22 July 1846.

In this solitude I have already been reading fairly diligently. I first chose Baur's treatise on John in which up till now I had only browsed. I am pleased to say that despite the fact that this work touches me personally, in a rather disagreeable manner, I can still heartily praise it and wholly acknowledge its conclusions in the fullest possible way. Now, but only now, has this ghost of the alleged John, which has again and again aped me and others, and always returned when we believed we had exorcized it, been banished. It has been banished because Baur has declared the answer to its riddle, the *constituens* of its being. No objection against the arguments is possible, because Baur's key fits in all the key-holes of this astonishing building and opens all – or, at any rate, almost all – the rooms. Also the work is very well planned and has the advantage over his book on Paul in that it rises to a climax whose highest peak, the final investigation into the authorship, leads into an area where the deepest psychology is at the same moment the highest poetry. He who can deny the conclusions of this work (and he who only denies outwardly, that is, lies consciously, is here, to be sure, more acceptable to me than he who has gone so far as to be able to deny it inwardly) of him it can be said, he has lied to the holy Spirit of science.

I myself, in Baur's treatment, am often considered in a polemical manner and my standpoint for the fourth Gospel is described as unsatisfactory. That is fair enough and Baur is completely right where he opposes me. This can hurt a person, but it cannot offend him; he will not feel vexed with the one who expresses this judgment. But now Baur always puts me on a par with Lücke[15] etc.; nowhere

[15] G. C. F. Lücke (1791–1855) was professor of theology at Bonn (1818–1827) and Göttingen (1827–55). He was one of the most respected, learned and *avant-garde* representatives of the so-called 'Mediating Theology' which followed, in essence, the programme of Schleiermacher and sought to reconcile faith with knowledge and traditional theology with scientific criticism.

does he emphasize what the criticism of the Gospels – and even the fourth – owes to me, and he shows a generally unfriendly, adverse attitude towards my works. I can explain this partly out of the matter itself; I am no historian; I have always proceeded from the dogmatic (alternatively, anti-dogmatic) interest, and he may rightly object to this from his historical-critical standpoint. But he should still consider just how natural and appropriate my method was for the beginning, and how, without my preparative work, criticism would certainly not stand where it stands today. When I now glance back, I actually nowhere find – even earlier – a complimentary word of Baur about my works – always rejecting, in parts quite laughably ignoring me; where it is a question of my ideas – such as in the doctrine of the atonement, where in the paragraph on the most recent period it hinges about the question: Christ, Individual or Humanity? – I am not even mentioned. I wrote over the passage at the time I was reading it, in a certainly not unjustified pride, the words of Tacitus (Ann. 3, 76): *Sed praelucebant Cassius atque Brutus, ad id ipsum, quod imagines eorum non viserentur.*[16]  In short: It is never pleasant for a teacher when his pupil makes a name for himself too early and, to a certain degree, before himself. You may say what you like against this statement, but it is still so, and from Steudel through Kern to Baur runs only a descending line. With the first this pupil-relationship has sharpened his hate; with the second it has decided his vacillations for the opposing side; with the third it has withheld acknowledgement. I am the son who left the business too early in order to establish his own, which in the beginning looked as if it might obscure that of his father. Therefore he did not lift a finger to help, and now that he with his *festina lente*[17] has progressed further than I, he says: See, you have your own business now. How completely different, how considerately, forwardingly, protectingly, like a hen looks after her chick, he treats his younger sons, Zeller, Schwegler, who at least have observed the courtesy of making names for themselves only after and in association with him, as younger partners in his business.

You see, I write in a city of commerce and in a house of business. Please don't take the matter too idealistically; remember that we are all men, that we – or at least I – would not even make it better. I must admit that because of this matter I find my personal relation-

---

[16] 'But Cassius and Brutus shone brighter by the very fact that their portraits were not seen.' The reference is to the funeral procession of Junia (sister of Brutus, wife of Cassius) in A.D. 21, in which the effigies of the most illustrious families were paraded. But those of Brutus and Cassius were not shown, either because they had been prohibited or simply as a matter of prudence.          [17] Hasten slowly.

ship with Baur has been disrupted; but on account of this I still praise his work as a masterpiece and model of criticism.[18]

Three months later he remarked in a letter to Vischer,[19] that so far as he was concerned, his personal relationship with Baur was at an end.

The situation deteriorated still further when Baur sent Strauss a copy of his latest work on the history of dogma,[20] the reading of which only strengthened Strauss' previous impressions: first, that Baur with his contrast of positive and negative criticism had painted a distorted picture of the theological differences between them, and secondly, that in classing his Dogmatics[21] along with the works of the rationalists, Baur had treated him in an off-hand and deprecatory manner. The letter which Strauss now wrote to Baur marked a definite break in their relations, and apart from the final expression of sympathy which he sent to the ailing Baur in the summer of 1860, there was no further correspondence between them. The tone in which Strauss poured out his bitter and wounded feelings is formal and courteous, but it does express all the indignation which had remained pent up inside him over past months and years. For Strauss had a keen sense of right and wrong and knew when he had been unjustly treated.

Most honoured Sir and friend,

Once again I have to thank you for a fine present which caught me here – wandering and fugitive as I now am on earth – on my return from Cologne only ten days ago. Next, I am quite embarrassed with the obligation which you place me under again and again, since I cannot console myself with any reciprocal gift which I could send you in the future; for – I do not know who may have cursed me – I am the fig tree of which it says in the Gospel that no one shall ever again eat of its fruit. Happily there is not much lost on this fruit, since it never consisted of sweet historical-critical figs, but of sour rationalistic wild grapes, as your *Dogmengeschichte* newly testifies. As regards my *Dogmatics*, I could bring forward as an apology for it that it never claimed to be a history of dogma, but only a Dogmatics historically treated; it never claimed consideration as a model in the question of the method in the history of dogma;

---

[18] Printed by Rapp, in: *BWKG* (1952) pp. 118–20.
[19] To Vischer, 13.9.46; quoted by Rapp, *BWKG* (1952) p. 120.
[20] *Lehrbuch der christlichen Dogmengeschichte* (Stuttgart, 1847).
[21] *Die christliche Glaubenslehre* (Tübingen and Stuttgart, 1840–1).

it could therefore reasonably be omitted from your book and it can owe its mention only to a quite special favour or intention. But as regards the negative conclusion for which you reproach me in your book, I can calmly ask, wherein are your dogmatic conclusions supposed to be more positive? Is somehow the one position supposed to be that in the eschatology one can point to the further development of dogma, which will show what is transient or permanent in this newest form of the consciousness? Or where in the doctrine of God, of the Person of Christ etc. is anything really positive to be discovered?

For here, in the realm of dogmatics, the double meaning of the expression 'positive', which in the field of biblical criticism can for a moment deceive, comes not once to our aid. When in your treatment of John's Gospel (which I truly admire as a masterpiece of criticism and agree with in almost every point, especially those made against myself) you distinguish your criticism from mine, as the positive from the negative, then on one hand I must say that you are completely right.

My object (in the *Life of Jesus*) was attained when I had shown that a narrative was not historical, and simply in order to make this conclusion more probable, I attempted to show (with how much or how little success is here not the question) how the narrative could have originated. Your main emphasis is on this last occupation, and in so far you may rightly call your criticism the positive criticism. But this is never a position in the sense of your opponents; in the present-day theological struggle in the Church, it is no criterion which would set you on one side and me on the other side. It is a false pass which you show to the watchmen of Zion when you always, again and again, assure them that your criticism is not negative like that of your notorious pupil, with whom to be confused is something you must strongly decline. How so? will the watchman ask. Do you also allow the Gospel histories to stand as historical? Certainly not, you will finally have to answer, but I show abundantly where, and from whom, they have been invented, and this task to which I devote so much trouble is indeed also a positive occupation. That's a pretty position! will cry the gate-keeper; the one says: it is not true; the other says: it is a lie and I know how to ascertain who fabricated it! Away with both into the same dungeon! However, you will say that you do not mean your 'positive' in this sense, that you have no desire to deceive with it, that you understand it not in an ecclesiastical, but in a scientific sense. But as I have already remarked, in your *Dogmengeschichte* – as regards the conclusions – even in the scientific sense, which there coincides with the ecclesiastical, you are not positive, and also in the criticism of the

New Testament my negation must precede your position. If I, in a born historian, as you are, can comprehend the aversion against a procedure such as mine, where history is simply the means to a dogmatic, i.e. anti-dogmatic objective – if I consequently understand the premeditated and almost provocative way in which you set yourself in opposition to me at every opportunity, without being able to comprehend that strategical, or better, diplomatic intention, I think I have the right to demand – especially from an historian – that he should see that the relevant critical questions of today could not be so calmly treated from a purely historical standpoint if the dogmatic point – I do not say by me, but through the whole discussion stimulated by me – had not been basically, and in the inner consciousness even of the orthodox, negatively settled. The acknowledgment of this, and that the present-day historical criticism proceeds along the road which I helped to open up for it – this is what I, from the beginning up till now, have never received from you. Whoever gets to know my works from your treatise on John must hold me for a continuator of Lücke and company; whoever gets to know me from your *Dogmengeschichte* must hold you (according to the passage p. 42f.) in contrast to me, to be a colleague of Dorner.[22] The mirror which reflects the figures in such a distorted way has no true surface.

And to what end have you so represented me? Use – the position which you seek to give me cannot make it more possible[23] for you and your present school; the Church lords and those who set the theological fashions have too fine an instinct to let themselves be deceived; this instinct is becoming continually stronger and if it sets me among the goats, it will not set you among the sheep. But on the other hand detriment – it could not have been detrimental to your position, your renown, even if you had done me justice – what I must hold for justice. He who laughs last laughs best. The laugh is long ago with you and will never again come to me. If I became famous somewhat too early for you, then I am for this act now forgotten; the most appropriate punishment for the all-too-early beginning is an early cessation. You live and thrive, I don't decline any more, but am already dead and have become so accustomed to this role of a deceased person that I certainly would

[22] Isaac August Dorner (1809–84). Dorner was a conservative mediating theologian whose theological views were generally opposed to those of Baur.

[23] Strauss meant that Baur sought to represent himself as positive in order to make his position less vulnerable to orthodox criticism, and the position of his younger disciples, Zeller, Schwegler etc., easier as regards academic promotion.

not have uttered what I here utter – indeed would scarcely have perceived it – if it had been a stranger who had so met me. But since it is you, then it is not literary sensitivity – which was always on my part, in moderation – but it is irksome for me to have to make our former friendship tally with an attitude which I myself would find hostile and unjust in a stranger. Now nothing could be more disagreeable to me and more against the purpose of this letter, were you to understand this declaration as meaning that I wanted to hear, by a corresponding opportunity, an open favourable word from you, or even just a suppression of the unfavourable. That is further from my mind than anything. Among so many things that I must see perishing in me and about me, I also calmly witness the crumbling of the little bit of literary renown which I acquired; its end will come whether now my friends accelerate it with the enemies or not; I have, however, the consolation to be able to take flight from one affliction into the other, and each time to be able to forget the one in the others which oppress me.

It will be difficult for me to find a conclusion to this letter; I would most of all prefer to leave it out since it can in no way profit or better our mutual relationship; the matter between us lies as it lies and neither these lines nor any answer from you can make it otherwise; however I had to say this to you sooner or later, in writing, or orally, and I close with the assurance that all the (in Rom. 8, 38f.) enumerated powers will not extinguish in me the respect and gratitude with which I remain

Your most devoted pupil (may I say that?)

D. F. Strauss[24]

Heilbronn 17 Nov. 46

In this difficult situation Baur decided to write to Märklin, who had resigned his pastorate in Calw and accepted a position as teacher in the secondary school at Heilbronn.

My honoured friend,

Permit me, trusting in your friendly disposition towards me, to turn to you in a delicate matter. Have the goodness to read the enclosed letter from Strauss, written against me from a most bitter heart, and judge for yourself what an impression such a letter must have made upon me. He reproaches me that I have repeatedly

---

[24] The letter was printed by Barnikol in his article: 'Das ideengeschichtliche Erbe Hegels bei und seit Strauss und Baur im 19. Jahrhundert', *Wissenschaftliche Zeitschrift der Martin-Luther-Universität*, Halle–Wittenberg, x, 1, pp. 281–324; pp. 290–1. Also reprinted with minor corrections in *ZKG* (1962) pp. 117–20.

distinguished – most recently in particular in my *Lehrbuch der Dog-mengeschichte* – my standpoint as a positive from his as a negative. This is in general correct, but I have always touched on this differ-ence as briefly as I could, only where I could not avoid the question, and I am not conscious of mixing in anything irrelevant. What I said in my *Lehrbuch der Dogmengeschichte* is just this, that if one binds the history of dogma with dogmatics – as happens in most textbooks on dogmatics, and also in Strauss' – the history of dogma always receives too brief a treatment in that it appears that the dogma is only there in order to let itself be criticised and to be shown by itself that it has no validity. I could not let this method of treating the history of dogma go unmentioned. But now what injustice have I committed against Strauss' *Glaubenslehre* when I say that such a treatment of the teaching of the faith is too negative, and that the positive treatment, which also belongs here, is that one must see the impulse of a further historical development where everything has only a negative ending? Strauss himself concedes this when he says in his letter that he did not write his dogmatics as a history of dogma.

More important is our difference in the criticism of the Gospels, and here I frankly admit that I not only stand on a different stand-point than Strauss, but also that my investigations into the Gospel have the tendency to go beyond Strauss, and, to be sure, for the reason that I cannot believe that one can stop at such a negative conclusion. The Straussian conclusion is – in that he takes the Gospels all together and always refutes one with the other – in brief, just this: that all the narratives are alike untrue. I have sought to give a new twist to the question generally. The question is no longer, what have they narrated, but how have they narrated, i.e. how far generally did they want to narrate. When one so formulates the question, then he will soon be convinced that the majority of the Gospels are obviously tendency-writings, and one obtains the canon by this criterion, that the historical truth is most probably to be assumed where a tendency character shows itself the least. In this sense I call my criticism positive, in distinction from that negative criticism, because it does not deny the historical credibility of at least one Gospel,[25] but concedes it – certainly only in a relative way, as here everything is to be taken merely relatively. Now what injustice have I committed here against Strauss? There is at this point, certainly, a great difference between him and me, but I have never tried to emphasize it more than the matter warranted and I have never engaged in polemics against him out of any other

[25] The Gospel of Matthew.

interest except for the purpose of giving my view a scientific foundation. If he demands that I should not have raised this difference
at all, then he demands something impossible and thinks that one
should call a halt, unconditionally, at his *Life of Jesus*. I certainly
know as well as anyone how to value his great significance and have
also always acknowledged it in my writings, but I believe that I
also know as well as any other, what impulse his criticism has in
itself for further investigations. Also, he was in no way the first to
help me – as he gives me to understand in his letter, through his
*Life of Jesus* – to the dogmatically free standpoint on which I stand.
I have never – neither in my writings nor elsewhere – pretended to
the merit that he had anything to thank me for; on the contrary,
I gladly admit that I have learnt much from him; but why will he
only claim for himself, what I, least of all, refuse to renounce – that
I have attained my standpoint independently? Not one of my
worst opponents has ever attacked me from this side, and such an
assertion as I now hear from Strauss will find no great acceptance,
neither now, nor in the future.

If I now gladly look beyond all this, as beyond a scientific difference in which, up until now, I never thought that such a hostile
personal relationship could ever be found, Strauss indeed does not
stop at this point of flaunting this difference against me with all
severity and bitterness, but he goes even further and throws suspicion
even on my character, in that he insinuates that in this difference
lies the impure motive, I want to appear positive in contrast to
him, just in order to make it possible for myself and my friends.
Whatever he wishes to understand by this 'making-possible-for-
oneself', even you will concede that this is a reproach which could
not be more grievous to me. I cannot bear to say even another word
about such an accusation, or appeal to facts which could clearly
prove to anyone the opposite. If he can believe this of me, then he
may believe it. I am not conscious of such an impure intention.
This is the only thing I can say about it and I can only reject it with
indignation.

But where is all this leading? In that Strauss at the end of his
letter declares an answer from me cannot make the matter any
better, he clearly wishes his letter to be understood as a letter ending
the relationship from his side, since he also indicates his changed
attitude towards me through other things in the letter.

I know, indeed, that everywhere in this letter there speaks a
wounded disposition that must be handled with tender consideration and forbearance. I have hitherto always been able to think
of our friend – as often as I heard of his relations with his wife – only
with the most inward sympathy, and even this last letter, which con-

tains so much that is bitter for me, has only awakened in me the most melancholy compassion. But when a relationship between friends, which originated so long ago and which has always been valued and cherished by me, is severed in a manner which I will intentionally not describe more precisely, then there is also a boundary from my side which I may not cross over. I cannot write to Strauss any more because I will not obtrude myself on him. Therefore I now turn to you, honoured friend, not at all to trouble you with a commission for him, but only to present to you, as one of his close friends, the impression which his letter has made on me; I indeed feel the bitterness and vexation which this letter contains for me, but I can well set my conscience at rest; and if better days do not come and our friend does not perceive to which darker demon he has in his ill-humour devoted himself, then all that has happened will still not prevent me from overlooking the whole matter, and showing the sentiment which I have hitherto maintained toward him and which I will also preserve in the future.

There is still much pressing upon me which I would like to express to you, in order to soften the impression of the matter by explaining Strauss' behaviour in the kindest possible way. I can well imagine how Strauss will be struck by the changed form in which he will glimpse his own image in the mirror of the time, when, after so long a pause, he reconsiders his position more carefully in the light of the consciousness of the time and the questions which excite it. However I will not draw you further into a matter in which I must generally have doubts about making such great claims upon your participation.

How are you getting on yourself? I have heard with regret how you and your wife have recently been visited by serious illness, and I sincerely hope that you yourself with your dear family may be completely well again.

In that I have now only to apologise for burdening you with this disagreeable matter, I remain with the sincerest respect and friendship,

Yours most devotedly,

Tübingen, the 26th Nov. 46.        D. Baur.[26]

When we pause to reflect on these two letters, we see that there were two main issues. The first was that Baur had no

---

[26] Printed by Barnikol in 'Das ideengeschichtliche Erbe Hegels', pp. 297–8. Märklin consulted Strauss about certain points and sent a cautious reply which conceded none of the theological points which Baur had made. This letter, of which the end is missing, adds little to the two letters which lie before us. It is printed by Barnikol, pp. 292–3.

intention of being linked with Strauss' anti-supernatural standpoint and had no desire to find himself under the same stigma
which lay upon his notorious pupil. He therefore emphasised
the positive side of his writings in contrast to the negative criticism of Strauss, so that the fact might be forgotten – or, at least,
covered up as much as possible – that he too accepted Strauss'
anti-supernatural principles. What we must understand clearly
is that Baur used the words 'positive' and 'negative' in a double
sense. In 1836 when he described the *Life of Jesus* as negative,
he meant that Strauss had simply demolished the traditional
view of Jesus, had shown what Jesus was not, but had produced no positive construction and had not shown what Jesus
was. By 1847, however, Baur had introduced another sense of
the positive–negative polarity, which derived its meaning from
his own so-called positive construction of Christianity. Strauss
was now described as negative because he had not taken the
sources into account, and Baur's new tendency approach, by
which he examined the character of the New Testament documents, was, in direct contrast, to be labelled positive. The
older meaning of negative is naturally included along with the
new, but Baur was now able to claim a new positivity which
had not been possible earlier. And over and above both these
meanings, the positive–negative polarity possessed an over-
tone which those less knowing in theological matters would
have often understood as referring to the fundamental doctrines
of the Christian faith. When Strauss' theology was described as
negative, and Baur's as positive, then it was not difficult to
draw the conclusion that while Strauss denied the essential
Christian doctrines, Baur upheld them. Certainly Baur never
used the words positive and negative in this sense, but it was in
no way disagreeable to him if others should receive such an
impression. It is not too much to say that Baur misused the
word positive; he certainly made capital out of the ambiguity
of meaning which it contained, and he never went out of his
way to elucidate clearly that the word, for him, had no reference to the traditional beliefs of the Church. As Adolf Rapp
wrote:

What he (Baur) might have cited in order to show himself as
'positive' over against Strauss, was that he at any rate stood inwardly

much more positive to Christ and to Christianity than Strauss; but that, he would, indeed, not have wanted to say.[27]

In point of fact, Baur's positivity rested on a negativity which he shared equally with Strauss, for both denied that the super-natural narratives contained in the Gospels were historically true. As far as Strauss himself was concerned, once he had shown that the stories were unhistorical, then it was of no further importance for him when and where the stories origin-ated. On the other hand, if Baur wanted to examine the sources further in order to gain a clearer understanding of the origin of the Christian faith – and Strauss never denied the legitimacy of such a procedure – then he was perfectly welcome to do so; only he had no right to describe his approach as positive without first clarifying the meaning of the word. Nor was he justified in asserting a positive/negative distinction be-tween conscious and unconscious mythologising. Strauss had shown that the origins of the Gospel stories lay in an uncon-scious mythical process (an explanation which Baur also accepted as true), but Strauss, in turn, had also accepted Baur's hypothesis that conscious invention was also present. And if Baur laid more stress on this latter hypothesis, he never denied that the conscious invention was ultimately derived from the unconsciously composed mythical core.[28] When Baur, how-ever, asserted that his approach was positive, because he had shown where, when and by whom the stories had been con-sciously invented, and when he declared that Strauss' approach was negative, because Strauss had merely maintained that the narratives were untrue, but had gone no further, then Strauss was certainly justified in his belief that Baur had not been completely honest in the matter – a point which he made with the charming little couplet in which he lets Baursay:

> We are as no and yes, like storm and rainbow mated;
> He says: it is not true; I say: it's fabricated.[29]

The second issue was that Baur attempted to diminish Strauss' importance. He had, to be sure, described the *Life of*

[27] Rapp, *BWKG* (1952) p. 125.
[28] This is also confirmed in Baur's penultimate letter to Zeller (6.11.60) where he writes: 'Everything in the circle drawn by Strauss remains in its right...' See below, p. 112.          [29] *GS*, XII, p. 27.

*Jesus* as an important work, but a warm word of praise never flowed from his pen; his references to it were reserved and cool; his approval was a grudging approval, and it was this reserve – one can almost say stinginess – which wounded Strauss most. It is true that Baur had to be careful not to give any toehold for criticism from the orthodox, but even in his letters he was critical, and when in 1846 he classed Strauss' *Dogmatics* in a line with the Dogmatics of the rationalists (however much this designation may be true), then it was, against Strauss, a deprecation and provocation which cannot be described as unintentional.

In the summer of the following year (1847) Baur made his bitterest attack on Strauss. In the introduction to his work on the Gospels[30] he re-emphasised the differences separating himself from Strauss, and the tone throughout is quite deprecatory – as if he had decided to let Strauss know that from his side also, the personal relationship was now at an end. Strauss' critical approach was once more described as negative, because he had made a criticism of the Gospel history without a corresponding criticism of the Gospel sources, and almost the only complimentary word which Baur had for the book was that it acted as a mirror in which the age saw its own reflection. And for this the age hated both him and his book. Here, certainly, a measure of recognition comes to view, but it is quickly dampened by the disparaging attack on the book's originality.

If there is any book which is constructed as much as possible only on the work of predecessors, which simply summarizes conclusions from a string of various investigations long ago conducted by so many others, which merely, but consistently, draws the last conclusions from premises about which one had already been agreed, then it is the Straussian *Life of Jesus*. In this dependence, the work itself is laid out according to its whole plan and content. Its procedure everywhere consists at each point in presenting and evaluating the various opinions about the matter in question, those of the rationalists and supernaturalists, the former being set in opposition to the latter, and after this procedure has allowed the views and assertions – which are mostly opposed to each other – to dialectically grind themselves away on each other, then it brings the unhistorical result with the somewhat problematic assumption of an historical

---

[30] *Kritische Untersuchungen über die kanonischen Evangelien* (Tübingen, 1847).

remnant to the more fitting expression of the mythical view. What then, in the whole work, is new and unprecedented? Where is even one assertion to be found in it that is first here put forward, and has not already been dared by other theologians whom no one can accuse of an anti-Christian direction. One needs only to remember how long ago even Schleiermacher passed sentence on the most important facts of Jesus' life – birth, resurrection, ascension. And just what else is this mythical view – which is here for the first time worked out in detail – than the old tradition-hypothesis merely conceived in a more living, concrete and deeper way, in the spirit of the ancient way of viewing things. When one considers the Straussian work from this side, then one in fact has trouble finding it conceivable how it caused such an extraordinary sensation in its first appearance, not at all just among the uninitiated, but especially among those to whom the most of what has been said here could have been long since no secret.[31]

Coming so soon after Baur's protestation to Märklin that he knew as well as anyone how to value Strauss' great importance, one must indeed say that there is here surprisingly little trace of this esteem. Baur could so easily have given a positive tone to his words by asking: 'Where could one find a book which systematised everything in such a penetrating and open way?'[32]

Relations between them were not completely broken off. When Zeller became engaged to Baur's daughter Emilie, in January 1847, Strauss wrote to him expressing his joy over the engagement and also, 'for our common papa'. 'For he remains that to me, even if he may have turned away from me, as a half cast-off Simeon, to you young Josephs and Benjamins.'[33]

In 1849 Strauss wrote his biography of Märklin in which Baur was presented in the best possible light, and at the end of 1851 they both met again on friendly terms in Ulm, where Zeller and his father-in-law were staying. Yet however friendly the outward relationship may have been and however much they both respected each other, there always remained beneath the surface a dissension and discord which was never healed.

---

[31] *Ibid.* pp. 46–7.     [32] Rapp, *BWKG* (1952) p. 126.
[33] To Zeller, 1.2.47; *AB*, p. 190.

The last piece of correspondence which passed between them was the letter which Strauss wrote a few months before Baur's death.

Heidelberg 5 Sept. 1860

Most honoured friend,

I felt deeply the old kindness which you showed anew in sending me the second edition of your work on Christianity during the first three centuries, and apologise for postponing the expression of my thanks for so long, until the news of your illness compelled me to wait no longer. I need not assure you that I have awaited the news concerning your state of health, which friend Zeller has now and then communicated to me, with concern and sympathy; nor do I need to assure you of my joy, which his last letter evoked in me, that you feel yourself in so far better, that you are able to undertake the journey to Baden for the completion of your restoration. My most inner wish, that the hot springs might accomplish the same service for you as the oil vessel once accomplished for its apostle and patron saint,[34] accompanied you thither.

For truly, it is urgently necessary for our decrepit theology that you remain and dedicate your rejuvenated and rejuvenating service to it still longer. As you perhaps may have seen from the preface to the *Gespräche* of Hutten,[35] which will have been sent to you by my publisher, I have, after many years of wandering, once more looked around in the old theological home country and have scarcely been able to wonder enough at the so greatly altered state of affairs. While you in your writings and in your scientific school have established a mighty fortress,[36] the flat land of theology has sunk into a condition of incredible degeneration. That useless apologetic climbing weed, which seeks to hinder the steps of research, grew in my time, at most, up to the ankles, while one must now wade through it up to the waist. Especially since the day when you took the beloved Gospel from its age[37] (for whoever seeks to remove the madness of one whose madness for a thing is equated with the thing itself, must have control of the matter), the theologians run hither and thither like an ant's heap which has been disturbed. In this respect, nothing has appeared to me more characteristic, than the sight of all the common theologians, after the so obviously artificial

[34] The reference is to John, of whom Tertullian reports that he had been immersed in boiling oil without suffering any harm.

[35] Strauss' translation of Hutten's *Dialogues* (Leipzig, 1860).

[36] An allusion to Luther's hymn: 'A mighty fortress is our God'.

[37] Baur set the composition of the fourth Gospel in the middle of the second century.

treatment of our friend Weitzel[38] in regard to the dispute over the Passover, like a herd of geese snapping at an apple core.

Among these men – and I can indeed now speak almost as a non-participant and yet as one not unversed in the matter – you appear as a watchman among dreamers, as a sober man among the drunken, as a man among boys, a giant among dwarfs. Indeed, you, if any, are called like the holy Christophorus to carry the Christ-child – but only its eternal and immortal part – through the burning of this time. For either theology and Church must stagnate and rot with one another, or the separation, the purification towards which you work, must really be resolved upon and carried through.

To work again with my modest powers for this end, is now my definite intention. If during the last 20 years of my roaming I have forgotten a good deal in the scientific realm, I have perhaps learnt a good deal as an author, and I hope that just this will be of use to me in my intention. For if I am not deceived, it is now time, along with the educated among the people, to step over the clergy. One must let the theologians remain as a *massa perditionis*[39] or as the hardened Jews in the time of the apostle Paul, and turn to the heathen who long for salvation, i.e. the laity. The facts are now (pre-eminently through you) so far brought into the light, that the laity *can* understand us, since the theologians indeed *will* not understand us.

So then most honoured old Commander, permit that a former officer who has however for a long time gone about in civvies, may now, in the changed circumstances of the time, enter once again into your corps as a volunteer, and may you soon, as the trusty General, hale and hearty, again lead us forward to the battle and to victory!

This the sincere wish of your
unchangeably devoted,
D. F. Strauss.[40]

In the summer of 1860 Zeller's long essay entitled 'Die Tübinger historische Schule' was published in the *Historische Zeitung*. It was indeed a comprehensive and carefully written picture of the 'school' and its aims, but Baur was not pleased by the important place given to Strauss. The essay began by depicting the inadequacy of the supernatural and rational

[38] The reference is to K. L. Weitzel's book *Die christliche Passafeier der drei ersten Jahrhunderte* (Pforzheim, 1848). Weitzel's views precipitated a long controversy on the subject of the Passover.

[39] Mass destined for destruction.

[40] Printed in *PJ*, 161, pp. 137–8; with textual corrections by Barnikol in *ZKG* (1962), pp. 123–4.

explanations, and the great commotion which the *Life of Jesus* had caused when it first appeared. Strauss, wrote Zeller, demanded that the Gospel narratives be examined in a scientific and purely historical manner, and not interpreted as accounts of supernatural and miraculous events.

He demanded not more and not less than what is obvious for any scientific theology: that the Gospel reports be treated according to the same basic principles by which we judge every other conviction; that the results of the critical investigation be neither wholly nor partly written in advance; that, much more, the determination of the investigation be alone and exclusively awaited from the investigation itself; that criticism, biblical criticism as well, should be, in one word, presuppositionless. A purely historical procedure and nothing else is what Strauss demands for criticism; he views the task of criticism as the determination of the historical facts from the reports, and expects, at any rate, also this, that the presuppositionless critic should not proceed from the presupposition of a belief in miracles.[41]

In employing this approach, continued Zeller, Strauss came to the conclusion that a large part of the Gospel narratives were unhistorical – not only the stories of Jesus' birth and childhood, but also the miracles he was supposed to have performed, and his resurrection from the dead. But there were two important shortcomings in Strauss' book, the first being that not all the narratives could be explained as having originated in the unconscious mythological process, the second, that Strauss had only shown what Jesus was not, but had not shown what he was. Only by a more positive critical approach could that be accomplished – by means of an investigation of the sources, their character, and the time and place of composition.

Here is now the point where the investigations of Baur in Tübingen enter the story. He had, to be sure, already begun these investigations before the *Life of Jesus* appeared, but their full and ruthless execution was first made possible through Strauss' critical effectiveness. If Strauss had come to his work from philosophy, Baur comes to his from history. If, for Strauss, the first concern was to get rid of untenable presuppositions, to free himself from the incredibilities of the supernatural interpretation and the tortures of the rationalistic, for Baur it was a case of attaining a satisfying view of the

---

[41] *HZ*, IV (1860) p. 100.

origin and initial development of Christianity. Now this is certainly impossible without previous or simultaneous examination of the tradition; Baur's historical construction is in so far determined by the Straussian criticism, and it could not earlier have come to fruition before that free road had been made for it. And yet in the procedures of the two men there always remains the distinction that for Strauss, the critical disputation of tradition was merely a means for the restoration of the historical facts, while Baur's positive view of history is only the product, and almost a secondary product, of his critical analysis.

This, their relationship, comes to view in characteristic way already, in their respective points of departure. Strauss, with his criticism, immediately devotes himself to those writings in which the miraculous and the improbable disturb him most, partly because it has mostly accumulated here, partly because it concerns the central point of the Christian religion, the Person and history of Christ. Baur seeks above all to obtain a firm foundation for further historical combinations...[42]

Baur was dissatisfied with Zeller's portrayal of the relationship between Strauss and himself, and wrote to Zeller expressing his views:

It seems to me that you have set the Straussian *Life of Jesus* far too prominently in the foreground and conceived the relationship to the actual object of the essay too little according to the side, which appears to me, to come mainly into consideration. I am certainly far removed from wanting in any way to cast doubt on the originality and great significance of the Straussian work; I have never dared to do it, nor to allude to anything which could let me appear, over against Strauss, as the founder of a school; but for just this reason it seems to me all the more important to emphasize sharply the distinction between the two directions. The Straussian tendency (you say) is the whole presupposition of mine – one does not actually think about this when one speaks of the Tübingen School of criticism. As I attempted to show in my essay on the Tübingen School – which is completely relevant here – and especially where I discussed the matter more carefully in the introduction to my book on the canonical Gospels, one can best define the distinction between Strauss' criticism and mine: Strauss' criticism is the criticism of history, mine the criticism of the writings which form the source of the history. This seems to me simpler and more definite than the distinction which you made (p. 106). My criticism is supposed

---

[42] *Ibid.* p. 106.

to be completely dependent upon Strauss' – but I had already, before Strauss, struck out on my own particular road, upon which criticism can first become strictly historical. It is conceded that the Straussian procedure is not completely satisfying, that it is deficient when everything is finally traced back to the mythical explanations; but where does this deficiency show itself more clearly than in the Gospel of John, in its relation to the Synoptics? This is the main point which, in my view, should have certainly been more emphasized if the characteristic of the Tübingen School, in so far as I am supposed to be its founder, is to be more exactly designated. Strauss himself conceded and acknowledged this; the Gospel of John made him, to be sure, vacillating, but he did not solve the riddle; he even says openly that I was the first to attain mastery over the peculiar magic of John's Gospel. Everything in the circle drawn by Strauss remains in its right, but one must also go beyond this circle; it is this turning point of the most recent critical procedure, which, according to my view, should be well held fast. The true and right view consists in not identifying oneself too closely with Strauss, but just as much in differentiating and separating oneself from him, and only then acknowledging the principal interpretation of the Tübingen School.

I must restrict myself to this small amount since unfortunately writing causes me so much trouble; I would gladly talk with you further about your essay, which has been read to me, parts I have read myself; I would best of all like to discuss it with you some time. Since I had to compose this letter as briefly as possible, I would ask you not to take the expressions I have used too strictly and to interpret everything in the best sense.[43]

Here, in the letter, we again see the two points which lay at the root of the dissension between himself and Strauss. First, that Baur attempted to diminish the importance of Strauss' theological achievement and was unwilling to accept the fact that he owed anything to Strauss. Secondly, and more important, Baur did not want to be identified with Strauss, but rather attempted to cover up the common anti-supernatural basis, which they in fact shared, by emphasising his positive, in opposition to Strauss' negative, approach. The problem was that Zeller had outlined the fact that Baur held to the same negative anti-supernatural principles as Strauss *too* clearly, especially when he had written:

[43] To Zeller, 19.10.60; *PJ*, 161, pp. 137–8.

The miracle and the historical consideration of things exclude each other; whoever will hold to the latter cannot grant the former – in this conviction Baur is fully agreed with Strauss.[44]

That was the really embarrassing statement! But what was Baur to say? He could not deny what Zeller had written; all he could do was to fall back on the old, hackneyed cliché emphasising the positive and negative difference as regards the sources.

Zeller's reply was a model of diplomacy.

I was terribly sorry that my essay did not completely satisfy you in just that point in which I believed myself to be in perfect agreement with you. Perhaps however a further consideration will convince you that the difference in our conceptions is not so great as might appear from your letter and one's first impression of it; and it is certainly my fault if I have not expressed myself clearly enough, in order to make this appearance impossible. As regards the first, the placing of the Straussian *Life of Jesus* before your writings, I have here, in the arrangement of the material, followed the same course – which is inherent in the nature of the subject – as you in your criticism of the Gospels. I have first discussed the book, which in time preceded your main works and, as regards the standpoint, represents only a first step to your criticism, in order to elucidate the stage of the investigation into which your investigations broke in an epoch-making way. But I believed I had taken adequate care to ensure that no one should conclude from this that your accomplishments were dependent upon those of Strauss, when I expressly emphasized that you had already found the basis of your view before Strauss came on the scene, and when I discussed in a detailed way the deficiencies of the Straussian standpoint which have been corrected by you. When I said that your construction of history is, in a certain respect (in so far), conditioned by the Straussian standpoint and could not have come earlier to fruition before that free road had been made, I meant this to be understood only in reference to an *undergirding* of your investigations. This, at any rate, seems to me to correspond to the facts of the matter. For so certain it is that criticism of the historical development remains imperfect, as long as one has not orientated himself in the source-material through investigations such as yours, so impossible is it, on the other hand, for these investigations to be carried on with scientific freedom, before the appearance has been destroyed that these writings are

44 *HZ*, IV (1860) p. 109.

E

straightforward historical books. This appearance however – even
if others might likewise have been able to destroy it – was indeed,
actually, and before the eyes of the scientific world, first destroyed
by Strauss, and you found this state of affairs when your criticism
proceeded from the New Testament letters and Acts to the Gospels.
But to go further, to explain satisfactorily the origin of the Gospel
reports by a positive view and to trace out a positive historical
picture of the earliest Christianity – this, Strauss was not able to do,
and just for this reason, in the introduction of your investigations
into the Gospels, you designated his view as the negatively critical
and set over against it your view as the historical (or as you also say:
the positive) criticism. Now my treatment says exactly the same
thing. Strauss, it says, wanted first to free himself from untenable
presuppositions; you wanted to attain a satisfying historical conception of Christianity; with Strauss the positive view of history
is only a secondary product of his critical analysis – he shows us
only what Christ was *not*; on the other hand, if we ask what he was,
then we do not pass beyond a few indefinite surmises. But with you,
conversely, the critical disputation of tradition is only a means for
restoring the historical facts; you are distinguished from one
another in that you, far more definitely than Strauss, proceed
towards a positive view of the origin of Christianity and its oldest
writings. In this respect there is certainly no essential difference
between what I have said and what you yourself have said, but at
most, such a distinction which touches the form and the magnitude
of the expression. But also my treatment did not omit the further
point, that Strauss wants to give a criticism of history without a
simultaneous criticism of the historical sources, even if it could have
emphasized this point even more clearly than it did (p. 103f), where
in this respect, just this – the omission of the particular literary
character of the Gospels – is designated as the first main short-
coming of the Straussian criticism while, conversely (p. 110), one
of your most essential services is found in the criticism of the
New Testament writings. Yet I must admit that radical as this
distinction is, it still seems to me that the contrast between the
positive-historical and the negative criticism, which also precedes
your introduction, is even more fundamental. For in the last analysis, wherein does the worth of the literary criticism lie except in the
fact that it enables us to attain a true picture of the historical
development itself, by means of writings from this period which –
correctly understood – are its records. Yet on this question there
is no difference in our views and even the appearance of a difference, which could be present elsewhere, will on closer investigation
be almost completely resolved.

At the most, what may remain over is that the significance of the *Life of Jesus* may perhaps appear greater to me than to you. We of the younger generation experienced from this book an effect which you could scarcely experience, because it did not first need to liberate you from the presuppositions on which the theological world then suffered. You may have been much stimulated by it personally, but you received no new standpoint; we had to thank it for opening – to us – a completely new breadth of vision into the area of criticism and for unshackling our courage to be critical. But the theology at that time was generally in the same position, and it is a question whether it is not more relevant to the facts of the case when one measures the historical significance of that book, not by its use for the Master who has progressed ahead of his time, but by its effect on the inexperienced and the beginners.

Pardon this long discussion, in which you will see nothing else than a proof of the most fervent wish to remove everything which could disturb you, as far away as possible.[45]

Even now Baur was still not satisfied.

The substance of the matter is still that Strauss carried through the already long present view of the unhistorical reality of miracles methodically and basically to a purely negative historical view, where, however, he also remained; between his *Life of Jesus* and his concluding dogmatic treatment lies an infinite cleft, beyond which, with his standpoint at that time, he could never pass. Only through a completely different criticism can his view descend from its negativity to a base on which there is also a true and real history. I believe that this should have been brought out with even more definite emphasis and should have been designated as the main point of the distinction.[46]

Baur died on 2 December 1860. Strauss did not attend the funeral on the ground that it was to be pre-eminently an academic occasion; but he wrote a warm obituary, and in a letter to Zeller declared that with Baur, 'the last great theologian has gone to the grave.[47]

Zeller and his wife asked Strauss if he would write Baur's biography, but Strauss did not have the heart. The rift over the years had been so deep and painful in its effects that even his great admiration for Baur's scholastic achievements was

[45] To Baur, 23.10.60; *PJ*, 161, pp. 138–40.
[46] To Zeller, 6.11.60; *PJ*, 161, pp. 140–1.
[47] To Zeller, 4.12.60; *AB*, p. 423.

insufficient to heal the wounds from which he had suffered for so long.

When you ask yourself whether indeed Baur would have been in agreement, if someone had proposed to him that I should be his biographer, so will you both – and especially you – certainly not be able to answer yes. Baur always looked on me as his Reuben (Gen. 49, 3–4), and this Reuben was at least honest enough, with his whole heart, not to begrudge you the position of Joseph, and even to confirm the verdict of our patriarchal father so far as you were concerned. But now consider what inner opposition my work must generate in the consciousness when I should set my hand to work as one uncalled, and when I should see the picture of the deceased confronting me, instead of with friendly beckoning finger, much more with raised parrying hand.[48]

[48] To Zeller, 15.5.61; *AB*, p. 432.

# 11

## THE THIRD EDITION OF THE
## *LIFE OF JESUS*

Strauss felt considerably more at home in Stuttgart than in Ludwigsburg, yet even here he could not rid himself of the feeling that he was reckoned as a heretic. For at this time the Church was so bound up with society that he was ostracised in both circles and could not openly visit his friends for fear of bringing them into disrepute. Cordial relations with acquaintances were continually restricted and sometimes had to be given up; thus the annoyance which he expressed in a letter to Rapp is quite understandable. 'This experience of the insidious poison by which the Church interdict gradually gnaws away all relationships, set me in a kind of painful rage.'[1]

The main problem confronting him was the question of his future sphere of activity. His hopes of obtaining a theological or even philosophical chair were slim; all that remained open to him was a position in a secondary school teaching languages – and he had no desire to spend the rest of his life in such an occupation. Certainly the two editions of his book had provided him with a small revenue, but that would not last indefinitely and it was imperative that some other means of income be found. In Bern, Schneckenburger exerted himself on his behalf, but the best possibility of obtaining a position appeared to lie in Zürich, where since 1831 a more liberal government had been in power. Here, Ferdinand Hitzig, a cousin of Binder's and professor of Old Testament, made two attempts to secure him a theological chair, but the majority were not yet won over and both attempts came to nothing.

It was probably all these factors combined – the ecclesiastical and social ostracism, the failure of the attempts to gain a

---

[1] Ziegler, p. 261.

117

professorship and the numerous pamphlets and books written
against him – which caused him to waver in his views. No one
supported him openly; he stood completely alone. Even his old
teacher Baur had expressed his disagreement over his denial of
the authenticity of John and it was only to be expected that
Strauss would be beset by doubts. 'Are you alone right and the
whole Church – orthodox, rationalists and liberals – wrong?'
And so, in this difficult situation, surrounded by uncertainty
and stunned by the torrent and force of the reaction which his
over-optimistic mind had under-estimated, he faltered, and in
the third edition conceded certain points to his critics.

The central issue in the whole discussion concerned the
authenticity of the fourth Gospel which Strauss, in the first
edition, had denied to be the work of an eye-witness or apostle.
It was on this point that friend and foe alike were in agreement
against him, and one could even say that it was almost regarded
as a test of one's orthodoxy. Baur in his defence against Hengstenberg protested that he had never and nowhere denied its
authenticity; de Wette declared that the matter could not be
decided, and even the rationalist Bretschneider had withdrawn
all his former objections against its genuineness, so that Strauss
was left completely in the lurch. With these doubts having
been planted in his mind, he now expressed his uncertainty
about his former views in the third edition which appeared in
1838–9.

The changes which this new edition offers are more or less connected
with the fact that a renewed study of the fourth Gospel, with the aid
of de Wette's commentary and Neander's *Life of Jesus*, has made me
once again doubtful of my former doubts concerning the authenticity and credibility of this Gospel. Not as if I had been convinced
of its authenticity; only that I am no longer convinced of its unauthen-
ticity. Under the so particularly opposed and contradictory criteria
of credibility and incredibility, of nearness and remoteness from the
truth, in this most remarkable Gospel, I emphasized with polemical
zeal, in the initial composition of my work, only – as it seemed to me
– the neglected, adverse side: in the meanwhile, the other side has
gradually attained its rightful place in my thinking; only that I am
not immediately in a position to sacrifice the contrary observations
to it, as almost all the present-day theologians down to de Wette do.
Through this situation my work, as it now appears, has lost in unity,
both in comparison with its earlier form, as with the newer works

of others written from a contrary viewpoint: but I hope that it has gained against both in truth.[2]

No longer now did he flatly deny the possibility that some of the events recorded in the Gospels were historical. The disciples, he admitted, might have so been chosen by Jesus; it may have been true that Jesus had seen Nathaniel under the fig tree, by means of an extraordinary gift of far-sight which enabled him to perceive distant objects impossible for normal-sighted men to see; he may also have possessed the gift of a supernatural clairvoyance which enabled him to discern the true state of the life of the Samaritan woman whom he met at Jacob's well; and as regards the healing miracles which Jesus was supposed to have performed, he was now prepared to grant the possibility that such healings had actually occurred as a result of certain mesmeric and psychic powers which Jesus had employed.

Even the pre-existence of Jesus was no longer emphatically denied as in the first edition. Certainly Strauss had no intention of accepting the traditional view, but he now conceded that the idea of Jesus' pre-existence may not have been merely invented by the biblical narrators, and that Jesus himself may have actually believed that he had had a former existence before his earthly life.

Accordingly, since the idea of a pre-existence of the Messiah is found in the higher Jewish theology directly following the time of Jesus, it is not too much to suppose that the same idea was also already present in the time in which Jesus developed, and that if he once conceived himself as the Messiah, then he could have transferred this feature of the messianic conception – which would ring in the peculiarity of his religious consciousness – to himself. It is however remarkable and suspicious that only the author of the fourth Gospel, who has an intimate acquaintance with the Alexandrian doctrine of the logos, puts the assertion of a pre-existence into Jesus' mouth: and from this side it will always remain open to doubt, whether this conception belongs to Jesus' actual view about himself, or is only the reflection of the fourth evangelist about him.[3]

As regards Jesus himself, Strauss was now prepared to make more positive statements instead of, as formerly, maintaining

[2] Preface to the third edition, pp. iv–v.    [3] *LJ* (3rd ed.), I, p. 542.

that Jesus' whole life was hidden in the mists of history. Thus Jesus was now considered as a genius, in the same class as Napoleon, Goethe, Raphael and Mozart, but with the added distinction that the religious genius occupies a higher place, since the divine Spirit is present in the consciousness *directly*, and not merely *indirectly*, as in other geniuses and heroes:

For me also is Jesus the greatest religious personality which history is able to point to; in the section dealing with Jesus' development I also explicitly expressed my conviction that his natural talent plays the greatest part in his greatness: by virtue of his genius he must indeed – as I have already conceded in the second edition of my *Life of Jesus* – have attained the conviction of his messiahship a good deal earlier than one could suppose according to certain hints in the Gospel – particularly the Synoptic – reports. His power over souls, with which perhaps a physical power of healing was also bound up, which we may interpret somehow by the analogy of a mesmeric power, achieved cures which must have appeared to be miracles; his standpoint, on the highest level of the religious self-conscious-ness, expressed itself in noble speeches; his purely human mind in instructive addresses; his originality in ingenious sayings; from the beginning to the end of his life his fate was, as his Person, extraordinary.[4]

This declaration satisfied the orthodox just as little as his final words in *Vergängliches und Bleibendes im Christenthum* (*The Transient and Permanent in Christianity*), where he maintained that so long as 'the highest' in religion remains, i.e. the con-sciousness of the true unity of the human with the divine, which is most perfectly revealed in the life of Jesus, then the historicity of the Gospel narratives is a matter of complete indifference.

So then, we need not fear that Christ might be lost to us when we find ourselves compelled to surrender much of what was formerly called Christianity! He remains for us, and for everyone, all the more sure, the less anxiously we hold fast to teachings and opinions which can become a stumbling block to thinking, leading us to fall away from Christ. But if Christ remains for us, and if he remains for us as the highest that we are able to know and think in a religious relationship, as he without whose presence in the soul no perfection

[4] *Streitschriften*, III, pp. 152–3. This passage well illustrates the same thoughts which Strauss expressed in the third edition of the *Life of Jesus*.

of piety is possible, then the essential element of Christianity indeed remains for us in him.[5]

In spite of all the criticism heaped upon him because of these changes, Strauss had not conceded so very much – the possibility that some of the narratives might be explained by unknown mesmeric, psychic and natural laws; that Jesus might have thought of himself as having had some kind of prior existence; that what could be known about Jesus was not so veiled as he himself had originally thought, and that Jesus could be considered as the greatest religious genius – all these concessions taken by themselves were not of such great significance. But what they did show was that Strauss was no longer certain about the full applicability of the mythical principle to the New Testament, and he himself finally realised that were he to concede even one of the miracles to the rationalistic explanation, then the unity of the whole interpretation by the mythical principle would be shattered, in so far as one could never distinguish between what was to be viewed as mythical and what had an actual historical basis. Previously all had been simple: every narrative showing traces of the miraculous or the supernatural had been regarded as mythical – regardless of whereabouts in the New Testament it was found. Now, however, he had compromised and retreated back to the same solutions on which he had formerly poured his scorn; the mythical principle was no longer independent of the sources, as it had been previously, and was automatically excluded wherever a narrative was given a rational explanation.

No one was satisfied. The orthodox were jubilant that Strauss had begun to contradict himself; the rationalists and liberals thought the concessions practically worthless, and Strauss himself, weary of strife and realising his mistake, decided to take them all back and return in the fourth edition of 1840 to the pure and unadulterated mythical interpretation which had been the basis of the first edition.

The jumble of voices of opponents, critics and supporters, to which I made it my duty to listen, confused the idea of the work in my

[5] *Zwei friedliche Blätter*, p. 132. Strauss' *Vergängliches und Bleibendes im Christenthum*, written in 1838, was reprinted the following year in *Zwei friedliche Blätter*.

mind; in the diligent comparison of divergent opinions I lost sight of the matter itself. Thus I was led to make alterations over which – as I once more looked through this last revision in a more collected frame of mind – I had to shake my head in wonder, and by which I had obviously done myself an injustice. In all these passages the earlier readings have been restored and my work in this new edition has, so to speak, simply consisted in removing from my good sword the notches made in it rather by my own grinding, than those hewn in it by the blows of my enemies.[6]

[6] Preface to the fourth edition.

# 12

## THE CALLING TO ZÜRICH

### THE ZÜRICH REFORMS

The Revolution of 1830 had brought about a profound change throughout Europe. No longer were the people prepared to sit passively under the thumbs of their aristocratic overlords and endure the miseries of poverty and subordination. They demanded freedom to think and to express their ideas; they wanted new governments which would permit greater freedom of thought, and progress in all areas of life. Those who were prepared to follow out such radical theories were men who had drunk deeply from the heady wine of the Enlightenment; reason was now placed above revelation and intellectual progress was seen as the new and true religion of the people. Emancipation and progress – those were the key words of the radical party.

In the Canton of Zürich, a new radical government replacing the old privileged city aristocracy had come to power in 1831 and in the remarkably short period of 8 years had achieved amazing results in the fields of education, law, administration, economics, taxes and a host of others. New roads had been built, schools established, factories erected, and in almost every sphere of life reforms had either been pushed through or were contemplated in the near future. Naturally, with so much progress in so short a time, there were bound to be mistakes, and sometimes not enough time was allowed for the necessary adjustments to be made. Then again, it was inevitable that antagonism should be aroused among those who found the new measures detrimental to their own vested interests. Thus in 1832, for instance, the recently founded weaving factory at Uster was burnt to the ground by a crowd of enraged peasants, who saw the income from their own hand-weaving endangered by the new mechanical looms.

123

Most of the trouble, however, stemmed from the educational reforms. The new government with its enlightened views had introduced compulsory education for children, and a new teacher's training college was established at Küsnach under the direction of Thomas Scherr. The old teaching system had become decrepit and many teachers did not possess the necessary qualifications. Examinations were therefore held to determine those fitted to teach, and the 104 failures were henceforth dismissed – a fact which could not fail to cause much resentment against the new college and its director. But not only the former teachers were hostile; the compulsory education also antagonised the factory owners who had formerly been able to employ the children as a source of cheap labour and who now saw themselves compelled to pay higher wages. Farmers resented the fact, that for a large part of the day their children were hindered from working on the farms, and there was also resentment among some of the clergy who, formerly occupying the position of village teacher, were now replaced by the qualified teachers from the new college.

All things considered, the reforms were good and necessary, and no one today will deny the foresight and perspicacity of the radical party. But the real and underlying grievance of the orthodox Christians was that this zeal for education was also bound up with an intense aversion against all forms of established Christianity – not only against the established Church, but against the Christian faith generally. The doctrines of the divinity of Christ, the virgin birth, atonement, resurrection, etc. were now to be thrown overboard, and even the existence of God was quietly and surreptitiously abandoned as the relic of an unenlightened age. The absurdity of such beliefs was slowly but surely to be demonstrated through intellectual enlightenment, i.e. through education, and to this end the training college at Küsnach served as a centre for the new atheistic policies. There, the radical ideas were imparted to all the future teachers, and even Ziegler admits that under the enthusiasm of Director Scherr, 'a free – an extremely free spirit was blowing'.[1]

It was, then, only natural that the orthodox clergy and believers throughout the Canton should regard the educational reforms with growing suspicion and hostility. Even one of the

---

[1] Ziegler, p. 294.

new geography books contained a passage describing the individual confessions of faith, in which was found the provocative statement:

Protestants are generally tolerant and worship only one God: but among these, the pious or pietists, who worship three Gods – God the Father, God the Son and God the Holy Spirit – must be excepted.[2]

and the new radical government was viewed as the root cause of the slowly continuing demoralisation of the people. Dancing, hunts, public performances on Sundays and religious festivals – all these were seen as resulting from the permissive laxity of the liberals and designed to turn Zürich and Winterthur into Sodom and Gomorrah.

Up until 1839 the new government had carried out reforms in all areas except one – the Church. Here the radicals knew that they had to tread extremely warily, but reforms were projected, especially a revision of the Catechism. It was just at this point that the calling of Strauss to Zürich assumed a significance which went beyond the importance of the professorship in itself, for the radicals saw in Strauss a theologian who would be able to help in carrying through these desired reforms. Had this not been the case, Strauss would never have received the support needed for his appointment. His nomination became a battle-ground between radical and conservative factions, and only as a result of the backing of the radical party was that calling effectively accomplished. The nomination in fact symbolised the government's intention of undertaking these necessary Church reforms, and it was for this reason that the Church mobilised all its resources to quash the appointment. The conflict was seen, on both sides, not merely as a dispute over the appointment of an heretical theologian, but as a struggle for control of the Church,[3] and, in the eyes of the

---

[2] Hausrath, I, p. 349.

[3] Cf. the letter of Alexander Schweizer in which he wrote to Strauss: 'Be assured that it is not primarily a question which concerns you as a person – neither among all your friends, nor among the majority of your enemies – but the struggle against a kind of radicalism which – I have long been convinced – you would not hold to. You immediately became the banner which should lead that party to new victories; hence the so widespread resistance which wants not only to keep both you and your theological

orthodox, as a struggle between the armies of God and the armies of Satan. Such then was the setting in which 'The Calling of Dr. Strauss' was to be played out.

## THE CALLING

Two previous attempts had been made to secure for Strauss a theological chair at Zürich. When Rettig, professor of Church history and dogmatics had died in 1836, Hitzig and the philologist Orelli had hoped that Strauss might be won for Zürich. However, apart from the rationalist Schulthess, there appeared to be no one else who showed any enthusiasm for the idea. Even the liberal theologian Alexander Schweizer, whose views were certainly not very different from those of Strauss, was adamant that Strauss should be proposed for the philosophical, and not the theological faculty. The result was that Strauss received only 4 of the 15 votes and a fellow Swabian, Elwert, subsequently received the appointment. Even so, the hope was not lost that one day the minority might be turned into a majority, and it was even reported that some weeks later at an academic gathering, a toast was drunk to 'Strauss and the future' by one and all.

At the end of the same year (1836) Schulthess died and Strauss was asked if he would consider accepting a position as assistant professor with a salary of 800, and possibly 1200, francs. He initially and cautiously indicated his assent with certain provisos – among which was one, that he should not receive less than 1200 fr.; however, in a second letter he withdrew this assent and stipulated that he would come to Zürich only on the assurance of a full professorship and a salary of 2000 fr. Thus the attempt failed for the second time although the general mood of the faculty appeared more favourable.

In 1838 Elwert became ill and resigned his position in order to retire to a small pastorate in his native Württemberg. Thus the chair of Church history and dogmatics again became vacant. Hitzig seized his chance and proposed Strauss for the position, expressing the hope that the appointment might help

---

views far away, but also, at the same time, to bring about a victory for Christian moral principles over this radicalism.' *Biographische Aufzeichnungen* (Zürich, 1889) Beilage III, p. 102.

Strauss to follow a more positive direction. Schweizer, however, and the majority of the faculty, still opposed the nomination on the ground that the chair of Christian doctrine could not be occupied by one whose theology was so critically negative, and merely on the hope that Strauss might be induced to follow a more positive direction.

The matter, in the first instance, was to be decided by the Council for Education where the opinions of the members were fairly equally divided between those wanting Strauss, and those desiring the conservative Landerer from Württemberg. The outcome of the vote was therefore somewhat uncertain, although the general opinion was that Strauss would not be chosen. Certainly it was emphasised that in the third edition of the *Life of Jesus*, Strauss had not been so negative as in the two preceding editions, and had even made certain concessions to his critics; but whether this fact would influence those whose minds had not yet been made up was anybody's guess, and no one was completely sure which way the decision would fall. The Council met on the 26 January 1839 to decide the issue one way or the other; the vote was tied – 7 voting for Landerer, 7 for Strauss – with Bürgermeister Hirzel, one of the leaders of the pro-Strauss party, having the casting vote. He naturally decided for Strauss and thus by one vote the radical party emerged victoriously triumphant. The first round had been won![4]

Five days later, on 31 January, the Great Council assembled to consider the matter. There was a long and serious debate lasting ten hours in which the speakers on both sides presented the pros and cons, with Alexander Schweizer again warning of the serious consequences which would result if the decision of the Council for Education were upheld. As before, it was

---

[4] The circumstances were related by Strauss two weeks later in a letter to Vischer. 'Thus – as was well known – the decision of the Education Council depended upon one vote (that of the teacher Ruegg who resides outside of Zürich), which remained undecided up to the day of the debate. Now what does the Bürgermeister do? He plants himself at the coach stop at the time when Ruegg must arrive, and as he alights, takes him home, entertains him to a meal and doesn't let him get up from the table until he has given me his vote. My opponents for their part complain bitterly about this – and justifiably; but for my part this story brings me much pleasure – likewise justifiably.' (To Vischer, 9.2.39; *AB*, pp. 79–80.)

widely believed that the Great Council would not uphold the previous decision and that the calling of Strauss would be the last straw which would break the back of the radical party. Late in the evening the vote was taken and when the result was announced, to the horrified astonishment of the orthodox party, the Great Council had endorsed the earlier recommendation by 98 votes to 49. Two days later the Governing Council, having ratified the decision by 15 votes to 3, appointed Strauss professor, with a salary of 2000 fr.; Strauss, in a letter from Stuttgart on the 18 February, accepted the call and sought to soothe the doubts of the orthodox concerning his radical views:

Your highly-esteemed President, Herr Bürgermeister Hirzel, has already, by public statements, sought to allay the various fears which have been expressed among your people on account of my religious views, and I thankfully acknowledge that the content of those statements is perfectly in accord with my own thoughts. I do not, in fact, count among the most difficult tasks which I will have to solve in my new post, that of calming the minds of those who suppose me to be a man who intends to use the position assigned to him at your university to undermine the existing religion. Fears such as these must disappear as soon as people see, that far from wishing to encroach upon unfamiliar territory and disturb the Christian community in its religious faith and practice, I will completely restrict myself to the limits of my academic calling; and in this too, I will work towards the end that the divine, fundamental truths of Christianity shall be respected, and, in the spirit of this respect, shall be continually purified by human proofs.[5]

By now the protest had grown into a great clamour against the appointment. Pamphlets and articles flooded from the press – even the Catholics took up the orthodox side. 'Strauss says in his book that Jesus was a fictional character invented out of the Old Testament, that the virgin birth, atonement, resurrection and ascension are all without historical basis, that heaven and hell are absurdities which no modern man can believe, that a life after death is an illusion and that God is to be conceived as a developing process which exists only in thinking.'[6] With such summaries of Strauss' views were the people aroused to the danger confronting them, and the title of one of

---

[5] Hausrath, I, Beilage VI, pp. 27–8.
[6] Cf. Hausrath, I, pp. 366f.

2 The original of this caricature, which is in colour, was drawn in the early 1840s. The cleft in the ground from which fire issues symbolises the barrier separating the upper class from the common people, alternatively, the pious from the unbelievers. On the left with the axe stands Strauss [Strauss in German = ostrich] attempting to fell the cross, while the common man (the man in the wooden shoes, badly clothed with a padlock in his mouth) lends support by pulling upon a rope. Pulling from the other direction are the pious [the sheep] exhorted on by E. W. Hengstenberg [Hengst = stallion], editor of the conservative Protestant Church journal, the *Evangelische Kirchenzeitung*. Above on the tree sit King Wilhelm IV of Prussia reading in his Bible and holding a basket containing decorations of honour which his Minister for Education, Johann Albrecht Eichhorn [Eichhorn = squirrel], is dropping to those helping to defend the Christian faith against the attack of the unbelievers led by Strauss.

*Photo by courtesy of the Schiller National-Museum, Marbach, which possesses the original drawing.*

3 Christian Märklin, 1834     4 Friedrich Theodor Vischer, 1845

5 Ernst Rapp, about 1870     6 Ferdinand Christian Baur, 1859

8 Agnese and children
(Georgine and Fritz),
about 1852

7 Agnese Schebest, about 1838

9 Strauss, about 1852

10 Strauss, about 1860

gez. v. Adolf Neumann

11 Strauss, 1865

the pamphlets: 'Strauss may not and shall not come!' became the motto of the opposition, an opposition which was hardly to be pacified by the blandiloquent pleas of Bürgermeister Hirzel:

My esteemed fellow citizens in town and country, be not any longer angry with us that we have made it possible for Professor Strauss to let his God-given gifts shine among us! Be not angry, but kind-hearted!...Just get to know this intelligent, moral and believing man. Who knows, the handsome stranger whom you now think that you hate, may yet become very dear to your hearts.[7]

The orthodox now began to make ready for battle. A network of committees was formed which spread throughout the whole Canton and a central committee of 22, among whom were 7 clergymen, became the focal point of the opposition party. On 1 March a petition was presented to the government demanding the annulment of Strauss' appointment and the calling of a professor whose views were of a decisively orthodox direction. The government was further informed that the radical tendency of the teaching in schools, and especially in the new training college, was distinctly displeasing, and the petition closed with a thinly-veiled threat of revolution were the demands not met:

Finally, we ask the esteemed government to consider the consequences which the refusal of our demands must necessarily have for themselves and for the whole land, and conclude by assuring the government of our whole and undivided respect.[8]

On 10 March the petition was circulated in all the churches of the Canton. Almost every eligible person voted and the strength of the opposition was shown in that 39,225 signed their approval while only 1048 voted against.

At this point, Strauss again entered into the fray with his 'Open Letter to Bürgermeister Hirzel, Professor Orelli and Professor Hitzig in Zürich', which he wrote at the request of these three friends. It was in fact a great mistake and only poured more oil on the fire. What indeed were the Bürgers of Zürich to think when Strauss, having summarised the

---

[7] *Ibid.* 1, p. 373.

[8] *Adresse der vereinigten 22 Deputirten an den H. Regierungsrath des Cantons Zürich* (Zürich, 1839).

traditional orthodox view of the Christian faith, then con-
descendingly and politely, gave them to understand that it
was all nonsense.

This is the old Christian faith. And who would be insensible to its
beauty, its uplifting and comforting qualities? Certainly not us,
but...[9]

Or when, for example, the miracles were simply brushed
aside with the plea that all miracles are simply to be regarded
as part of one great miracle.

The miracles, in the sense of the old popular belief, can only have a
particular value for the person who is incapable of recognising the
power and wisdom of the Creator in the natural order of the world;
and we, who are accused of not believing in those miracles which
God performed in the land of the Jews at the time of Moses and the
prophets, Jesus and the Apostles, do not esteem these as important
because, to us, they are lost like a drop in the ocean among the
innumerable miracles which God is performing daily and hourly in
all parts of the world which he created and preserves. 'Behold the
finger of God', they cry to us – 'His finger stopped the sun and moon
in their courses in the time of Joshua!' 'His finger?!' we reply, 'We
recognise his whole hand, his strong arm, which not only stopped
the sun and moon once, for a few hours, but which holds, bears and
guides in their rightful courses all suns, moons and earths – the
whole host of heavenly bodies – from the creation of the world until
now.'[10]

Nor was Strauss' explanation of the divinity of Jesus calculated to soothe the indignant feelings of Zürich orthodoxy:

But the Saviour – is he then no longer extraordinary? Has not the
Son of God become merely an ordinary man? A man, a true man:
Yes! but an ordinary man? No! And he remains the Son of God
for us also – only not in the crude sense which must always remain a
stumbling-block to reason. Tell me: in the Scriptures is Christ
called only the Son of God? Is he not just as often called the Son
of Man? And does it not follow that one must be able to be the Son
of God and the son of man at one and the same time? Thus Christ
is for us the son of two pious parents, Joseph and Mary: but God
sanctified the fruit of their union; he breathed into it the beautiful
and pure soul, the high and mighty spirit which already, at an early

---

[9] *Sendschreiben an Bürgermeister Hirzel, Prof. Orelli und Prof. Hitzig in
Zürich* (Zürich, 1839) p. 12.
[10] *Ibid.* pp. 13–14.

age, manifested itself in the child; and for that reason we are fully
justified in calling the son of man also the Son of God.[11]

In his treatment of the resurrection and ascension we find
the definite beginnings of a modern existentialist interpretation:

According to the old Christian faith Christ rose again from the dead
and ascended into heaven. And according to us too; only not merely
once, and not first of all at the end of his life. But he rose at all times
from the dead whom he commanded to bury their dead (Matt. 8, 22)
and he awakens now, to this life, this side of the grave, all those who
follow him; as he himself says: He who hears my word and believes
him who sent me, has eternal life, and has passed from death to life
(John 5, 24). Likewise there was no necessity for him to be taken in
a cloud to God in heaven at the end of his life on earth, since he
raised himself thence during his lifetime in every prayer...[12]

But finally, Strauss made it only too plain that the old
Gospel stories could never be acceptable to modern scientific
thought.

We rejoice in the piety and child-like simplicity of the authors and
in the deep significance of their narrations, even though we must
recognise these as legends or poetic inventions.[13]

And it was hardly surprising that the Bürgers were incensed
when they read:

My words have been directed towards others who cannot know
these things as well as you, and who may perhaps still be prepared
to receive instruction from that incensed mass which glows with a
positively unchristian hatred of heretics, and who are resolved to
defend all other possible worldly interests under the cloak of piety.
I have nothing to say to these people, remembering the words of
Christ which expressly forbid us to cast the jewel of religious conviction before such people.[14]

and that the passage was interpreted as meaning that Strauss
considered his Zürich opponents as swine before whom he
refused to throw his pearls.

The orthodox realised only too well that were Strauss
appointed, his influence would be like a spring of poisoned

[11] Ibid. pp. 14–15.                     [12] Ibid. p. 17.
[13] Ibid. p. 21.                        [14] Ibid. p. 22.

water, whose lethal effect would gradually spread through all the lakes and streams of religious life in the Canton. Thus the hue and cry increased. 'Strauss may not and shall not come!'

Two ways out of the dilemma were proposed. Either Strauss could be pensioned off, or, a second chair might be created for an orthodox professor appointed alongside of Strauss to appease the feelings of the orthodox. The Council for Education were unwilling to pension him off and merely suggested the latter course. This did not satisfy the Governing Council which called the Great Council into special session on 18 March. Again there were sharp debates, but the mood had now completely changed from that in which the Council had met previously; the former decision was now completely reversed and it was decided by 149 votes to 31 that Strauss should be pensioned off with a yearly pension of 1000 fr. An attempt to create a second chair found little support, and the conservative theologian J. P. Lange, who had written a book against Strauss, finally received the appointment. Thus ended the whole affair for Strauss.

For the people of Zürich, however, it was not the end and the Canton remained split into pro- and anti-Strauss factions. What rankled the Zürich citizens – and especially the poorer ones – was that they should have to pay 1000 fr. every year to a man who had done nothing for them but cause division and bitterness. One newspaper even suggested that Strauss' supporters should pay the money out of their own pocket. The Central Committee, elated by their success, resolved not to disband, but to continue the struggle with the radical and atheistic Government, to which end they demanded the removal of Scherr and the elimination of the radical views in the realm of education. The sequel to these demands – how in the summer of 1839 a civil war fomented, how the orthodox and conservative Bürgers under the leadership of Dr Bernard Hirzel marched on Zürich, how the Government collapsed in confusion after the storming of the city, how Scherr was finally dismissed and the radicals suspended from office – these events belong rather to the history of Zürich than to that of Strauss, and need not be related here.[15]

[15] See Heinrich Gelzer, *Die Straussischen Zerwürfnisse in Zürich von 1839* (Hamburg and Gotha, 1843) pp. 317f.; Hausrath, I, pp. 395–423.

When we look back over the whole episode it becomes plain, that the protest of the Zürich citizens was not the groundless protest of religious fanatics that Ziegler claimed it to be.[16] Even the liberal theologian Alexander Schweizer declared that Strauss' views were quite incompatible with the orthodox Christian faith, and that his appointment could only result in conflict and bitterness. To give Strauss his due, he would probably have shown himself more conservative than most expected and attempted to honour his pledge not to disturb the faith of the people; but how long he could have 'held out against the demands of the radical party who wanted to use him for their own destructive plans',[17] and how long he would have been content to uphold the orthodox doctrines while at the same time denying them by means of a theological sleight of hand – such questions must ever remain in the realm of speculation.

In a letter to his brother just after the final decision had been made known, Baur expressed his regret that Strauss' appointment had been terminated.

The Strauss episode has certainly had a very sad ending. I feel very sorry for him, since the affair will also spoil his chances for the future.[18]

Baur was certainly correct in his presentiment. Any hopes that the notorious Dr Strauss might ever again find a position in a German university were not to be reckoned with.

[16] Ziegler, p. 326.
[17] Baur to L. F. Heyd, 7.2.39; *PJ*, 160, pp. 502–3.
[18] Baur to F. A. Baur, 25.3.39; *PJ*, 160, p. 503.

# 13

## THE DOCTRINE OF THE
## CHRISTIAN FAITH[1]

The reversal of fortune at Zürich was a severe blow to Strauss' hopes of ever obtaining a professorial chair, and the death of his mother in the same month disheartened him still further. Now he became embittered against the orthodox theology and theologians, and in this acrimonious spirit he retracted all the concessions which he had previously made in the third edition of the *Life of Jesus* and the *Two peaceable Writings*. From now on it was war to the knife against the orthodox theology.

So then, let the believer leave the intellectual to go his own way in peace, as the intellectual does the believer; we leave their faith to them; let them leave our philosophy to us. And if the over-pious should succeed in shutting us out of their church, then we will count this as gain; there have been enough false attempts made to mediate; only separation of the objects can lead anywhere new.[2]

The two-volume Dogmatics, containing almost 1500 pages, was the companion work to the *Life of Jesus* and marked Strauss' definite break with all and every theology which could claim to be based on the Bible. It was a Dogmatics from which, as Strauss wrote to Rapp, all theism was excluded.

I have here encircled and attacked theism from every side and have come out quite openly with pantheistic language. The only consideration which caused me here and there to moderate my language more than I would have liked is that my book should not be banned.[3]

---

[1] *Die christliche Glaubenslehre in ihrer geschichtlichen Entwicklung und im Kampfe mit der modernen Wissenschaft dargestellt* (2 vols.; Stuttgart, 1840–1). [The Doctrine of the Christian Faith presented in its historical Development and in its Struggle with the modern scientific Criticism.]

[2] *Ibid.* 1, p. 356.  [3] To Rapp, 27.2.40; *AB*, p. 90.

The idea of a Dogmatics, as we learn from the third *Streitschrift*, stemmed from the time of his visit to Berlin.

In the general consideration of the relationship between the religious representation and the philosophical concept, the idea of a Dogmatics developed in me and my like-minded friends, in which not merely the uppermost fat should be skimmed off – as in the Dogmatics of Marheineke – from the dialectical cauldron in which the ecclesiastical dogmas had been cooked up, but where, from the outset, all the ingredients would be on display and the whole process undertaken before our eyes. First of all, we thought, the biblical representation should be expounded; then it should be shown how this representation had evolved into the dogmas of the Church, through interaction with the one-sided heresies; the dogmas would then immediately disintegrate under the polemics of deism and rationalism and then, purified, again be restored through the concept.[4]

This plan, however, had had to be shelved, on account of the writing of the *Life of Jesus* and the subsequent *Streitschriften*, but the idea was not forgotten. In preparation for the anticipated summer semester in Zürich, Strauss had prepared a course of lectures in dogmatics; it was presumably this further engagement with the material, and perhaps the desire to justify his views against all attacks – especially from the Hegelian right – which again awakened the old interest lying dormant within him.

The form of the work follows the normal pattern of the time, with the various doctrines being considered individually, beginning with the doctrine of God and then treating of sin, Christ, the atonement, predestination, the Church and the sacraments, and finally, eschatology. The content reveals the influence of Schleiermacher, but owes most of all to Daub's Hegelian Dogmatics,[5] which had appeared several years earlier. Written in a difficult style and using the abstruse speculative terminology, the book had been almost entirely neglected, and Strauss regarded it as his duty to extract the essential core and spirit of the work and to mediate it afresh through his own writings.

One other fact of real importance should be noted – that

---

[4] *Streitschriften*, III, p. 58.
[5] Karl Daub, *Die dogmatische Theologie jetziger Zeit* (Heidelberg, 1833). Daub (1765–1836) was professor of theology in Heidelberg.

although the Hegelian thought forms constantly emerge throughout Strauss' Dogmatics, Strauss had actually given up his former view that religion is simply the outward and imperfect manifestation of the Absolute Spirit. Previously he had believed that it was possible to reconcile the religious representation with the philosophical concept – that they were merely two different forms of the one reality – but this view is now abandoned, as is shown by a letter to Märklin in 1839.

You quote in your letter against this judgment of mine, some earlier statements which I made. Firstly, the preface of my *Life of Jesus*, and here I admit quite openly, that I now no longer hold to that Hegelian standpoint and would no longer care to speak of the virgin conception of Christ, his resurrection etc. as eternal truths...Do not misunderstand me; I do not want to make inward success dependent upon outward, i.e. exhort that we should direct our scientific endeavours towards where they find approval – but I am showing the outward side only as the reverse side of the inner nature of the matter. And in this respect I stand by my opinion – and back it up by the result of your own sincere self-examination – that our co-operating with and giving philosophical support to the Christian dogmas is vain affectation, that no simple religious feeling that we have clothes itself naturally in a Christian form any more – indeed, that all the religious feelings may flee away from us rather than allow themselves to be forced into the old stinking cage of ecclesiastical doctrine – however nicely decorated it may be outwardly.[6]

A detailed exposition and criticism of the work is unnecessary for understanding the basic and essential idea of the Dogmatics as a whole, and we shall therefore confine ourselves to a brief summary of the more important features, which will also have the added advantage of relieving the reader of a long and tedious theological discussion.

In general layout the composition of the Dogmatics follows a form similar to the *Life of Jesus*, with a traditional, critical and dogmatic consideration of the individual doctrines. The biblical foundation of each doctrine is first presented and its historical development outlined, beginning with the Fathers and working through the Scholastics to the Reformers and Protestant orthodoxy – all this being interspersed with penetrating comments from Strauss. Then follows the critical sec-

[6] To Märklin, 3.11.39; Ziegler, pp. 333–4.

tion in which Strauss allows the objections of Spinoza, the Socinians, Arminians, and the rationalistic theologians of the Enlightenment to further demolish the traditional interpretations. Thirdly and lastly comes the restorative dogmatic section, where the speculative philosophy is employed as the key to interpret correctly the old traditional beliefs.

After an historical introduction to the work, the first (apologetic) part deals with certain basic problems such as the relation between philosophy and theology, the problem of history, the miraculous, the inspiration and authority of Scripture and the relation between faith and knowledge.

He who is unable to determine his own self, seeks to be determined by an authority; he who is not yet mature enough to trust in reason, remains trusting in revelation. Here, a gulf is fixed between two classes of human society, between the intellectuals and the people, i.e. the non-philosophically minded of the higher as well as the lower classes; and this gulf will, perhaps, never be bridged. If now the intellectuals have never dreamt of wanting to prohibit the non-intellectuals from expressing their faith and uttering the hardest condemnations of the intellect, it is, on the other hand, quite common for the believers to demand that the intellectuals should not be permitted to express their intellectual belief, or, from this point of departure, their judgment about the faith.[7]

The discussion of the various doctrines begins with the doctrine of God, which takes up the remainder of the first volume. Here Strauss deals with revelation, the nature of God, the divine attributes and the creation. God is no longer conceived as the personal God of traditional theology, not one person among many, but as

the eternal movement of the Universal which continually makes itself subject and which first comes to objectivity and true reality in the subject, thereby abolishing the subject in its abstract being-for-itself. Because God in himself is the eternal personality itself, he has eternally allowed his other quality, nature, to proceed forth from himself, in order to return eternally to himself as self-conscious Spirit. Or, the personality of God must not be thought of as individual personality, but as universal personality; instead of personifying the Absolute, we must learn to conceive it as the Absolute which personifies itself into the Infinite.[8]

[7] *Glaubenslehre*, I, p. 355.          [8] *Ibid.* I, p. 523.

The second volume opens with a consideration of the doctrine of sin, in which Strauss criticises the traditional theories, but has nothing at all constructive and positive to set in place of the old ideas. Then follows a lengthy section on the Person of Christ, in which he attempts to explain the metaphysical Christ without reference to the historical Jesus.

In his *Life of Jesus*, Strauss had already shown that little could be known about Jesus himself; but of one thing Strauss was certain – that Jesus was no divine, supernatural personage, and, on this account, he could have no place in a Christian Dogmatics. This attitude is well illustrated by a passage in the above-quoted letter to Märklin.

Christ, for himself, may have been who and what he likes; that is a matter of indifference to our religion, because we no longer need a Reconciler, an oracle outside of ourselves.[9]

Thus Strauss' view of Jesus remained substantially unchanged from the speculative views which he had elaborated in the concluding section of the *Life of Jesus*. The unity of God and man had been poured out, not into one specific individual in history, but into humanity; the divine predicates, which the Church had ascribed to Jesus, belonged to mankind as a whole. Two concessions which Strauss had formerly made in *Vergängliches und Bleibendes in Christenthum* are now taken back. Previously he had declared that Jesus was the highest and most-exalted personality who had ever lived and that he could never be surpassed by any other. He now asks whether such a statement can be verified, for in his reconsidered opinion, the assertion is entirely without foundation. The second concession which he had previously made was that without the presence of Jesus within our consciousness, no religious piety is possible – a statement which he now simply abandons.

The other doctrines – the Work of Christ, justification by faith, the sacraments etc. are similarly drummed out of court, and all future events transferred to the here and now. Thus the last judgment is viewed as a continuing and present judgment on our earthly life, in which we create our own heaven and hell. As for a second coming of Christ – such an absurd idea requires no discussion and is simply omitted.

[9] Ziegler, p. 334.

The doctrine of immortality, on the other hand, was rightly understood as one of the central doctrines of the Christain faith.

This doctrine of immortality is the soul of the present emotional and mental religiosity: the educated pious person would rather have his God and Christ taken from him, than the hope of a life after death. What use is a God to me, what reason do I have for taking Christ's yoke upon me, if death is the end of everything? According to the Kantian view of the old world of ideas, God, freedom and immortality remained, these three; but the greatest of these is immortality.[10]

The main argument in favour of this dogma – viz., that all right and wrong upon this earth requires a corresponding reward in the next world, otherwise all is unjust, is countered by the assertion that every man receives his true reward during the present life, although this is not always clearly observed to be the case. For, according to Strauss, the wrong-doers and the wicked ones are in fact not happy, while those who suffer righteously exude peace and joy from their hearts. The other arguments for immortality are likewise quickly disposed of and the work ends with a summary of the viewpoint which plays a prominent part throughout the whole – viz., that every supernatural and other-worldly doctrine is to be interpreted in a natural and this-worldly sense.

The word of Schleiermacher: in the middle of the finite to become one with the infinite and be eternal at every moment, is all that modern knowledge can say about immortality. With this word, our business, for the present, is ended. For the other-worldly realm, in its future form, is certainly, among all others, the one final enemy against whom the speculative criticism has to wage war, and, where possible, to overcome.[11]

That, in brief, is Strauss' Dogmatics. It was, in fact, Christianity no longer mysterious, but an exposition of the Christian faith without a personal God, without a divine and supernatural Jesus, without any miraculous events and without any life after death. And just at this point, the argument is seen to be circular, for these results were actually the presuppositions from which Strauss had written his Dogmatics – or rather, they were the logical consequences of Strauss' initial premiss, that there is no personal, no transcendent, other-worldly God.

[10] *Glaubenslehre*, II, p. 697.     [11] *Ibid.* II, pp. 738–9.

For those like Theobald Ziegler who accepted this premiss, the book possessed a certain liberating power from the constricting bands of ecclesiastical orthodoxy.

*The Doctrine of the Christian Faith* is a fine, and also extremely instructive, book from which, as Strauss himself testifies, even today one can learn much – much, that is, about the history of dogma. And it is a liberating book. I can testify to this myself: Strauss' *Doctrine of the Faith* has made me a free man; as I read this work it was as if scales fell from my eyes; as if freed from chains and fetters I could henceforth be up and about.[12]

On the whole, however, the book received an apathetic reception. With such presuppositions the result was a foregone conclusion and few people expected anything different: in this sense, then, the book contained nothing new, and was as negative as Strauss' earlier *Life of Jesus*. All the traditional theology had been demolished, but nothing substantial had been rebuilt in its place.

Its neglect stemmed also partly from the fact that theological interest had been somewhat diverted in other directions: a new king had ascended the throne of Prussia and political questions were to the forefront of the time; then there were other theological and philosophical controversies which had arisen and which claimed the attention; but above all it was the right-wing Hegelians, Bruno Bauer and Feuerbach, who were creating the stir. Bauer's attack on the Gospel sources was published during this same period (1840–1), and his wild and irresponsible assertion that the Gospel of Mark was the product of a single mind which had invented the whole story out of thin air, was even more radical than the views of Strauss. Feuerbach went just as far in a slightly different direction, and flatly rejected the Hegelian metaphysics: God was no longer the Absolute Spirit – that too, like all forms of God, was simply a projection of the human mind. The true essence of religion – its beginning, centre and end – was man himself. Christianity was henceforth to be anthropology. That was all clear and straightforward, whereas Strauss' ideas were still, to some extent, clad in the abstruse and complex Hegelian phraseology. The radical Hegelians had now completely broken with their Master and

---

[12] Ziegler, p. 354.

regarded Strauss as being outmoded, and – worst of all – as standing half-way. That was the most humiliating thing for him: he who had wanted no compromise solutions and had himself accused others of being inconsequent, now found himself in the dock. For almost a quarter of a century he remained quiet. He had, he insisted, nothing else to say. Feuerbach had dotted the i, which he as pioneer had omitted to do. And what more was there to say? Without God there could be no theology – only philosophy and anthropology.

Strauss was now sick and tired of intellectual arguments and wanted only to get away from all theological disputation. A new situation now confronted him which was to dominate his whole life for the next six years, and even beyond: marriage!

# 14

## ROMANCE AND MARRIAGE

A romance between a young university lecturer and the daughter of a Tübingen inn-keeper might have provided the theme for a famous novel, but Minele Schweickhardt was never more to Strauss than a youthful first-love, and apart from odd moments where dreaming superseded reality, marriage was never seriously considered.

Strauss' second love affair was even more fleeting. In the spring of 1837 as he was residing in Stuttgart and busily engaged on his *Streitschriften*, a young girl developed an infatuation for him, and while staying with relatives in Stuttgart, took the opportunity to visit him. He related the episode to his friend Rapp.

Just imagine – a young and pretty girl, not from Stuttgart, falls in love with me on account of my book and the controversy over it; while visiting relatives here she has come to see me often, for this very reason; she tells me all this so naively and is satisfied in the most innocent way when I cool down her delightful declaration of love to an assurance of friendship. Let no one say that we live in an unromantic age!

On one occasion she came again, regretted that I had not been in, and I had to go and visit her. The relatives had nothing to do with the affair; on one occasion I was led through their midst to her room, without being introduced to them, whereby I had exactly the same feeling as one of Horace's lovers, who at every moment has to fear being torn to pieces by a husband who comes storming into the room. But what really makes the affair so delightful and dear to me is that it has become so evident how the whole story rests on a purely naive basis: here is a young girl, brought up in the country (in a small town), who envisages a much-criticized young writer – somehow like the hero of a novel – as her ideal, and goes to him for this very reason without caring about what people think or propriety. So finally a proper declaration of love was made, but so innocently, that when I made it extremely clear that the affair could be nothing more than a friendship, she was quite content, as if she had not actually desired anything more. With such naivity, I am now almost sorry not to have hindered the several visits to my room, since she could so easily be made the object of gossip – and it would pain me terribly if this so charming story was profaned in the mouths of the people.[1]

Much more serious was his relationship with Emilie Sigel, a young lady of high-minded ideals and intelligent nature, whose interests were very much akin to those of himself. 'She has a dainty figure', wrote Mörike, 'pale, refined features; beautiful blue eyes contrast strikingly with dark hair and eyebrows. She speaks gladly and without shyness.'[2] Strauss used to spend two or three hours with her during the week and Emilie helped him greatly by her sympathetic and understanding concern. 'She is one of those natures, whose lively intellectual life powerfully opens up another's personality and stimulates conversation.'[3] Here, then, was a serious friendship which might have formed the basis of a marriage had not a new passion burst into Strauss' life in person of the opera singer Agnese Schebest.

The daughter of a Czech father and a German mother, Agnese Schebest[4] was born at Vienna in 1813. The father was killed in an accident when Agnese was only three years old and the mother decided to move to Theresienstadt, where the young Agnese received her early schooling. Through singing in the church choir, her musical talent and excellent voice were discovered and so highly appraised, that it was arranged for her to receive further musical training in Dresden. By the age of 15 she was singing independent roles and 2 years later the whole of Dresden lay at her feet. In 1832 she began to tour the leading musical centres of Europe – Budapest, Vienna, Graz, Nuremberg and Karlsruhe; everywhere was a triumph and her singing was enthusiastically acclaimed night after night.

[1] To Rapp, 10.4.37; Ziegler, pp. 364–5.
[2] Cited by Adolf Rapp in his article: 'David Friedrich Strauss in einem bedeutsamen Abschnitt seines Lebens 1835 bis 1842'. *Zeitschrift für württembergische Landesgeschichte*, XII (1953), pp. 147–68; 271–300. Cited henceforth as *ZWLG*.
[3] To Rapp; undated letter about summer 1837; *ZWLG*, p. 155.
[4] An account of the years before her marriage to Strauss is found in her autobiography *Aus dem Leben einer Künstlerin* (Stuttgart, 1857).

It was in December 1836 that she first visited Stuttgart[5] but at that time Strauss was working furiously on his *Streitschriften* and not until April did he attend one of her concerts. The first impression was obviously arresting. 'Saw Schebest yesterday', he wrote to Vischer. 'The most charming appearance.'[6] Strauss, who was friendly with the actors and artists in Stuttgart, lost little time in making her acquaintance and there is a rather amusing account of their first meeting, according to which he was introduced as the famous Dr Strauss; Agnese, who was a Catholic, confused him with the pious editor of a well-known devotional magazine and replied: 'I know, I know all about you; I've read much of your writing and am very pleased to meet you personally at last.'[7]

Strauss was soon smitten by her charm.

Soon after that the singer Schebest arrived here; I was greatly attracted by her appearance at the theatre; half pushed, half pushing myself, I helped her last Sunday to arrange a dinner party in Cannstatt for a company of several actors and friends of the stage; I drove there with her in the same coach and since that time a fire has been kindled within me. Only yesterday I composed a sonnet to her which, as evidence of your friend's strange state of mind, I will not withhold from you.[8]

However, there was no great response on her part. At the age of only 24 and at the height of her fame, Agnese was surrounded by a bevy of admirers and it was hardly likely that Strauss, at that time, could have won her heart. He was not rich, had no position, was certainly well-known – indeed notorious – but socially ostracised; and how could she, a leading figure in the social world, tie herself to a man in a relationship which must have certainly brought her into the same disrepute? As an admirer he was to be valued, along with his friend

[5] *SVBr*, I, Anm. 41.

[6] To Vischer, 20.4.37; *SVBr*, I, p. 31.

[7] Hausrath, II, p. 38. The same error was often repeated, and also in reverse. The preacher at the Court of Potsdam, also Strauss by name, was once introduced by a lady of society as the famous author of the *Life of Jesus*, and as he disavowed the honour, the lady rejoiced even more to be able to present the famous composer of waltzes. The worthy gentleman, now a little impatient, replied: 'He also I am not, nor am I the Strauss who lays the egg, but the court-preacher Strauss from Potsdam'.

[8] To Rapp, 7.5.37; *AB*, pp. 36–7.

Reinhold Köstlin, but only as one of a number of possible contenders for her hand.

Yet Strauss did not give up hope and when Agnese returned in October 1837 his passions were again aroused. He attended all her concerts and wrote two ardent reviews for the local newspaper. The attraction for her grew ever stronger and thoughts that he might win her increased.

With respect to the beautiful singer, I must take back the assurance that I gave in the second last letter, or have actually already taken it back in the last letter; I am again fairly well inclined to her. I have been visiting her again these last few days and have been powerfully impressed by the strict classical style of her beauty as well as by her artistically-cultivated form and movement. Her speech, too, is thoroughly noble and intelligent and she always receives me with a warm friendliness, which tells me that she holds me for an understanding and good fellow, who is honourably devoted to her and ready to herald her praise at every opportunity. She earnestly invited me to call again and this shall certainly not be long deferred.[9]

But soon rumours began to spread and we may be sure that the following conversation, reported to have taken place in Tübingen, found similar echoes in Stuttgart.

Silcher:    And do you also know who the two enthusiastic reviews of Schebest in the *Deutscher Courier* were written by?
Wachter:   By Köstlin?
Silcher:    No, by Strauss.
Schrader:  Ah!
Wachter:   Ho, ho!
Bahnmayer: By which Strauss?
Silcher:    By etc. etc.
Schrader:  One can easily see where that's leading.
Bahnmayer: The fellow must have sunken completely; in losing his religious faith he must have lost all moral sense as well.[10]

It was, in fact, widespread knowledge that Strauss was flirting with the singer, and the brother of Emilie Sigel, concerned lest his sister should become the object of public scandal, gave

[9] To Rapp, 9.11.37; *AB*, pp. 42–3.
[10] To Vischer, 20.11.37; *AB*, p. 45.

F

Strauss to understand that he was no longer welcome to visit them.

Relations between Strauss and Minele, which had hitherto remained on a fairly platonic basis, were also somewhat disturbed. Strauss, not wishing to become more deeply involved with her than he already was, wrote to her declaring that he could not contemplate any more serious relationship than their present one, and Minele was hurt by what she considered to be the cold tone of the letter. However, the difference between them was gradually smoothed over and they remained friends, Minele finally marrying a professor in Tübingen.

At the end of 1837, just before Christmas, he received another visit from the 'unnamed', which he recounted in a letter to Rapp.

When I returned home last Tuesday afternoon from the library, where I had been looking up some things in Polybius and Diodorus, I ordered the heating to be turned on full, on account of a spell of cold weather which had just come upon us. Then there came a knock on my door, at first so light that I hardly heard it, and then once again, somewhat more clearly: I could hardly have expected anything less than that my 'unnamed' from last spring should be standing there. And yet there she was, sent here to Stuttgart to purchase Christmas necessities. At the beginning it was somewhat formal, since the affair had receded pretty much into the background, and I sat down, not beside her, but on the stool opposite her. However the ice soon melted and I couldn't resist trying a few of the kisses which had tasted so good in the spring. On the following day she came again, since she had some things to buy in the shop below, and told me that a young civil servant has asked for her hand; she said he had very good testimonies but refused to concede that he had made any personal impression upon her, whereby I – caressing her as she lay in my arms – encouraged her to consent to the marriage – a situation which seemed to me alternately funny and sad, frivolous and innocent.[11]

Agnese had already left Stuttgart on another concert tour and had given no indication that she was serious about him. For although he and Köstlin were her two foremost admirers in

[11] To Rapp, 18.12.37; Ziegler, p. 367; AB, p. 48. The 'unnamed' eventually declined the proposal and began writing to Strauss, so that the situation became somewhat of an embarrassment; however, her letters did not please him and gradually the relationship withered away.

Stuttgart, she had a host of others in the many cities where she had sung, and the prospect of making many more; thus during the following four years communications ceased between herself and Strauss, and Strauss gradually put his dreams of marrying her out of his mind.

After Agnese's visit to Stuttgart, meetings with Emilie Sigel appear to have been few and far between, but in 1841 Strauss attempted to resume the old relationship and Emilie's interest in him began to increase – a problem of which Strauss was not unaware. He tried to remain aloof as much as possible and to 'balance the relationship on a middle course between friendship and love',[12] for he knew how much he owed to this friendship between them both. 'In the relationship with her, which is of inestimable value to me, the thing which oppresses me – as it must do every upright man – is that I receive more than I can give.'[13] Even so, relations between them were seriously impaired by Strauss' moodiness, and as the year 1841 wore on, he tried to see her as little as possible and to sustain the friendship by letter rather than by meetings. Emilie, naturally piqued by Strauss' attitude, reproached him with coldness towards her, and the discontent between them reached such a pitch that Strauss burnt one of her letters, in which she had criticised his ill-humour and peevishness towards her.

This bad temper of Strauss, which was felt by all his friends, must always be taken into account in judging his relationships with others. He knew his faults but could not bear to have them pointed out; he felt, as he wrote to Emilie, like 'a small wheel, soon worn-out in the machinery of time'.[14] A marriage with Emilie would never have been successful and was apparently never seriously considered by Strauss. With all that they had in common, there were still great differences between them, and a marriage would probably have been as disastrous as that upon which he was now about to enter.

It was four years since Strauss and Agnese had said farewell to each other in the winter of 1837-8. From Stuttgart Agnese had travelled to Munich, where she experienced a tremendous reception, with 'thousands' of bouquets being thrown on the stage; Trieste, Venice and finally La Scala Opera in Milan –

[12] *ZWLG*, p. 281.    [13] *Ibid.* p. 282.
[14] *Ibid.* p. 295.

everywhere in Italy she was applauded and cheered by enthusiastic audiences. In September 1839 she arrived in Zürich,
at the height of the revolution, and probably it was only then
that she began fully to realise that her Dr Strauss was a figure
of international renown. From Zürich she toured the north-
German cities and Warsaw and finally, after further concerts
in south Germany, she returned to Stuttgart in the spring of
1842. For Strauss, her arrival was quite unexpected and he had
almost forgotten her – or at least attempted to forget her. Now,
suddenly, the old feelings were again awakened and his former
love once more burst into flame:

Yesterday a note from Schebest announcing her return flashed into
my peaceful existence, like lightning from the blue sky. Went to her,
therefore, and found her more beautiful and charming than ever;
am also again just as bewitched as ever. She was in Zürich during
the revolution against me, saw me being burnt and dared not admit
that she was a friend of mine. However, on her travels in North
Germany she was able to profit from her friendship with me. She's
singing Romeo on Wednesday. This time I kissed her as much as I
wanted to; when she was here previously I was never so impertinent.[15]

and a letter to Georgii on the following day reveals his feelings
even more expressively.

Schebest has been here since the day before yesterday; she let me
know straight away and I have already been to see her twice. Am
also naturally in raptures. On Wednesday, i.e. tomorrow, she is
singing Romeo. It is a great burden on me that I shall have to fall
in love with her again, yet it is inescapable. One should let the
dead rest peacefully, and I was one such. It is cruel to summon
them back to life, to make them to dance to the pipes, and then lay
them back again in the grave as they were before. Include my poor
soul in your Christian prayers.[16]

Agnese's return was not simply fortuitous, and the fact that
she allowed Strauss to make love to her on their first meeting
shows that she had made up her mind to marry him. Moreover,
her decision is explicable just as much in terms of the head as
of the heart, and there were certain very good reasons why at

---

[15] To Rapp, 11.4.42; *AB*, pp. 129–30 (incomplete); *ZWLG*, p. 298.
[16] To Georgii, 12.4.42; *Briefe* (ed. Maier) p. 40.

this juncture she found it so advantageous to give up her career and settle down to her new role of housewife. To begin with, her career was now in decline[17] and she obviously saw marriage as providing the best possible ground for retiring from the stage. Secondly, she was not well-off financially[18] and the money which she had earned over the years had somehow slipped through her fingers. Thirdly, she had just come from an unhappy experience[19] – which is probably to be interpreted as an unsuccessful love-affair; thus the peace and quietness which she would have in a home of her own, away from the rush and bustle of the world and the continual necessity of travelling from one city to another, must have appeared most attractive to her. And finally, she was now almost thirty; she had seen the world and experienced its pleasures; if she waited longer the chance of marriage might be lost. In short, now was the time to act, to act without delay, and she saw in Strauss the answer to all her problems. For he had money, good breeding, intelligence, fame, and would be able to provide the secure home which she desired.

But if the marriage had advantages for Agnese, it was also what Strauss himself required, and he was now in a position to marry. The death of his father in the previous year had left him with a considerable amount of money, and if he was not the wealthiest of men, he was at least well-off and had no need to be concerned financially about the future.

Even more important was the fact that he had become apathetic and morose; marriage, as he saw it, was the only thing which could raise him out of the lethargy in which he found himself. Four years previously he had written to Rapp:

I feel in the most definite way that the days of my youth are over. I no longer find any enjoyment in the kind of society which comes through taverns and the like. Now I remain at home and spend my evenings and other free time in reading, or walking back and forth. This, however, is unnatural and leads to souring. I should, therefore, have a family life for which – as you once, rightly, wrote to me – my nature is completely suited. It is not my financial position which stands in the way of establishing such a life; for if a wife had only as much property as I have, then – quite apart from my further literary works – we could already live off the interests. But the

---

[17] Hausrath, II, p. 43.　　[18] Ziegler, p. 393.　　[19] *Ibid.* p. 394.

obstacle is this: I have for a long time, and also at present, stood so far outside those circles – family circles and public circles – where young ladies of cultivated taste are to be met, that I have to fall in love with inn-keeper's daughters and actresses.[20]

and a few weeks later to Märklin:

The only thing which can save me from this completely bankrupt life is – as I see things, and certainly rightly – the establishing of a family life; I have perceived this for a long time previously, before I was able to pluck up courage and put my feeling into words. Finally I did it, with definite reference to an object: but it was too late and unfortunately I learnt too late that it was too late – and therefore the annoyance of which I spoke at the beginning. It would not have affected me so much at any other time as just at present, when I have in fact tied the saving of my whole mental existence from the unavoidable fall into hypochondria and nausea to such a way of escape....

Now I want to ask you in all sad seriousness, today, unfortunately, without any humour, without which I could certainly not have spoken in this manner, whether you are acquainted with any possibility in Calw that could help me out of this decline into desolation and isolation, and whether you would be able to get the affair going, perhaps by a visit, which I would then make to you.[21]

The problem, then, was to find someone suitable, and apart from Emilie, with whom he often became moody and ill-humoured, the only other serious possibility was Agnese. Now she was back, and his for the taking.

But the engagement was disapproved of by almost all his friends, and Frau Kauffmann, who knew both parties well, saw the tragedy which lay ahead were they to marry. She expressed her fears to Emilie in the following letter.

My dear Emilie,
The reason that I have kept quiet for so long after receiving your lovely letter, which Strauss (to whom I read it) declared exquisite, is simply because of my love for you. A number of things have happened in the last weeks that I could not have kept quiet about had I once written to you, and I feared in so doing that I would cause you pain. If I could think that you were still at the same point on which you stood in Ludwigsburg – cured and finished with

[20] To Rapp, 2.3.38; *ZWLG*, p. 165.
[21] To Märklin, Easter Day 1838; *AB*, pp. 63–4.

Strauss – then my news would not greatly disturb you; but you have already so often relapsed that I do not trust your feelings. I implore you therefore: recognize that your rich spirit is not for Strauss, because he himself has spirit enough; understand that your deep personality and simple, but glowing, love is likewise not for him who wants to be charmed and dazzled – which can only be achieved with artistry, or in the flush of youth. Be strong, be still and listen: Strauss is unofficially engaged – engaged to Agnese Schebest. I am sure that either this engagement will be broken before the marriage, or, if the marriage takes place, it will bring only disaster for both parties; Kauffmann, Märklin and Schnitzer are also of the same opinion after more sober consideration, which Agnese's dazzling and really bewitching presence did not at first permit. If this woman had not appeared to me as your rival I could have formed a love for her, for she seems to me so wonderfully talented and richly endowed with natural and artistic gifts. Both Kauffmann and I were enraptured by her musical performances; there is unimaginable depth and passion in her voice and so much elegant grace in her behaviour that I am convinced you also would be favourably disposed towards her. But she is still not deep-minded enough to understand Strauss and he does not possess her queenly nature; in short, they are suited to one another only in so far as they are both exceptionally nice people, but there is no point of contact between them. Strauss praises the fact that Hardegg, in his friendship with Strauss, behaves in such a sympathetic manner and furthers Strauss' attraction to Schebest.

We all made an excursion into the country together and several times I mentioned your name and made remarks about you, which Strauss took with the greatest friendliness. 'Who is then this Emilie?' asked Schebest. 'A friend of Herr Doctor and one of the most highly gifted women.' With that Strauss expressed his full agreement and said: 'Just read Bettina, there you have your Emilie.' I looked at him sharply and if my eyes can speak, then they said: Fool! that woman had a glowing love for you and you have spurned her for the sake of this woman, who neither understands nor loves you, but who takes you so that her fame, which will soon be extinguished, will be ignited by yours. My eyes became wet; he perceived it well and for a long time said nothing more.[22]

Frau Kauffmann was not the only one who saw the dangers. Both Märklin and Rapp counselled against the engagement and this led to a strong difference of opinion between them. Letters

[22] Frau Kauffmann to Emilie Sigel, 15 May (not March, as Hausrath dates it) 1842. *Deutsche Rundschau*, 141, pp. 40–1.

were exchanged in which they all expressed their views plainly and bluntly, and before the end of April the three friends journeyed to Wildbad in the Black Forest, where the pros and cons of the situation were discussed into the early hours of the morning. To marry or not to marry – that was the question. If he did not marry now, he would be in a worse position than before, and it might be his last chance lost; but to marry was, as Märklin expressed it, an even greater gamble.

Certainly, on the whole, my judgment now about the affair is no longer the same as it was at the beginning, but even so I am still not satisfied with the matter as it stands. Either you marry Schebest or you don't. If you take the latter course, the affair cannot be allowed to go on in this way indefinitely, and it can only come to a tragic ending for you. You will afterwards feel your situation in an even more painful way than previously. But if you marry her, well, good – you know how we three recently exhausted ourselves in discussing the matter; but I have only given a qualified approval. You must be certain that she really loves you and sure that she is really worthy of your love.[23]

The whole affair caused a good deal of high feeling between the three friends, for Strauss was irritated by their criticisms, and they on their part were only trying to protect him from the possible disaster which he did not wish to recognise. Even less in favour were Strauss' brother Wilhelm and his wife, who were worried about the rumours they had heard concerning Agnese. What then were these rumours, and what was it that caused so much apprehension among Strauss' friends about the possible consequences of such a marriage?

It could not have been religious differences; for although Agnese was a Catholic, she appears to have been quite unconcerned about religion and it was never a point of dispute between her and Strauss. Nor could it have been Agnese's education. Certainly she was not so well read as Strauss, but neither was she uncultured, and Strauss himself could say of her: 'That Schebest in all essential things, among which – apart from her physical nature – I understand the spirit and personality, is worthy of the finest man and capable of making such a man happy, of that I am completely assured.'[24] Hausrath saw

[23] Märklin to Strauss, 30.4.42; the original is in the Schiller Nationalmuseum in Marbach.     [24] To Märklin, 2.5.42; *AB*, p. 132.

the fatal difference between them as lying in their respective careers – he a theologian, she a woman of the world. 'When one has been educated in the Tübingen seminary, one may not marry an opera singer.'[25] But this view is too superficial and they both had a great deal in common, especially music, for Strauss was a passionate lover of the older baroque style of Haydn and Mozart.

There were probably two main objections against the engagement, the first being the feeling that the marriage would just not work because of the difference in their personalities; this really boiled down to the question of whether Agnese could successfully cope with Strauss' apathy and ill-humour. The second objection concerned Agnese's own moral character. It would appear that Strauss' friends were apprehensive because they regarded Agnese as a woman of doubtful reputation, who was seeking to marry him because of her declining career, because she had lost most of her money, because Strauss was rich, because he was famous etc. etc. – but not because she really loved him. That these objections were not without foundation is shown by Ziegler's remarks that she was a 'light-living Austrian' deeply caught up in the 'delusions and confusions' of a famous public life.[26] The rumours floating about at that time probably concerned her former love-affairs; Strauss himself knew about these rumours, but was not particularly concerned about Agnese's past. It was the future that mattered; he needed a wife and Agnese might be his last hope. What did it matter anyway? It was a case of win or lose. If he did not marry then he lost; if he did marry then there was a chance of success, and, after all, what had he to lose anyway? 'Better to drown than pine away.'[27] 'If there's a tragedy – well, it could not be evaded. But in the quietness of my heart I have a better hope.'[28]

And so through the month of May, Strauss, not knowing what to do, was driven hither and thither by the advice of his friends. Märklin wrote to Wilhelm and then visited him in Cologne, where a plan of action was agreed upon. In late May or early June Wilhelm came to Stuttgart and persuaded Strauss

---

[25] Hausrath, II, p. 44.      [26] Ziegler, p. 383.
[27] To Rapp, 25.4.42; *AB*, p. 131.
[28] To Märklin, 2.5.42; *AB*, p. 132.

to return with him to Cologne, so that he might have time to cool off and come to a more sober frame of mind. Here the whole matter was again discussed, with all the doubts and dangers being weighed against the consequences of renouncing the present opportunity, which Rapp also expressed in an undated letter of about this time.

The time has come – it's either now or never. I share this doubt with you as few others do, and in spite of that I give you my advice. If life is to remain life, then I know of no other way out. After this love, there would be only annihilation for you. *It is your last love!* You have reached the goal. So then sparkle up, get cracking![29]

Strauss determined that he must see Agnese once more and discuss the matter with her again. She was at that time giving a series of concerts in Aachen and they arranged to meet at Coblenz. Here, Strauss' fate was sealed and by the following day the affair had been finally settled. Agnese had triumphed[30] and Strauss brought his new fiancée back to Cologne, from where he wrote to Märklin.

I cannot cease to believe, but that my good guardian angel extends his hand to me here – for the last and the first time simultaneously – in order to lead me out of my abstract existence and raise me up to a true human life. You will say that's daring; but daring wins and what stakes do I play with in the game? What have I to lose? Having gone through every conceivable doubt, I am now calm and at peace – you may be the same.[31]

The marriage ceremony was held in the church in Horkheim, near Heilbronn, on 30 August. The service was conducted by Rapp, with a sermon making no reference to anything specifically Christian, and Kauffmann at the organ played excerpts from Mozart's opera 'The Magic Flute'. After the service the guests returned for the wedding breakfast to the large house (formerly a small castle) in Sontheim, which Strauss had rented as his new home. The breakfast itself was a jolly occasion with poems from Kerner and others. Rapp dressed as a cook and

[29] Rapp to Strauss, undated letter about May 1842; original in the Schiller-Museum.

[30] Much of the story of the engagement was covered up by Strauss' biographers and since the letters most relevant to this period were destroyed, one must read between the lines.

[31] Strauss to Märklin, 19.6.42; original in the Schiller-Museum.

gave a humorous recitation and Kauffmann was active both at the piano and at refilling the wine glasses. Strauss' bachelor life was now over – a new life had begun, and the words which he had written to Rapp a few days previously expressed his optimistic hopes for the future.

I am contented and really quite proud about the whole affair, like one is proud over a job which has been well accomplished; and I am pleased that here I followed my heart, without allowing myself to be led astray by following the warning signs, which were here plentifully present for my cautious and simple nature. It must, it will go well – where it doesn't, the blame must lie more on me than on her.[32]

For the first few weeks of their new married life everything appeared to be running smoothly and Agnese applied herself to the task of learning to run a household – to cook, sew and do the washing – things which she had not been accustomed to do and probably had not done for years. But the isolation slowly began to be a strain upon them. Whereas previously Agnese had been a central figure in the social world and Strauss had had a certain amount of social life, now they were both shut up in a large mansion, in a small village, with no regular communication with the world at large. There was no academic stimulus for Strauss except from books and occasional visits from friends, and there was no social life for Agnese. Already in November, Frau Kauffmann wrote to Emilie:

For some time now in Strauss' marriage, things have not been going as they should...Strauss often asks Kauffmann about you and seeks to justify himself against reproaches which might be made against him concerning you. You would scarcely recognize him any more, so thin and pale he has become. There you prophesied falsely; she no longer even makes out that she loves him. If she did then he would not so soon be deadly bored in her presence. He now wants to move here to Heilbronn, at any price, where he can spend at least the evenings with his friends. She is offended about it and expresses herself in her honest manner quite frankly to us all – that his inclination to her was simply a craze which the possession of her has cured, that she is too dumb for him, that he is a miser, a cantankerous intellectual with no love or feeling, a man with whom she can henceforth grow only in renunciation and humility – that, she

[32] To Rapp, 6.8.42; *AB*, p. 138.

claims, is the only profit which she derives from the marriage. In a word, it shows that she never loved him, that she does not understand him and that his love was based upon physical attraction; on this account, his love for her has considerably diminished, even if it always remains much greater than her love for him. If he were still madly in love with her, as he was, he would rejoice over her really praiseworthy exertions to be a housewife; in a word, if he idolized her, as she has always been idolized, then she would be content, and in the isolated village of Sontheim she would fancy herself as a romantic figure; but she has no idea that now it is her turn to live to please him, to guess his desires, to idolize him – what all men in the world expect from their wives. In addition she has a terrible inclination to jealousy, which – imagine it – extends even to me. For this reason she will on no account move to Heilbronn. That then is the fate of your friend. Our meetings together are in this way highly unenjoyable and take place only rarely. Constantly, complaints from both sides, and we can do nothing except try to bring about peace – which doesn't always succeed. If the birth of a child, which is expected in the spring, doesn't bring more harmony between them, then there is nothing more certain than that the marriage will break up or they will divorce. The shrewd Hardegg was right when he prophesied that a wife would have a difficult time with him; only one who loves him with a boundless love and constantly forgives could dare it with him, and no so pampered lady as she. I'm really very sorry for her, by the way, for she remains a true, upright woman, and her beauty and grace would bewitch even you; she seems, however, to have lost all control over him.[33]

The fault, however, did not all lie on Agnese's side and Mörike described how on one occasion when he was staying with the couple for a few days, Strauss became vexed with a remark which displeased him, lowered his eyes, and said nothing more for a long period of time.

Mörike also related how on another occasion Agnese had poured out her heart to him about Strauss.

At present I'm really concerned about him. He doesn't have any company with other men, not even a get-together in the evenings. What company can I be for him the whole day long, a housewife for a scholar? He is often so cross with me. The whole day long he sits there by the window with his book, reads till he is worn-out, and often never speaks. I cannot always accompany him on walks and

---

[33] Frau Kauffmann to Emilie Sigel, 13.11.42; *Deutsche Rundschau*, 141, pp. 41–2.

now ever less frequently; but to go alone is no pleasure for him; when
he ever does so, he is certain to return home more sullen and bad-
tempered.[34]

Strauss found the separation from his friends more than he
could stand and resolved to move to Heilbronn. However,
since the child was expected in early spring, he gave into
Agnese's wish to remain in Sontheim, hoping that the new
addition to the family might bring a new interest in life. For
Strauss had nothing to do; no book and no articles to write;
no real interest any more in theology: 'I do nothing because I
have nothing more to do.'[35] He could only read, but read to
what purpose? And the matter was made worse by Agnese's
continual nagging that he did nothing.

At the present time your friend lacks no good thing except a subject
to work on, for reading is not working, and when reading has no
definite publication in view, then I do it no longer as study, but
merely to while away the time.

> Under mountains of work, the young man sighed after life;
> Now in the river of life, the man yearns after work.

Doubtless also my wife would have more respect for me if I
worked as I did in the past; certainly I often lay my writings before
her and tell her that I have written all those – but soon she won't
even believe that any more.[36]

In the spring of 1843 a daughter was born and since the
birth fell on St George's day (23 April), she was appropriately
named Georgine, the baptism taking place a few days later.

Am now the father of a daughter, who was baptized 14 days ago.
Many pious people are almost angry that I deprived them of the
scandal which would have arisen had she not been baptized. As if I
were a fool! The pastor in Horkheim, a true-hearted old grenadier
who is quite unconcerned about theology, but vexed by the new
hymn book, introduced the ceremony thus: The following order of
service for Protestant baptismal services in Württemberg is prescribed by the Royal highly-esteemed Consistory: etc. etc. The
good man remained afterwards, completely merry in our heretical
fellowship, and had an admirable conversation with Uncle Hiller.
Kerner also came and gave the child his blessing. Kauffmann composed a cradle song for her. The little one thus cannot say that she

---

[34] Mörike to Hartlaub, 20.3.43; *Schwabenspiegel*, 1 (1907–8) pp. 115–17.
[35] To Rapp, 23.7.43; *AB*, p. 153.     [36] To Rapp, 2.12.42; *AB*, p. 143.

did not find a friendly reception in the world. Up till now she has put up with it well, and gives us much pleasure through her vitality.[37]

But relations between Strauss and Agnese did not improve and both became more and more irritable. At the end of 1843 they finally shifted to Heilbronn, where Strauss was able to meet more frequently with Kauffmann and Märklin. The change was undoubtedly beneficial for Strauss himself, but not for the marriage. The angry scenes increased and Agnese grew continually more resentful and jealous of the occasions which Strauss spent with his friends. For Strauss, the time was almost unendurable and only when Agnese travelled to Nuremberg for a holiday in the following year did he once again enjoy peace and quietness. On her return they both made a new attempt to make the marriage work, but with no lasting overall improvement in the situation. A son was born at the end of 1845, but there were so many faults on both sides that however much good will each brought to the trying situation, the bickering and quarrels continued to jar the nerves.

Strauss decided it must end. He could not take any more and decided upon a divorce. This, however, was not so simple, for the whole affair was even now a well-known scandal and to go to court would have made things far worse. Moreover public opinion was definitely on Agnese's side, and if Strauss wanted divorce it would have to be on her terms – that Strauss should give up the children until they were seven, and pay her the enormous sum of 30,000 fl. – which was indeed quite out of the question.

In 1846–7, after Agnese had been away on holiday, the matter came to a climax when Strauss refused to take her back into the house. Agnese took legal action, and in 1847 the affair was finally settled to Strauss' disadvantage. He conceded Georgine for ever, Fritz until he was seven, and agreed to pay 1050 fl. per year (about three times the amount of the Zürich pension), of which Agnese received 750 fl., the remaining 300 fl. being divided equally among the two children. In addition he yielded to Agnese's desire to live in Stuttgart, although he himself would have preferred to remain there.

During the following year he lived in Heilbronn, but at the

---

[37] To Käferle, June 1843; *AB*, p. 152.

end of 1848, after his election to the Württemberg Assembly, he again resided in Stuttgart, where he received visits from the children and could not help coming into occasional contact with Agnese.  That was what he found most painful, for although he could not bear to meet her, although at times he had even begun to hate her, yet a residue of love remained which he could never extinguish.  One evening at a concert, as he sat in the darkened gallery above the main body of the auditorium, he caught sight of her below and knew that she was thinking of him.

### At the Concert

I sit there in the gallery,
In darkness, with a heart that yearns;
She sits below where one can see,
Where many hundred candles burn.

The music flutters through the air,
Like tiny birds in joy and glee;
I think of you my torment fair,
My heart assures, you think of me.

We hear the same sweet harmony,
Our thoughts accord and oft repeat;
O could our hearts not once more be
United in the same heart-beat.

Yet deep and deeper, spirit-torn
I sink in dreams of kith and kin,
Perceive instead of flute and horn
The song of pain and grief within.

The music ends and two by two,
The couples go to where they dwell;
I go alone, she goes alone,
We both return to lonely cell.[38]

He was now a lonely man, with no position, no desire, and no aim.  Hardest of all, he now had no wife and could only see his children at certain times, when Agnese was not present, or when they were brought to him by Emilie.  Without consolation, with no sympathy from the world around him, he was left with only sad memories.

### West-Eastward

I longed to travel, now I do not leave,
But whether I shall stay, I do not know.

[38] *GS*, xii, p. 63.

That I'm a stranger in this land is certain:
But where my homeland is I do not know.
I think I once had two beloved children,
But whether t'was a dream I do not know.
A wife I spurned – did love to hatred turn?
Or hatred turn to love?  I do not know.
They say that once upon a time I'd written books:
But whether truth or scorn I do not know.
I hear, an unbeliever I am called,
I know not if I am not rather pious.
The thought of death has never caused me fear,
I know not if I have not long been dead.[39]

[39] *GS*, xii, p. 64.

# 15

## THE POLITICIAN

> Here, in accord with my whole nature and my best
> conviction, I had to swim against the stream, and,
> moreover, against an extremely turbulent and wild
> torrent.[1]

The accession of Friedrich Wilhelm IV to the Prussian throne
in the spring of 1840 provided new hope of liberal reforms.
The new emperor was certainly not lacking in intelligence and
was imbued with the Romantic spirit, whose quintessence he
found supremely in the writings of Novalis. Theological understanding was another quality which he possessed in good
measure and his sympathies lay with the orthodox-pietist
party of Hengstenberg, so far as was compatible with the
smooth running of the Church, of which he saw himself as the
visible head.

At the beginning of his reign some minor concessions were
made to the liberals – a relaxation of censorship and the re-
habilitation of some teachers and writers who had suffered on
account of their views – and as a result political activity slowly
began to revive, culminating in the revolution of 1848. Friedrich Wilhelm now found himself compelled to make further
concessions. He agreed to the calling of a newly elected Parliament in Frankfurt at which all the German states would be
represented and also seemed prepared to agree to the unification
of Germany under the hegemony of Prussia.

The election of representatives to the Frankfurt Parliament
provided the opportunity for Strauss to enter into the new
sphere of politics. On 16 April a delegation from Ludwigsburg
arrived in Heilbronn and asked him to stand for election as
the liberal candidate. Strauss hesitatingly, reluctantly and
rather indifferently agreed: 'At times I get amused, at other

[1] *GS*, 1, p. 19.

times I get irritated', he wrote a few days later to his brother in the middle of the election, 'the outcome is doubtful, yet, at any rate, the attempt is interesting.'[2]

One may well ask what qualifications Strauss possessed which enabled him to enter on to the political scene, considering that he had spent the greatest part of his life reading and writing on theology and the six preceding years absorbed in the problems of his marriage. He was, however, not ill-prepared for his new political career. To begin with, he had read widely over the years and possessed an extensive knowledge of the history and politics of the past. Nor was he unacquainted with the important political issues of the day for Church and State were at that time so bound together that matters which concerned the Church were often also political questions. Thus he possessed a good general understanding of political affairs and if he lacked the practical experience of politics, he was certainly not devoid of a sound theoretical knowledge of the current political situation.

As regards the election itself, Strauss had the support of the liberal party, but the radical party, who knew him only by reputation, also gave him their backing on account of his attack against the established Christianity. On the other hand, however, his religious views were a distinct disadvantage, since right from the beginning the orthodox made his denial of the Christian faith a focal point of opposition. Thus one of the key issues over which the election was fought was the question of Church and State, and one could almost say that the whole election was determined by one's attitude to religion, rather than to politics. Strauss, it was declared, would try to destroy orthodox Christianity, would undermine the teachings of the Church and attempt to replace religion by morality; some even went so far as to say that if Dr Strauss were elected, he would abolish baptism of infants and Bible reading. This, of course, Strauss strongly denied, and pointed to the fact that his own children had been baptised in the Church. On the contrary, what he demanded was the separation of politics from religion and complete separation of Church and State, so that one could believe what one chose without being subjected to any political or religious discrimination.

[2] To Wilhelm Strauss, 22.4.48; *AB*, p. 209.

Two words summed up the burning political issues of the time – freedom and unity. Freedom meant primarily the right to determine the policies of the nation by means of democratically elected representatives, but this in turn was tied up with the whole question of the unity of the German nation. At that time Germany was split up into a number of states or duchies, of varying size, each having their own ruler and system of government. If democracy was to be established throughout the whole land then the various states would have to be united into a confederation which would obviously be dominated by the largest and most powerful of the states. Two of these vied for hegemony – Protestant Prussia in the north and Catholic Austria in the east. The smaller unaligned states were not enthusiastic about such a confederation since they desired to retain their independence and had no wish to be swallowed up into a nation: but without such a confederation there was little hope of a representative democratic government for the country as a whole, and the undemocratic and aristocratic rule in each separate state would remain as before. To accept Austrian hegemony of a possible confederation was completely unacceptable to the Protestants; the alternative was Prussian hegemony under the monarchy of Friedrich Wilhelm IV, and although Strauss had criticised the King for his medieval views,[3] he was inclined to accept this plan as the best of several unsatisfactory solutions.

But freedom and unity were of little comfort to the people when they were hungry and cold, and Strauss was also intensely practical in advocating a lessening of the people's burdens through financial aid, better education, help for the sick and aged, and a betterment of conditions generally – all of which, at that time, were quite radical reforms.

The campaign itself was a lively one with the speeches of the candidates, especially in Ludwigsburg, being frequently interrupted. Strauss' main opponent was the pietist Christoph Hoffmann, the brother of Wilhelm, his friend of student days. Christoph Hoffmann was indeed a doughty opponent, one of the acknowledged leaders of the pietists in Ludwigsburg and a director of a private educational college in the town itself. This college was the centre of the pietistic activities in the

[3] *Der Romantiker auf dem Throne der Cäsaren* (Mannheim, 1847).

district, and through evangelisation in the surrounding areas, Hoffmann had become well known and had the support of the majority of the people. In the town itself, however, where Strauss' supporters enjoyed a roughly two-thirds majority, the rowdier radical party were not averse to using intimidating tactics on the quieter conservative citizens. The Jews, perceiving that Strauss was regarded as the enemy of Christ, stood behind him to a man and even the Catholics found the unbeliever preferable to the pietist. Enthusiasm grew as the election approached and the final gathering at which the contestants spoke was not without a spirited and impassioned interest, described by an eye-witness as follows:

Hoffmann spoke first and then Strauss arose to be greeted by the jubilation of a thousand voices. For a long time he was scarcely able to start speaking on account of the continually resounding cheers, but when it at last became quiet, he made a fine, calmly-delivered speech, whose political ideas have already been set forth. Every striking word was accompanied by tumultuous applause. After him Dean Christlieb from Ludwigsburg mounted the rostrum. From the beginning I had an unhappy feeling about the line he was going to take. I recognised only too well the doubtful position which the otherwise popular man had adopted. Accordingly, he began by praising the clarity of Strauss' speech and the political beliefs expressed in it (Bravo!); he extolled the high-minded spirit of the speaker (Bravo!); 'but – (but what?), he does not possess the confidence of the people. (Yes he does!) You are not the whole people. (Yes we are! Down!) Strauss wrote a book in which – (Down! Pietist! Hypocrite! Pharisee!) – and now began a storm of which you can have no conception. In vain did the chairman ring his bell; in vain did Christlieb remain quietly standing; the whistling and howling increased in a frightening way; scythemen overturned the rostrum and the Dean had to get down. Now came Deacon Hackh. He was allowed to speak in peace so long as he spoke in general terms; but as soon as he arrived at that desperate 'but', the storm began again and he too had to get down. And now everyone cried Strauss! Strauss! The summoned one climbed on to the stage amid jubilant shouts and began his stirring words: 'My friends, the Pharisees once approached the Lord and asked him: "Is it right that one should pay tribute to Caesar?" He answered: "Show me a coin": and they handed him a denarius. And he said to them: "Whose image and whose inscription is this?" They answered: "Caesar's". Then he said to them: "Therefore render to Caesar what belongs to

Caesar and to God what belongs to God". So also some of you are
asking: Is it right that we should send this and that man to the
Parliament in Frankfurt? I ask in reply: Whose is the image and
inscription of this Parliament? You will have to answer me: The
emperor's, i.e. the determination of the Parliament is political.
Therefore I tell you: Vote according to religious considerations
where it concerns religion, but according to political considerations
where politics are concerned'. As he ended with his voice raised
high, a ray of sun broke forth from the dark clouds and a voice cried
out from below: 'The sun of truth!' Mighty jubilation.[4]

The jubilation of the Ludwigsburg citizens, however, quickly
vanished. On 28 April the people gathered to choose between
Jesus and Barabbas, between the pietist Hoffmann and the
antichrist Strauss, and the result was a victory for Hoffmann
by 5851 votes to Strauss' 3365, although in the town itself
Strauss gained 2162 votes to Hoffmann's 1516. Strauss' supporters in the town were so annoyed and embittered by the
outcome that it was feared that a riot might break out. The
town was bedecked with symbols of mourning and Strauss
himself came from Stuttgart to implore his followers not to
make trouble. A guard was posted at the houses of Hoffmann
and Christlieb and although no disturbance eventuated, it was
some time before the agitation died down and things returned
to normal.

There were hopes among his friends that Strauss might be
elected to the Parliament as the representative for neighbouring
Baden, but the Baden citizens showed little enthusiasm for
Strauss' candidature. However, Ludwigsburg had its own
seat in the Württemberg provincial Parliament and the citizens
of the town resolved that Strauss should be chosen to represent
them. Since the vote was this time not influenced by the
pietistic element in the surrounding districts, the result was a
foregone conclusion and Strauss was elected with 103 of the
126 votes of the citizens in the town council.

The great day of the vote (20 May) began early in the
morning with music echoing from the towers. At 7.30 a.m.
the council gathered together to vote, the result being greeted
by cheers from the assembled crowd and the firing of the cannons.
Strauss, who arrived later in the morning, was accompanied

---

[4] Ziegler, p. 435.

through cheering supporters lining streets decked out with flowers and the colourful black, red and gold national flags. At midday a great meal for 200 guests – not all of whom found places – was held in a local restaurant and this was followed by another procession through the town to a large garden, where speeches and toasts were the order of the day; the jubilation lasted well into the night.

For Strauss, however, this taste of honour and success soon subsided and he quickly sank back into the same melancholy state which had possessed him since the breaking up of his marriage. Frau Kauffmann, who visited Heilbronn at the end of July, described her meeting with him:

I went to see a friend of Märklin's, in their garden, and soon after me Strauss, who had just returned from a walking trip, also arrived. He looked morose and greeted me like a stranger. I said to him in my most natural voice: 'I believe you don't know me', whereupon he, in a more friendly manner, answered: 'Certainly I do, although I haven't seen you for a long time', whereby he put his hat and stick aside and began speaking with Märklin. As he heard from Märklin that Sautter was in Heilbronn and was planning to depart that same day, he dashed off because he had to speak with him. Meanwhile Märklin came with Georgii and as I was about to go, since I heard that it was Märklin's birthday, Strauss returned and spoke with me in a somewhat more friendly manner; yet on the whole he seemed in a bad mood and when he again left after quarter of an hour, I remained a little while longer so as not to go along with him. On Sunday Kauffmann returned and I complained to him about Strauss' cold demeanour; I came to the inner conviction that he could be bad-tempered, cold and hard, and that he lacked feeling. Yesterday evening he came so softly to my door, with the most friendly countenance, and as I somewhat seriously told him that Kauffmann was not in, he replied, 'I know that well', and marched into the sitting room even before I had bidden him enter. He sat down quite inconspicuously, by the window opposite me, listened to an account of Kauffmann's journey, told me about his own and finally spoke of his own state of mind and his suffering; he allowed me such a deep gaze into his soul that Kauffmann is completely astounded. How unjust I have been to him and how the world mis-understands him when it accuses him of having no feelings. He has a rare depth of feeling and he is so highly-strung that it is from this that his pronounced bad-temper springs, not from ill-breeding.[5]

[5] Hausrath, II, pp. 145–6.

Strauss decided that a change was necessary and resolved to spend August and September in Munich where he could devote some time to examining the art treasures there. The new environment was indeed beneficial for him. He visited the museums and art galleries, made numerous excursions into the surrounding countryside and composed several poems. The time flew by only too quickly until his return to Stuttgart on 18 September, two days before the opening of the provincial Parliament.

The citizens of Ludwigsburg expected great things of their new representative who had already shown himself to be the most radical critic of the Christian faith before Bruno Bauer and Feuerbach had appeared on the theological scene. But Strauss' *Life of Jesus*, written 13 years previously, was a scholarly and scientific investigation into the historicity of the Gospels, and his Ludwigburg supporters were soon to learn that there was a world of difference between religion and politics.

The divisions in the Württemberg Chamber soon became clear and Strauss was quickly repelled by the uncouthness of the radical party.

Relations in the Chamber formed themselves right from the beginning in a way which could not be attractive for me. A radical majority prevailed, which repelled me just as much by the roughness of its appearance as by its motives – the purity of which I doubted. I saw only a lust to destroy, but little constructive understanding, and I could not expect any salvation for the people in general from incited masses under ambitious leaders among whom I was able to discover just as little political integrity.[6]

To the disillusionment of the radicals Strauss now attached himself to the conservative right, to a political friendship with those who had once been his sworn enemies in matters of religion. That was the ironical part of the whole thing. In the new political situation the old religious differences were now forgotten, or at least swept into the background, and Strauss was now to be seen in the company of Dr Kuhn, professor of Catholic Theology at Tübingen, who, as Strauss remarked, would have gladly burnt him as a heretic had he lived 400 years earlier, but who now heartily supported the views of his

[6] *GS*, I, p. 19.

'friend' Strauss. The other notable personality with whom
Strauss came daily into contact was Dr Wolfgang Menzel, who
had formerly reckoned Strauss among those in danger of committing the unforgivable sin. It was against Menzel that Strauss
had written a good portion of his second *Streitschrift*; but now all
was different, as Strauss related in a letter to Märklin:

We have now, more and more, cultivated a club in which, besides
myself, are the two Wiests, Menzel, Adam from Ulm, Seybold,
Weber, Reyscher etc. and I can say that these men have gradually
given me their trust, indeed even a devotion, which does my soul
good. They would give me precedence in everything and think that
nothing is too difficult for me; I, unfortunately, know the true state
of affairs better. The most remarkable thing is my relationship to
Menzel. We have come together in a 5-man commission chosen
from our club and have thereby become quite intimate. Menzel has
understanding for politics and is well-versed in parliamentary
matters; in this respect it is good and profitable to associate with
him. We were at first reserved towards each other, then courteous
and now friendly. I can take this attitude because now that I can
see him with my own eyes, I am able to accept him as a completely
different man from the one whom formerly I learnt to know only
out of books. Perhaps he's experiencing the same thing in regard
to me.[7]

The first sally which Strauss made against the general
opinion came a few days after Parliament had opened, when
the radicals protested that the sending of troops to quell a disturbance at Schwäbisch Hall was quite unwarranted and only
saddled the people with unnecessary costs and burdens. To
objections that many of the citizens had been in grave danger
from unruly mobs, there was only laughter and jeers from the
radical party and it was in such a tense atmosphere that Strauss
rose to defend the Government who had ordered the operation.

Gentlemen, I strongly doubt whether our members – I mean the
better part of them – share these misgivings. By the better part of
them I mean those who would rather work than talk; those who do
not want continually incited agitation and unrest, because they
thereby have something to lose – be it possessions or opportunity to
serve. These people, I believe, are grateful to the government for its
measures. Certainly it is said that these were unnecessary, but when

---

[7] To Märklin, 3.11.48; *AB*, p. 226.

the sending of troops has hindered the open outbreak of the rebellion, were they then unnecessary?[8]

The representative for Schwäbisch Hall declared Strauss' speech to be a vote of trust and not mistrust towards the Government, but then others rose to support Strauss' views and to express their agreement with the Government action. Then the representative for Blaubeuren declared his anti-Government views with the cry 'I am a Republican', and the resulting roars of approval and disapproval raised the debate to an even higher pitch. Certainly the Blaubeuren representative found greater applause in the newspapers, but honour of the day belonged to Strauss, who alone had made the first important attack on the radical policies. Even the King complimented him, remarking: 'That he has courage I have always believed, else he would not have picked a quarrel with the clerics',[9] and asked if Strauss would be willing to undertake the editorship of a new Government political journal. Strauss replied that it would probably be of more use were the King to make him Colonel of the palace guards.

Only occasionally did he side with the left against the right – once on the issue of the abolition of tithes for the Church, the other time in protest against laws which permitted the rich to hunt on their great estates while restricting the poor to their own small plot of land. In all other debates his sympathies lay with the so-called 'moderate party' and after a slashing attack on the radical newspapers and especially the Heilbronn '*Neckardampfschiff*'

with its insolent scorn, its abandoned character which bares its envious teeth, with its deep hatred against every educated man who has raised himself above the masses, not to speak of the cynical, loathsome tone of its pages. It is well known throughout the country that the best men who rise up against such mischief are branded as aristocrats, pulled into the dung heap and doused with filthy water. The better thinking citizens are reproached with the charge of passivity; but just this situation of the press is most to blame for this passivity; many fear being thrown into the dung more than being wounded.[10]

his credit with the radicals had practically sunk to zero.

[8] Hausrath, ii, p. 155.
[9] Ziegler, pp. 454–5; Hausrath, ii, p. 156; GS, i, p. 23.
[10] Ziegler, pp. 442–3.

In November arose the outcry over the death of Robert Blum and the ensuing speech of Strauss was to play a decisive part in bringing his political career to a close.

Robert Blum[11] was a true son of the proletariat, by birth as well as by sympathy. A year older than Strauss, he was born in 1807 at Cologne, where his parents were poor working-class citizens. He received his education in a Catholic school run by the Jesuits after which he worked in a lantern factory, studied literature, wrote poems, attended the theatre and finally decided to enter the publishing trade. In the political unrest in Leipzig during 1845 he became prominent as a public orator with scarcely an equal, and from him exuded a power and a magic which held the people entranced. Elected to the Frankfurt Parliament as the representative for Leipzig, he visited Vienna with other members of the Left in order to meet with the revolutionary elements there. He was well aware that the Frankfurt Parliament was now losing its momentum and in Vienna, inspired afresh by the new possibilities, he came to believe that the fate of the revolution would be decided here in the Austrian capital. Thus he leant his whole support to the revolutionary cause, not merely with words, but with weapons, proclaiming the fight with all the rhetorical power he possessed and taking an active part in the *Corps élite*.

The revolution, however, was not destined to succeed and the Austrian General Windischgrätz, with his superior artillery, tightened his grip on the city, which finally fell after the barricades had been stormed and taken. The leaders of the revolution were arrested and executed. Blum pleaded his immunity as a member of the Frankfurt Parliament and Windischgrätz was in fact prepared to have him deported from the country in order to avoid diplomatic problems. However, the Austrian Count Schwarzenberg argued that Blum deserved to be shot and would be better out of the way for ever. This counsel prevailed and early on the morning of 9 November Blum was awakened from his sleep, informed of the decision, given the opportunity to write letters and to speak with a priest; at 7.30 a.m. he was executed by firing squad.

[11] On Blum see Veit Valentin, *Geschichte der deutschen Revolution von 1848–49* (new edition, Aalen, 1968) I, pp. 220–3; II, pp. 204–16. Hans Blum, *Robert Blum* (Leipzig, 1879).

The execution created a storm of protest all over Germany and especially in Blum's own province of Saxony. Hundreds of thousands signed petitions against the shooting; everywhere mass meetings and memorial services were held and in the service at Dresden alone, it was estimated that 8000 participated. Primarily the protests were led by the radicals and not everyone was agreed that Blum's execution merited a memorial service. In Munich the Catholic Church forbade such services and Ziegler relates the experience of his father:

My father also, then a clergyman in Göppingen, was to be compelled to hold such a service. He was conservative and therefore declared: Yes, I will hold for you such a commemoration service for Blum, but you will have to hear me telling you that he was justly shot. Thereupon they naturally renounced his participation and in the evening broke the window panes in our house. The shattering of the glass is the earliest recollection of my youth.[12]

The Württemberg Chamber gathered for the purpose of framing a protest against the high-handed action of the Austrian Government. The speeches were all extremely hostile to the abhorrent act and it was resolved that an Address should be sent to the National Assembly in Frankfurt.

Sovereign German National Assembly,
    In Swabia, as in the whole of Germany, arises a cry of horror and indignation over the bloody violation of our national laws, which has been perpetrated by an Austrian General in the violent execution of a representative of the German nation...This shot goes right through the heart of the German people...The unity of the German people is at stake; therefore the National Assembly and the National power will and must take those measures...which the German people have the right and the duty to demand.[13]

Even the more conservative members of Parliament dared not raise any protest, for the situation was dangerous, with the extreme radicals threatening violence against all who opposed their views. The clerics in the Chamber all fell in line and one of the higher ecclesiastics declared that the Assembly must express its deepest abhorrence of the act. Strauss, too, did not at first withhold his assent to the resolution, but on later reading over the proceedings, he became dissatisfied with his former

[12] Ziegler, p. 443.          [13] Hausrath, ii, Beilage i, pp. 3–4.

acquiescence and decided to wipe the slate clean by openly declaring his abstention.

He began by expressing his regret about the shooting, which, in his view, was more of a mistake than an injustice, because it made Blum a martyr.

That, from my standpoint, I can also regret, and in so far we would all have cause for protesting against this execution if we could only change what has happened. But since it has happened, what is the use of our protesting? One will answer: to avenge the honour of the German National Assembly, which, in the person of the deputy Blum, has been violated in the most shameful way by the Austrian commander. But was Robert Blum in Vienna as an emissary of the German National Assembly? The Assembly sent completely different people there. He was there off his own bat, as a representative of opinions which are miles apart from those of the National Assembly. Therefore Blum was not in Vienna officially, and in so far, the examples quoted by the deputy Notter are completely irrelevant. But I know well that a member of the German National Assembly, as, in general, every representative of the people, is inviolable as regards his person so long as his mandate lasts, not merely at the place of the Assembly, but everywhere, and that he can only be judged by the Assembly itself to which he belongs. But how, Gentlemen, how does the matter stand when such a deputy engages in things which are not compatible with his position as a deputy, when his character as a deputy not only lies idle, but when he has stripped off his deputy's cloak and put on the blouse of a barricader? Gentlemen, a man who appeared in Vienna as leader of the revolutionaries ceased in that same moment to be a representative of the National Assembly. Both positions are incompatible and when he was captured in the conquest of the city as a rebel leader, then the conqueror had a right to judge him as a rebel. (Protests from all sides.)

He was in Vienna not as a deputy, but as a guerrilla, and from of old the victor has always made short work of guerrillas.

Gentlemen, in the first days of our present Assembly we heard the news of the ghastly murder which was likewise perpetrated on two members[14] of the German National Assembly in Frankfurt. There was at that time no motion tabled to express our abhorrence of this abominable deed; we believed that we could confidently leave judgment to be passed, on one hand, by the courts, on the

---

[14] Auerswald and Lichnowsky, two conservative members of the Frankfurt Parliament who were caught and murdered by a mob on 18 September. See Valentin, *Geschichte der deutschen Revolution* II, pp. 164–6.

other hand, by public opinion. And yet, Gentlemen, these deputies had not left their posts or overstepped their authority: it was only their speeches in St. Paul's church which had brought hatred upon themselves, and when no motion was tabled by us over the abominable murder of these two men, no resolution passed, are we now to vote a resolution of disapproval of the court-martial and murder of a man who left his post in Frankfurt and took up arms against the legally constituted power in Vienna? Are we to do what at that time we omitted to do, because the two who fell in Frankfurt belonged to the right wing of the Assembly while he who was executed in Vienna belonged to the left, because the execution of Blum was carried out by the plenipotentiaries of a sovereign prince while that in Frankfurt by those who reckoned themselves as part of the sovereign people? Were demonstrations against anarchy at that time not at all in place, shall now a demonstration against the reaction be in place? If the bullet in the heart of Robert Blum was a bullet in the heart of German freedom, was it not this very same German freedom which was torn to pieces in Auerswald and Lichnowsky? If we were silent then, then we have no right to speak now; to have neglected to do it then and want to do it now would be partiality, dangerous partiality! For this reason I must refuse my assent to the motion.[15]

The members who had supported the resolution were naturally enraged and criticised him bitterly. Strauss, the apostate son of freedom, they cried, was heartless and without feeling, to which Strauss replied that in his view, to be without heart was far better for a politician than to be without sense. The papers attacked him with most hostile and insulting words and some of the citizens, disillusioned with the representative they had themselves chosen, formed themselves into a 'Fatherland-Association' and sent him a petition expressing their disapproval of his views. The petition, however, was only signed by 25 of the 126 delegates of the town council and this minority had to be bolstered up by a further 90 signatures from the ranks of the ordinary citizens. Strauss was not impressed and wrote a pungent reply:

To the Fatherland-Association in Ludwigsburg.

I have finally received the Association's declaration with its 90 signatures, which has long been announced in the newspapers, wherein the Association lets me know of its strong disapproval of the

[15] Hausrath, II, Beilage II, pp. 5–6.

way in which I have expressed my views in the Württemberg Chamber, both earlier against the misuse of the press, and more recently against R. Blum. What the Association actually intends with such an explanation is not completely clear to me. If it thinks that because it disapproves of the position I have taken in these two matters, that I also will now disapprove of the position and repent, then it errs. On the contrary I stand by my own political judgment and am free to do so, even over against the 90 authorities of the Fatherland-Association in Ludwigsburg; and I am proud of the fact that I expressed my conviction without fear of being unpopular with the fashion-setting public, an unpopularity which on account of my speeches, as I could easily see, I should draw upon myself. Or does the Association hope that because of its declaration I will go into my shell and change my position in the Chamber in order to make myself worthy of its applause in the future? It errs there likewise and may well know that it is mistaken. I have always gone my own way, might it please or displease whom it would, and I intend to continue so in the future. So incorrigible as I am supposed to be, the declaration of the Fatherland-Association could only attain a practical object if it succeeded in moving me to lay down my office, to which end even in the Assembly on the 20th a motion was tabled. Even so, as sorry as I am about the whole matter, I must still say that even the declaration which has been handed to me is not enough to accomplish this end. But in this matter good intentions are certainly not lacking on my part; I did not apply for the position of deputy, but accepted it only on the pressing wishes of my fellow-citizens, and I would – were I to follow my own inclinations – give it up today rather than tomorrow. But this post was once entrusted to me and so I may not forsake it without breaking my obligation, so long as the same majority which entrusted it to me does not relieve me of it. If the petition which I received had come from the majority of the electors – and I would immediately acknowledge it – if it had been signed by the majority of the citizens in the town, then I would not for a moment hesitate to hand in my resignation. However, out of 126 Ludwigsburg electors, only 25 signed the petition, and from the whole of the citizens, only 90. The Association would first have to produce a good many more signatures than that, to make my withdrawal possible. But perhaps there will soon be a new opportunity for achieving this end when I – as I purpose – continue just as previously. Certainly when the electors among the under-signed take offence towards my appearance in the Chamber, it only makes me wonder, and will make other people also wonder, that they elected me. For in the speeches which, to be sure, had the election to the Frankfurt Parliament in view, but the election to the Württemberg Chamber as a consequence, and which fortunately were printed, I have so repeatedly and decidedly declared that I wanted freedom only with good order, that no one, with any ground, could have expected me to have expressed myself on a subversive press or the inflammatory action of a German deputy in Vienna other than I did. And anyway, whoever wanted to have a mere yes-man of the daily opinions should not have voted for me; for I have been just the opposite throughout my whole life. When therefore under the often-referred-to petition, someone signed himself as a 'deluded elector', then the man was certainly, as his signature shows, caught up in a cruel delusion; but that is charged to his account and not to mine. I have remained thoroughly true to myself and will also remain so. If this does not please the Fatherland-Association then it may take more purposeful measures than its statement of disapproval, which I herewith indifferently lay aside.

Stuttgart 20th Nov. 1848

Deputy Strauss[16]

By now Strauss was sick of parliamentary life and wanted to resign. Only the entreaties of his friends prevented him from doing so, but he looked forward to a suitable opportunity when he could at last lay down his mandate. This opportunity arose during a debate over a new law for a Constitutional Assembly. Strauss found the proposal of the radical representative Seeger 'ambiguous' and Seeger, taking this as a slight on his character, protested. The President of the Chamber declared that Strauss should abstain from using such expressions, to which Strauss replied:

Where, in the course of my theological studies, an expression remained unintelligible, I found each time by a more careful investigation that one either wanted to hide something which was there, or present something which was not there. So it seemed to me as if there is something in the motion which one does not want to completely deny, but also  not to conceed.[17]

and after acknowledging the ability with which Seeger had imported another meaning into his words, he continued:

That I have spotted his clever trick does not detract from his artfulness and if I have not thrown a 'Yes' upon his plate, so many others have done so, that he could still be satisfied.[18]

[16] Ziegler, pp. 446–8      [17] Hausrath, II, p. 175.      [18] *Ibid.* p. 175.

The President demanded that Strauss retract his statement. Strauss refused, left the Chamber and that evening handed in his resignation. He saw, as he expressed it in an explanation to his Ludwigsburg constituency, little hope that anything essentially worthwhile would emerge from the deliberations, because the radical majority was solely bent on destroying the old, while having nothing constructive to set in its place.

Every new election of a commission, almost every following vote showed the increasing majority pursuing a policy which wanted to drive down the slope without brakes, with the express intention of overturning and wrecking the old state-coach while leaving the passengers to manage as best they could; a policy which with boyish petulance rejoiced over every hole that it succeeded in knocking in the former legal basis, without considering on what other basis than that of law and respect for the law a future state should be grounded. In such a way, mostly voting fruitlessly with the minority and simply, as it were, placing my protest on record against resolutions which were bound to be passed – that was a position from which I believed myself permitted to retire.[19]

That was the end of Strauss' political career. The whole basis of Strauss' political convictions was the preservation of law and order. He hated mob rule and anarchy because moral principles were violently thrown aside and cultural values trampled under foot. This moral and cultural point of view ultimately determined his political convictions, and those who cannot share the fundamental moral principles of his thought must necessarily disagree with his political views in general. All that threatened the moral order of society was intolerable to him. He could still have existed under Russian despotism, but mob rule, he declared, would destroy him. '*Odi profanum vulgus et arceo*',[20] he wrote to Vischer,[21] 'is and will remain my motto.'

On the whole it is true to say that Strauss had little interest in the people and their needs. As a member of the upper-class he sought to preserve the moral, social and cultural values of the society to which he belonged and he was strongly opposed

---

[19] Ziegler, p. 453.

[20] I hate the rabble and stay well clear of them. (A much-cited line of his favourite Latin poet, Horace.)

[21] To Vischer, 13.4.48; *SVBr*, i, p. 213.

to anything which threatened to destroy these values. It is not true to say that he was opposed to the betterment of living standards for the people, but he believed that this betterment should come gradually, through legal and peaceful means, and not by violence and revolution.

Strauss was not a politician in the usual sense of the word. Compared with the great political figures of the time he lacked the political acumen and foresight which characterise the true politician. He was no outstanding orator or debater – as he himself admitted – and he had no great political aptitude. He was and remained essentially a scholar, a man of letters, and not a political activist. Nevertheless, he had more political understanding than he is usually given credit for, and no other member of the Württemberg Assembly showed greater courage in openly expressing his opinions. True political thought is based primarily on truth and not on a superficial rhetoric deficient in this essential. What Strauss possessed was an honesty which placed moral convictions before everything else. He was not simply prepared to follow the prevailing mood, to be a mere 'yes-man'. He valued truth above political success and was not prepared to compromise. In Bismarck's Government he could have been happy and might even have made an important contribution towards the running of the country; but in the Württemberg Chamber he was forced to swim against the stream, which naturally demanded a corresponding negative attitude to the prevailing political opinions. The politics of the radicals disgusted him and he therefore associated himself more and more with Menzel and his friends – not because they too were of the upper-class, but because he recognised them as men of character and integrity. These virtues he did not find in the other members of the Assembly.

In the final analysis political and social attitudes are governed by moral principles; and whatever may be thought of Strauss' political views, no one can deny the honesty and integrity with which he upheld his own personal convictions.

G

# 16

## THE LITERARY WANDERER

With his resignation from Parliament a great burden fell away from Strauss' shoulders. 'I breathed more freely with every mile as I journeyed on Three Kings Day once again to Munich',[1] and with these words he begins another chapter in his life, which may be described as the wandering years.

In Munich he lived with the ethnologist Neumann and his family and felt well at home. In earlier years Neumann had spent some time in China, and on account of his interest in this country and his study of Chinese language and literature, he was often jokingly referred to by his friends as 'the Chinaman'. He possessed much in common with Strauss, the greatest difference between them lying in the fact that Neumann thought all music little more than an irritating noise which disturbed his Chinese studies, while Strauss revelled in attending the theatre, music concerts and the opera. But all the outward attractions were unable to cure his inner depression; he was moody, irritable and likely to flare up at the least provocation, so that even the few friends which he had, began to find his company a trial and a strain on their nerves. This morose side of Strauss' nature is revealed in the following letters of Ludwig Steub, one of Strauss' friends at this period;[2] it would, of course, be kinder to Strauss to omit these passages – as Ziegler does – but if we would have a true picture of Strauss as he really was and not simply the portrait of a hero with all his defects omitted or softened down, then this other side of Strauss must also be included.

[1] *GS*, i, p. 23. (Three Kings Day is 6 January.)
[2] Strauss later broke off the friendship, but there is no reason for doubting the truth of Steub's description.

The evening gatherings in the Museum[3] with the celebrities of Munich, were, according to Steub, no substitute for the company which Strauss had enjoyed with Märklin and Kauff-mann in Heilbronn.

His shyness before the world never allowed him to be warm in it. He never entered into conversation and when anyone asked him his opinion he was alarmed, and the answer was usually below expect-ation.  He could have certainly got to know all the other men one after another, but since he did not seek an intimate kinship with any of them, they too in a short time became accustomed to treating him with respectful indifference.  His closer friends, Professor Neumann and myself, quickly saw that he would not be able to stick it there for long and in order to try another experiment we took him on one occasion to Mittnacht's in the Fürstenstrasse – a tavern extremely quiet in the evenings.  'Ah, look at that', he ex-claimed after he had looked around a little, 'I like it here!  But the Museum is not for me, for', he added, in his best Swabian dialect, 'that there ain't no pub'.

So finally we had found the right tavern and sought to make our-selves at home.  We came on certain days, had our own special table and no other listener except Frau Mittnacht, who sat knitting by the other stove, and only joined in the conversation when there was a lull, which she sought to fill up with observations about the weather.  We two from Munich had soon agreed to treat our famous friend, on the one hand as our Master and Commander, on the other hand, as a convalescent who required care, and to treat him, moreover, with the therapy which he himself prescribed or seemed to wish.  Since his voice was somewhat weak we lowered our voices too and spoke secretively in whispers for a couple of hours.  If one of our acquaintances from the Museum managed to find us and sat with us, then the Master even left off his whispering and looked into his glass with despondent eyes until the other had left.  It was understandable that such a gentleman, who had hoped to have a bit of intellectual conversation with the author of the *Life of Jesus*, felt somewhat disillusioned and didn't come again.[4]

Although Strauss sometimes related his experiences in the Tübingen seminary or spoke about Goethe, he was unwilling to discuss theology, and the description concludes:

[3] The word has nothing to do with the English word; it was the usual name for the meeting place of upper-class society, roughly equivalent to the Victorian club.                    [4] Hausrath, II, pp. 187–8.

Certainly there was no lack of stimulus and instruction, but the subdued *sotto voce* conversation, the complete silence at the danger of an approaching masculine acquaintance, the anxiety that we might irritate our convalescent through an inadvertent word, the extremely restricted choice of subjects for conversation, the ghostlike pallor in which we had to veil every contradiction – all this made our tavern seem to me almost like a nun's room and did not allow me to forget the charm of a healthy, fresh association of men.[5]

In the autumn of 1849 Strauss suffered a great blow. He had expected a visit from Märklin, but instead came the heart-rending news that his closest friend was dead.

You can imagine how the news affected me, since I expected Märklin's arrival any day; his bed had been made up, to which however he preferred the grave. That was not unjust! Yet he should have waited a little for us. We are made all too poor through his death, especially I, since I only live for my friends.[6]

Strauss resolved to write a biographical sketch of Märklin's life, and the work, written during the winter months, was able to be published at the end of 1850. But his solitariness and loneliness did not abate; even a journey to Venice and Northern Italy did little to relieve his discontent.

However, in the autumn of 1851 came a new and heartening development. It had been agreed that when Fritz was seven he should come to the father, and now Agnese not only handed over Fritz, but also Georgine. There were probably two main reasons which induced her to take this step: first, that Georgine did not want to be separated from her brother, and secondly, that Agnese herself still had hopes of a reconciliation; with the children together she presumably hoped to see more of their father. Strauss was not to be deceived as to her intentions and decided to live away from Stuttgart. But where? Munich did not seem a suitable place to bring the children up; Heilbronn was out of the question because of his book on Märklin and because Kauffmann had shifted to Stuttgart. Moreover, he needed an educated children's servant who could help in their education. One possibility was only too clear. Emilie Sigel was deeply devoted to the children and ready to come and help him. That indeed was the perfect solution and if a divorce

---

[5] Hausrath, II, pp. 188–9.    [6] To Rapp, 28.10.49; *AB*, p. 249.

from Agnese could be obtained...But Agnese would never grant a divorce and reasons of social convention and Strauss' own personal feelings dictated that someone else would have to be found. A suitable woman was finally engaged and the family shifted to Weimar at the end of 1851. But Weimar, in spite of its historical and literary greatness did not particularly please him. 'No wine, no beer, my acquaintances drink tea', he complained to his brother, who attempted to alleviate his distress by sending him some bottles of best quality Rhine wine. Even the musical atmosphere was not to his taste since most of the musicians were crazy about a new composer called Wagner

so that even Beethoven himself is not modern enough for them, at least they prefer most of all to play his latest most complex works. I modestly asked the first violinist – a skilful, quite young virtuoso – whether the old Haydn might also be allowed to appear on their programme and this led on to a discussion whose upshot was that he promised – without my requesting it – next Sunday I shall hear a Haydn quartet from them.[7]

Strauss resolved to shift in the following summer to Cologne, where his brother and sister-in-law would be able to help him with the education of the children. But Cologne had even less to offer than Weimar, and Strauss, with no intellectual companionship, no library, and an unenjoyable theatre, was forced to endure a grimy industrial city and a townspeople which he considered to be a poor breed of men.

He employed his time by reading and sought avidly for a suitable subject in which he could carry out some original research. He was in luck. Having become interested in the sixteenth-century philologist and poet Nicodemus Frischlin, he cast his line into the Stuttgart archives and by chance the hook caught an unexpected fish; many of Frischlin's letters were there and a chest containing them, along with various acts, was sent to him in Cologne.

But when I had hammered the case open, who can describe my horror when I found that I could read absolutely nothing in Frischlin's letters and little in the other letters. A more abominable handwriting was scarcely ever written by a scholar; I thought that the cases had made their way to Cologne for nothing and that I

[7] To Wilhelm Strauss, 20.10.51; *AB*, p. 299.

would never in all eternity learn to decipher this writing. Yet within a few weeks I had learned it so well that only a few words remained incomprehensible. But unfortunately I must also believe that this work was one of the main causes of my eyesight being ruined, a process which began about that time. Yet the work gave me uncommonly great joy; I found how extraordinarily animating, how stimulating for the imagination it was, to reproduce from the actual handwritings and the old documents, the fortunes and events of times and persons long ago.[8]

Even in Cologne he was not free from his wife, who still had hopes of reviving the marriage; but he was extremely wary and had her every move anticipated. Still, there was a continual emotional strain arising from her imprecations, demands and threatened legal processes, since Strauss hindered her as much as possible from seeing the children. On one occasion during the holidays of 1853, the children were staying with the mother in Stuttgart and Strauss at neighbouring Ludwigsburg; when the time arrived for the return to Cologne it was found that Agnese had taken the children from Stuttgart and that their whereabouts was unknown. The state of mind of the worried father and the resulting bitterness and hatred may well be imagined. What actually took place cannot now be ascertained, but the children were at last brought to him at Mannheim.[9]

The blame for the unhappy situation cannot all rest on the side of Agnese and it would appear that Strauss was still seeking the necessary divorce which would enable him to marry Emilie; probably for this reason Kauffmann also finally broke off the friendship. But all Strauss' attempts to obtain the divorce were fruitless and he had to resign himself to the status quo.

The pressing need in Cologne was to obtain a suitable woman who could run the household and at the same time educate the children. This situation led Strauss to think of returning to Ludwigsburg, but a better solution soon presented itself. Fritz was sent to a private boarding school in Öhringen, where Strauss had friends, and Georgine was accepted into a well-run and highly-praised girl's college in Heidelberg; and in this charming university town, whither he himself shifted in the autumn of 1854, he enjoyed six of the happiest years of his later life. He lived quietly and comfortably, and Georgine was able

[8] *GS*, I, p. 29.                    [9] *SVBr*, II, p. 51.

to be with him every Sunday. Here also he found a true friend in Kuno Fischer, a lecturer in philosophy who, in consequence of a religious controversy, had had his right to lecture withdrawn.

Everything else also combined to make my stay in Heidelberg pleasant and profitable. One of the first visits that I made was to Dr. Kuno Fischer, who at that time lived there, but whose right to lecture in the University had been withdrawn. I had read an essay of his on Feuerbach a few years before, which seemed to me the best piece of criticism which had been written up till that time; and now, in consequence of the interdict which rested on him as the consequence of a theological denunciation, he was, in a certain way, a colleague of mine. I found a still very young man with bright blond hair and moustache, quick and sharp in his speech, and stiffly-erect like a North German in his bearing. So strongly contrasted as we were in all our nature and ways, he showed me right from the beginning such great respect and affection that I felt myself intimately drawn to him. His wife also, after we had come to know each other, contributed to make me feel at home in their circle. She was of French origin, but educated in Germany, and so tender and kind that she appeared to the Germans thoroughly as one of themselves. Also my daughter and my son – when he came home in the holidays – were accepted in the most friendly way into the family, which included a lively little daughter about 2 years old; and so a relationship developed which, although for a long time restricted by the distance between our towns, will accompany me – and I hope my children also – throughout the rest of my life.[10]

For almost three years, until Fischer received an appointment as professor of philosophy in Jena, the happy relationship continued and Strauss found help and encouragement in all his ideas and writings. There were also other friends such as Gervinus and Locher, who did not, however, share the same intimate place in his life as Fischer. And so the biographical writing quietly continued. *Frischlin* was finished and published in 1855 and then Strauss began work on his most important biography, the life of Ulrich von Hutten, which appeared at the end of 1857.

## STRAUSS AS BIOGRAPHER

For 20 years Strauss wrote nothing of a directly theological nature. His entire output during the years 1842–62 consisted

[10] *GS*, i, p. 32.

of biographical, literary, historical or political writings, and we must now quickly glance at this side of his literary career which occupies such an important place in his life. Who were the subjects of these biographies? Did Strauss portray and interpret them as they really were, or was his impression distorted? And how successful were these biographical writings in catching the attention of the public?

The year 1847, as we have already seen, was an almost unendurable year for Strauss, owing to the break-up of his marriage. He was listless and irritable; he had no topic to write on and nothing to do except read. In the summer of this year Vischer had been offered some 110 letters of the musician and poet Christian Schubart, and had thereupon bought them, intending to edit them himself. However, since time weighed heavy upon him, and knowing of Strauss' predicament, he sent the letters to his friend hoping that Strauss would find fresh impetus for writing. More letters of Schubart were also obtained from other sources and Strauss enthusiastically set to work on the task of editing them and writing a biographical introduction to the life of this extraordinary man. Who then was this now almost completely unknown musician and poet?

Christian Friedrich Daniel Schubart[11] (1739–91) was of an unruly and passionate temperament, extremely gifted in many ways, but incapable of a regular and organised way of life. He studied theology at Erlangen, but probably spent more time at his music, for he was, if not a genius like Mozart, at least an extremely able musician and esteemed as the best pianist in Erlangen. Nor was his poetical talent to be undervalued, as is shown by the perky and rollocking little gem:

*The Trumpeter's Assurance*

How lucky is the trumpeter,
How lucky, who can tell!
He'll come, when he departs this life,
O surely not in hell.
For God holds with his chosen few
A feast for ev'ry pray-er;
And since there must be trumpets blown,
God needs the trumpet player.[12]

---

[11] On Schubart see *Schwäbische Lebensbilder*, 1, pp. 492–509, which gives a bibliography.　　　[12] 'Zinkenistentrost'. Quoted by Ziegler, p. 494.

Schubart was to have sat his theology examinations, but was arrested for some misdemeanour and sat instead in the University 'lock-up'. However, his talent could not be suppressed and he obtained the post of schoolmaster in his home town of Aalen, where he was also made music director and assistant preacher in the church. He married in 1763 and decided to try his luck at the royal palace, where he obtained the position of court musician; but his loose mouth and insulting manner soon led to his dismissal, arrest and banishment. Back in Aalen he lived in adultery with his maid, and after some years in Ulm he was once more arrested in 1777 on account of his attacks and insults against clergy and royalty alike. Imprisoned in the military garrison of the Hohenasperg, where he remained for the next 10 years, he was, after an initial and severe imprisonment, soundly and solidly converted. Thereafter he became a convinced pietist, viewing his imprisonment not only as a punishment for his former sins, but also as a means of grace, whereby he had been brought from death to life.

Why then did Strauss find in Schubart such a congenial figure for a biography? The reason is that Schubart before his conversion had lived under very similar circumstances to Strauss. Schubart had been a rebel and a poetic rebel; he hated the organised religion, especially the clergy, and his battle cry which caused so much trouble for himself was 'freedom!'. It was Schubart the anti-cleric and poet whom Strauss admired, and Schubart the Christian and pietist was an unfortunate enigma for whom Strauss had little regard.

The book[13] was not a success. Few people in those revolutionary days had time to read the letters of an obscure Swabian poet and musician whose name was hardly known outside Württemberg, and most of the edition remained unsold.

The next biographical sketch composed by Strauss was his life of Märklin[14] which provides a delightfully warm and intimate picture of Märklin's life and thought. This book also found little acceptance, although Strauss had the satisfaction of knowing that it created quite a lot of indignation and anger in

[13] *Christian Daniel Friedrich Schubarts Leben in seinen Briefen* (Berlin, 1849).
[14] *Chri*,*tian Märklin. Ein Charakterbild aus der Gegenwart* (Mannheim, 1851). The book appeared at the beginning of December 1850, but has 1851 on the title-page.

Heilbronn, where Märklin had waged his political struggle against the radical party. Two smaller essays were written in 1849 – on A. W. Schlegel and on Karl Immermann – and then Strauss was once more at a loss for a suitable subject. At Weimar he wrote nothing of importance and not until the chest containing the letters of Frischlin was delivered to his door did he again find a topic to which he could whole-heartedly devote himself. But why Frischlin? Who was this obscure scholar?

Philip Nicodemus Frischlin[15] (1547–90) was a philologist and poet known primarily for his latin verse and commentaries on Virgil, which were, in fact, an important contribution to the scholarship of the time. He was born in 1547 and educated at Tübingen where in 1568, aged only 21, he became professor of poetry and history. On account of various religious and political indiscretions he was forced to leave Tübingen in 1582 and spend the next few years teaching in various German towns. He lived a rather unbridled and immoral life, committing adultery and writing insulting and libellous letters against clergy and nobility. On account of a rather stupid attack on the Duke of Württemberg he was arrested in 1590 and imprisoned in the fortress of Hohenurach near Reutlingen, from which he attempted to escape by letting himself down from the walls. The sheeting was either not long enough or tore under his weight, and Frischlin plunged to his death on the rocks below.

Here again it was Frischlin the anti-cleric who awoke the sympathetic chord in Strauss' affections. Frischlin had been hounded from pillar to post by his enemies and Strauss was by no means unacquainted with such experiences. That the biography[16] would have little success on account of its unknown and unimportant subject was fully anticipated by Strauss and he was not unduly concerned at the lack of response.[17] For

[15] On Frischlin, see *ADB*, VIII, pp. 96–104.

[16] *Leben und Schriften des Dichters und Philosophen Nikodemus Frischlin.* The book appeared in October 1855, but has 1856 on the title-page.

[17] Even Vatke was unimpressed, as the following dialogue between the two friends in 1860 reveals.

Vatke: You have also written a boring book – your *Frischlin*.
Strauss: I'm sorry you think so, *Frischlin* is my best book!
Vatke: It's too specifically Württembergian for me; shame that a man like you should expend so much industry on such material.
(Benecke, 492).

him, the book had been a source of interest and pleasure, providing him with a badly-needed topic. He had written something constructive, something created out of original sources and it had been well worth the effort, even if only for the satisfaction which he had derived from writing it.

From Frischlin it was only a short step to Strauss' most important biographical work – the life of Ulrich von Hutten.[18] Hutten (1488–1523) was descended from a noble family and had been well educated in the humanistic arts. Coming under the influence of Erasmus, he perceived the evils and abuses in the Church and demanded their reform. It was only after the Council of Worms, however, that his eyes were opened to the importance of Luther's theological conflict with Rome; from henceforth he determined to aid Luther in every possible way, in order to deliver Germany from the Roman yoke. With hopes that a protective league of knights might be formed which would act as a counterbalance to the power of the princes, he threw in his lot with Franz von Sickingen; but the forces against them were too powerful and Hutten was forced to flee to Switzerland. Weary and sick he finally arrived at Zürich where Zwingli provided him with shelter; but he had not long to live and died on the island of Ufnau in the lake of Zürich in 1523.

The book had a far better reception than any other which Strauss had written. He was fortunate in having access to a new critical edition of Hutten's works, and the resulting biography was a carefully organised and well written book which provided a full and detailed account of Hutten's life and thought.

But this work, more than any other of the biographies, was essentially concerned with the religious factor, for Hutten supported a religious cause and not merely a social and political Reformation; and where religion enters into the picture, Strauss' portrayal becomes untrustworthy, because he saw every situation to a large degree through his anti-religious spectacles. For the task of any biographer is not simply to relate the facts, but also to interpret them, and where religious issues are involved, then Strauss' interpretation is always suspect. In the Schubart biography, for example, the earlier Schubart is well depicted, but what was Strauss to make of Schubart's

<hr />

[18] *Ulrich von Hutten* (Leipzig, 1857). The title-page bears the date 1858.

conversion, Schubart the pietist? That was where Strauss was untrue, both to himself and to Schubart, for he suppressed the whole significance of Schubart's conversion as much as possible and regarded him as the victim of a pietistic brain-washing, which afterwards left him permanently incapacitated. But that was certainly not how Schubart understood his experience; this becomes abundantly clear when we read the poems composed in prison, and especially in the following extract from the military chaplain who carefully questioned him about his motives for wishing to partake of the Holy Communion.

I questioned him why he was pressing so urgently and continually for admission to the Holy Communion. His answer was that he perceived well, and more and more, how far he had strayed from God through the abomination of his character and life; that he had allowed himself to be led astray through the lusts of the flesh to terrible sins; that through his teaching, writing and life he had given great offence and caused much harm. He testified this to me with sorrow, repentance and tears and declared that he now wanted, that he sought nothing so much as to be again reconciled with his God, especially since he had been fully convinced from the Holy Scriptures that in Jesus Christ is to be found forgiveness etc. etc., even for a great sinner like himself; and he is also assured that he may receive this forgiveness in partaking of the Lord's Supper... He would gladly renounce wife and children, freedom and comfort and whatever else is pleasing to man, if he could only be reconciled again with his God and again obtain his grace.[19]

Schubart held to his new-found faith and remained a convinced pietist unto the end of his life, so that Strauss' assertion that Schubart's religious zeal declined after his release from prison[20] cannot be confirmed from Schubart's letters.

And just this same anti-religious bias is found in the biographies of Frischlin and Hutten; it is indeed unfortunate that so much of Strauss' interpretation in the latter work is unreliable because he so often attempted to avoid the religious implications of the Reformation and to interpret it in terms of social, moral or political motives. That the Reformation was intertwined with such non-religious factors is not in question, but the mainspring of the whole movement was certainly Luther's new discovery of the biblical doctrine of justification by faith.

---

[19] GS, VIII, pp. 273–4.    [20] To Emilie Sigel, 3.4.51; AB, p. 276.

And yet Strauss himself, to his great credit, recognised this. He understood far better than many later interpreters where the true centre of the Reformation lay. He even had thoughts of writing another biography – of Luther! Luther of all people! But finally he was forced to turn back. He made an attempt to study 'the less spiritual Zwingli', but as he read and pondered Zwingli's biblical theology he found he could proceed no further and the plan to write the Luther biography was also finally abandoned.

I reconsidered my intention once again and came to the conclusion that I had reckoned up the bill without the waiter i.e. that I had formulated a plan without considering my innermost nature and disposition. It was not merely my continuing alienation from theology at that time; even now – although I have overcome this and again written many more pages of theology – I could not write a biography of Luther. I respect the great liberator with inward gratitude; I admire his manliness, his courage so true to his convictions; I feel drawn by so many features of his complete, healthy human nature, which his life as well as his writings reveal; but one thing separates me from him in the most inward way and this – when I see it clearly – makes every thought of a biographical work on him impossible. A man in whom everything proceeds from the consciousness that he and all men are in themselves utterly corrupt, and subject to eternal damnation, from which they can only be redeemed through the blood of Christ and by trusting in its power – a man whose inner core is determined by this consciousness is so strange to me, so incomprehensible, that I could never choose him to be the hero of a biographical representation. Whatever else I might admire and love in him, this, his most inward consciousness, is so detestable to me that there could never be any question of sympathy existing between him and myself, which is indispensable between the biographer and his hero.[21]

It is just at this point that Strauss' honesty is so clearly seen in that he acknowledged the cruciality of the biblical doctrines of the atonement and of justification by faith. He perceived the impossibility of changing and modifying the supernatural and other-worldly categories into moral and this-worldly ones, but he could only shake his head in bewilderment and turn sadly away.

[21] *GS*, I, pp. 40–1.

I have started to read for the Luther biography...But now in order
to comprehend Luther one must clearly understand, must immerse
oneself in his teaching on justification and the inner conflicts which
led him to it. The latter is not easy to do, at least for me. First,
these inner dispositions are repugnant to me 'and their result, the
doctrine of justification, appears to me as nonsense. But now I
tell myself: these histories have changed the world; even you stand
in this tradition, with everything that is dear to your convictions;
it cannot therefore be plain nonsense; press under the surface and
dig out the meaning. Right, I'll do that and translate these conflicts
and their result into my language; but do I not falsify them in doing
so? are those still Luther's inner feelings? Luther's views? And yet
there must be a mediation through which, by means of a line of $=$,
and again, $=$, Luther's Law and Gospel may flow into Kant's cate-
gorical imperative and Schiller's aesthetic education of the human
race. You see on what knots I am toiling. Therefore I think: let
Luther be Luther and write 'The lives of German poets from
Klopstock to Schiller'. You will have more pleasure doing that; is
also easier. Easier! Just that throws me back again to the other task,
which lures me through its difficulty. Oh Rapp, what sort of foolish
friend do you have.[22]

[22] To Rapp, 19.11.57; *AB*, p. 373.

# 17

## THE RETURN TO THEOLOGY

The biography of Hutten was finished and Strauss needed a new subject to occupy his time. We have seen how he considered writing a biography of Luther but relinquished the plan after finding Luther's theological ideas too repugnant. Now he turned to the great literary figures of the past and expressed his hope of writing the biographies of Klopstock, Wieland, Lessing, Herder, Goethe and Schiller. He began work on Klopstock and completed a study of the poet's early years to which other studies of Klopstock's life and work were later added; but the whole biography was never brought to completion; it lay outside the realm of public interest and Strauss resolved to return to the burning theological issues which held the limelight during these years. What then were the reasons for this change of mind? Why did he suddenly decide to enter the struggle once again? For as late as May 1858 he had told Rapp that he was selling his theological books, since 'I shall certainly not read them any more.'[1] And yet, by the end of the same year he was again immersing himself in theological literature.

It is true that in one sense Strauss had always retained some connection with theology; his interest in politics had also been an interest in Church affairs since the two were so closely connected, and the biographies were of men who had been deeply involved in religion, either as friends or as foes. And yet one can certainly say that for most of the time since he had written his Dogmatics, he had so completely washed his hands of religion, theology and the Church, that the new preoccupation with these subjects marks a definite renewal of interest. There were probably a number of reasons for this and he himself tells us of two – his anger with the Church hierarchy, and his study of Hutten and the Reformation.

In the autumns of 1857 and 1858, Strauss and his two

[1] Ziegler, p. 554.

children spent their holidays in the village of Münkheim, where Rapp was the local vicar. Strauss was daily at the parsonage with Rapp and his family, but did not stay in the house, and lodged instead at the local inn. On Sundays he and the children attended Church and gladly listened to Rapp's sermons. Outwardly it appeared that there could be no objection to the visit, and to all intents and purposes Strauss was no more than an ordinary visitor. However, some members of the congregation had long been dissatisfied with Rapp, although they could find no charge to bring against him, since his sermons were always impeccably ethical with no doctrinal opinions which could provide leverage for a charge of heresy; even Rapp himself 'believed that the Church authorities could never convict him on any charge'.[2] But now Strauss was recognised and Rapp denounced for his friendship with the notorious Dr Strauss. The charge was transmitted through the official channels of the Church to Bishop Mehring, who, with Strauss, had been a member of the Stuttgart Parliament. Strauss, who had a very low opinion of the bishop, was furious about Mehring's actions and wrote to the Württemberg Minister of Justice, with whom he was personally acquainted. The Minister in turn took the matter up with the Minister of Culture, who wrote to Mehring criticising his actions. The charge against Rapp was not considered substantial enough to proceed with further, and Rapp escaped with a censure from his Consistory.

Soon afterwards, however, Rapp again landed himself in hot water when he declared in his religious instruction class at the school, that the resurrection of Christ was 'an old myth'.[3] And so the dispute flared up anew; the villagers were enraged, the Consistory and Bishop Mehring saw this as a confirmation of their former action, and this time Strauss could do very little to help.

The second and more important reason which Strauss gives was occasioned by his study of Hutten and the Reformation. In 1859, while engaged on the translation of Hutten's *Dialogues*, he once again turned his gaze back to the happy hunting-ground which had long ago been his preserve.

In the midst of this task I busied myself with all kinds of theological reading, especially with a survey in the field of the latest biblical

---

[2] Ziegler, p. 558.          [3] *Ibid.* p. 563.

criticism, of which I had read only the main works of Baur at the time when they first appeared, with well-merited admiration in spite of the way in which I was often unjustly treated. But the closer acquaintance with the mischief continually being carried on in this field was still insufficient to fan the embers, caused to glow by the words of Hutten and stirred up by the unfairness on the part of the Württemberg hierarchy, into a bright flame.[4]

A third motivation was the thought of a new edition of the *Life of Jesus*. Twenty-five years previously his book had shocked the world, and through its influence – both direct and indirect – the whole course of theology had been changed.

It is just a quarter of a century ago that my *Life of Jesus* entered into the world for the first time. The theologians will scarcely want to celebrate the silver jubilee of this book, in spite of the fact that it has helped more than one of them to all manner of pretty thoughts and then to position and honour. But many a better man, in every country, who dates the liberation of his mind from the study of this book, has been grateful to me for this throughout his whole life – I know it – and participates in the celebration in quietness, without actually thinking about it. Even I myself could harbour a grudge against my book, for it has done me (and rightly too! cry the pious) much harm. It excluded me from a teaching position in a university, for which I had a desire, perhaps also talent; it tore me out of natural relations with others and drove me into unnatural; it has made my whole life lonely. And yet, I reflect, what would have become of me had I suppressed the word that was laid upon my soul, had I stifled the doubts which worked within me; then I bless the book which outwardly, to be sure, has done me so much harm, but inwardly has preserved the health of my spirit and soul, and – I may console myself – that of many others also. And so, on this its day of honour, I testify to it that it was written from a pure impulse, with honourable intention, without passion and without secondary aims, and that I would like to wish that all its opponents, when they wrote against it, had been just as free from secondary intentions and fanaticism. I testify to it further that it has not been refuted, but only continued, and that if it is now read only little, the reason is that it has been absorbed by the education of the time and has penetrated into all the veins of present-day science. Finally, I testify to it that in the whole twenty-five years since it appeared, not a significant line has been written about the questions with which it dealt, in which its influence is not to be perceived.[5]

[4] *GS*, I, p. 46.                    [5] *GS*, VII, pp. 561–2.

And now, a quarter of a century later, Strauss again takes up the arms which he had long ago laid down. The preface to the *Gespräche*, written with all his old fire and brilliance, is his manifesto of war.

From no side do I find that one gladly says the last honest word. And why not? Is it still, among all people, only those who are to some degree educated and thinking people who know the long open secret, that no one believes the dogmas of the Church any more? He believes that he believes, that I concede; but really believes, that I deny. For nobody is the Apostles Creed or the Augsburg confession an appropriate expression of his religious consciousness any more. No one believes any more in any of the miracles in the New Testament (not to speak of those in the Old), from the supernatural conception to the ascension. Either one explains them naturally or conceives them as legends. And if this is the case with the thinking laity, the situation, as we have seen, is no better among the clergy. And to what end are these subterfuges? To what end the hypocrisy before others and before oneself? Is it worthy of a man in his relation to religion to resort to it like a cowardly and artful slave with half-truths and empty excuses? Why not come into the open? Why not mutually confess that one can only acknowledge poetry and truth in the biblical stories, only meaningful symbols in the Church dogmas, but that one remains devoted, with unchanged respect, to the ethical content of Christianity, to the character of its founder (so far as the human form is still able to be recognised within the miraculous casing into which he was placed by his first biographers)? Yet may we then still call ourselves Christians? I do not know; but is it then a question of the name? I do know that only when we confess these things will we once again be true, honest and enlightened, i.e. better men, than formerly. We shall also remain Protestants; yes, only then will we be true Protestants.[6]

The battle was not to be joined immediately, however, for Strauss required time to prepare his new attack and family concerns were especially to the forefront. Georgine had finished college and Strauss persuaded his friend Rapp to accept her into his household, in order that his wife might teach her the essentials of running a home. The experiment was not a success. Frau Rapp possessed little enthusiasm for the new probationer and relations soon cooled; with the marriage of Rapp's daughter Frida, the most warm-hearted member of the family departed

---

[6] *GS*, vii, pp. 559–60.

and Georgine experienced a most unhappy time. It was on account of this situation and the necessity of finding a new school for Fritz that Strauss decided to shift to Heilbronn, where he still had a number of close friends who would form a welcome substitute for the depleted society at Heidelberg. There Fritz would have the benefit of an excellent secondary school and Georgine would be able to keep house for the three of them.

But the most pressing concern was his eyesight, which had deteriorated since the writing of Frischlin's biography. An operation was necessary, which in those days was a rather fearsome prospect; but there was no alternative and the whole episode was related by Vatke in a letter (dated 15.11.60) to his brother with a freshness which requires no other commentary.

After all these things, at 10 a.m. on the 26th October Dr. Strauss from Heidelberg (he and his two children have just shifted to Heilbronn) unexpectedly appeared and requested me to take him to Professor von Graefe. He was suffering from double images over distances of 7 feet. He had introduced himself to Graefe when Graefe was passing through Heidelberg at the end of August, but since Graefe was not remaining there longer he referred him for an operation to Dr. Weber in Darmstadt, one of his pupils. The operation took place on both eyes in September (the cure lasted six weeks) but without the desired success. Strauss felt that not enough had been cut in the left eye, although the amount was adequate in the right. He therefore wanted to see the Master himself. But Graefe returned from a long journey only on the 3rd October, and therefore, in the meantime, Strauss could only introduce himself to Graefe's assistant Dr. Arendt, let himself be examined, and then wait until Graefe himself saw him on the 5th November. On the 6th November he entered the eye-clinic; on the 7th at 1.15 p.m. the left eye was operated on and immediately afterwards he could see everything as a single image. He is at present staying in the clinic and Graefe is observing the success; the right eye was not cut at all and Strauss hopes to be on his way home at the beginning of next week, satisfied with the result. This, in brief, is the history of the operation. Now a few details. I am the only old friend of Strauss in Berlin...Thus I felt it my duty to look after him as well as possible; he spent every evening with me from the 26th October to the 5th November and most afternoons. Then, at his request, I was with him during the operation and according to his own statement he owes it to me that the operation was performed. He was greatly afraid of the whole thing because he had heard the other

patients screaming, in spite of the fact that they had been chloroformed, and learnt that they had only been partly chloroformed.
As he waited in the operation room until his turn came, he suddenly hurried out of the door, put on his hat and coat and refused
to hear anything more about the operation. I remonstrated with
him that I must at least tell Graefe; I re-entered the room, talked
the matter over with Graefe and in the friendliest manner fetched
Strauss in, to whom Graefe also spoke. So he consented to the
operation, but with great struggle during the chloroforming since
he feared that one would lay hands on him before he had become
unconscious, and he called out loudly to me to help him. Yet after
5 minutes he became unconscious; the left eye was drawn by
instruments to the outer side, the musculus internus which lay
underneath exposed and somewhat more cut than Weber had
done. At most it lasted two minutes; yet Strauss cried out, as he
said afterwards, unconsciously. Immediately after the operation he
recovered consciousness; he saw a single image and was very happy.
Since then I have visited him every day, often 3 to 4 hours, in order
to shorten the time for him, since he is not allowed to use his eyes.
I wrote letters for him to his children, to his brother in Darmstadt,
and read him the letters which he received. When it appeared that
the right eye might also be operated on, not merely Strauss, but also
Graefe requested my presence in the operating room, because the
gentlemen, as Strauss said to me, have respect for my presence.
Praise God that the operation does not appear to be necessary.
The whole thing has cost me much time, but also given me much
joy, that I have such a friend to whom I have been able to show a
loving devotion.[7]

The operation was successful, although Strauss had to take
great care of his eyes and was not allowed to read by lamp-light.
His writings during this period were not profuse, the most
important being the long, 180-page essay on Reimarus' *Apology
for the rational worshippers of God*.[8] He had intended to edit the
manuscript, but having perused the work, decided against it;
the following paragraph from the Foreword reveals Strauss'
aims and objects in writing this extensive analysis of Reimarus'
work.

I had thought of editing the whole work, but after I had had the
manuscript in my hands, no more. Certainly it is one of the most

----

[7] Benecke, pp. 485–8.

[8] *Hermann Samuel Reimarus und seine Schutzschrift für die vernünftigen Verehrer
Gottes* (Leipzig, 1861); *GS*, v, pp. 229–409.

remarkable and sterling productions of the former century; certainly one must bitterly complain that it did not emerge at the right point of time, in order to break into the intellectual movement of the seventies with the full force of an entire, self-contained and scientific work. But if one now wanted to publish the work in its entirety, it would be difficult to find many readers. It has become so alienated from our time in its standpoint and attitude, its viewpoint and style. For our age the old Reimarus needs an interpreter, a go-between. I wanted to be this man. I wanted to make plain to my contemporaries who Reimarus was, how he thought and what he strove for. I wanted to dampen the arrogance of the theologians who would have liked to refute him with the objection that all these ideas had long ago been disproved. I wanted to guard against the offence which the harshness of his judgments about holy persons and things could arouse among the sincere laity. I sought to accomplish both these things simply by opening up the view of the contemporary state of biblical criticism, where the harshness and one-sidedness of Reimarus' views is toned down and supplemented, while the core of his views proves itself indestructable truth.[9]

The death of four friends, and of his brother Wilhelm, during the four years 1860–3 were keenly felt by him. Baur died on 2 December 1860 and although his death was regarded by Strauss as a great loss to the theological world, he did not feel it as such a personal blow, since they had never been intimate friends and were bound by ties more theological than personal. In the following summer he lost his friend Sicherer and also Emilie Siegel. Emilie's passing was especially regretted, although in her last years a difference of opinion on questions of religion had arisen between them and put a damper on their former friendship.

Our deceased friend Emilie, in her will, handed over to me in a sealed packet not only my letters, but also those of other people, among others also your letters; you can tell me what you want me to do with them. Through reading her letters and mine, I have now recapitulated a good piece of my life and also our common life (I mean yours and mine) from 1836 to 1842, when a breach in the dyke tore up all the seedlings once planted; then also the correspondence which was renewed from 1848, in which my children now constitute the main object of interest. But a change in

[9] *GS*, v, pp. 232–3.

Emilie in the course of the years is unmistakable. Her religious views in the earlier period, in conformity with her whole personality, had a fairly free direction. An insulting word against clerics and obscurantists did not at all offend her; she even permitted herself such a word. But that changed later on. Her earlier more natural piousness became continually more churchly. That she, before this time, had to read to her mother from the books of Moses with their sacrificial laws, preserved her in the opposition; but when she was no longer compelled, she read the books for herself. Conversation on religious matters later became impossible between us; she put up with my position only for my sake, as an exception, and that had to harm our intercourse; and yet I am now angry with myself that I did not treat the whole matter much more lightly. Such a treasure of love and faithfulness as is contained in these letters makes me indeed quite painfully ashamed of myself. I could not have rewarded her completely because I could not completely reply to her; but could I not yet have done far more that I did?[10]

On 21 February 1862 Justinus Kerner died, and the death of Strauss' brother exactly one year later, on 21 February 1863, was the heaviest blow of all, since the friendship between the two brothers had been such an intimate and untroubled relationship. Wilhelm had been a sympathetic confidant of all Strauss' plans and it was to him, even before his death, that Strauss had resolved to dedicate his new *Life of Jesus*.

My dear brother,
   Old as my literary activity is beginning to be, this is still the first work – apart from two addresses – which I have ever dedicated to anyone. I have never had patrons, nor have I sought them; my teachers – after I had caused offence with my first work – hastened, in conformity with the truth, to assure that those things which had aroused indignation, i.e. the best that I knew, had not been learnt from them; and I saw my friends and student companions, especially in our native Württemberg, exposed to so much embarrassment, discrimination and inculpation, even because of the mere report of their friendship with me – so far as they preferred not to sacrifice this friendship (which also happened) to the expediencies of the situation – that I felt bound by my conscience not to expose them to still further odium by a public memorial of our friendship.
   You, dear brother, are independent – that is the blessing of commercial enterprize; you do not have to worry about the favour

[10] To Rapp, 9.8.61; *AB*, p. 433.

or disfavour of clerical or lay superiors; it can do you no harm when your name appears before one of my writings.[11]

And to this new *Life of Jesus for the German People* we must now turn our attention.

[11] *GS*, iii, p. xv; ET: *A New Life of Jesus* (London, 1865) pp. iii–iv.

# 18

## THE *LIFE OF JESUS* FOR THE GERMAN PEOPLE

For the *German* people! This was an allusion to the *Life of Jesus* which Renan had written for what Strauss considered to be the banal religious taste of the French. Strauss' new *Life of Jesus* was to be the German counterpart – a book 'as suitable for Germany as Renan's is for France'.[1] But primarily the book was for the German *people*, i.e. the laity in contrast to the theologians.

In the Preface to the first edition of my *Life of Jesus*, which I wrote almost twenty-nine years ago, I expressly stated that the work was only intended for theologians; for the laity no adequate preparation had been made and the book was intentionally arranged so that they would not understand it in its theological content. This time, however, I have written for the laity and taken particular pains that no single sentence shall remain unintelligible to any educated or intelligent person: whether the theologians also (I mean those in academic positions) want to read me or not is a matter of indifference to me.

If we want to advance in matters of religion, then those theologians who are above the prejudices and vested interests of their academic position must reach out their hand – undeterred by the majority of their academic associates – to the intellectuals in the Church. And as the Apostle Paul turned to the Gentiles when the Jews rejected his Gospel, so we also must speak to the people, since the majority of the theologians will still not give us a hearing.[2]

Since 1835 there had been many new developments in the field of historical criticism, which the first *Life of Jesus* had been so instrumental in setting in motion. Strauss had long been considering a new edition of the earlier work which would take

---

[1] *GS*, III, p. xxx; ET, I, p. xviii.
[2] *Ibid.* III, pp. xix–xx; ET, I, pp. vii–viii.

these new developments into account. However, he had no desire merely to patch up the original work and decided to rewrite the book completely, incorporating the results of the most recent critical research, but leaving the mythical interpretation unchanged.

During the 1840s, Strauss, influenced by the slashing attack of Feuerbach on the Hegelian philosophy, slowly discarded his earlier speculative views. No longer could God be described as the Infinite Spirit – that was all delusion, like the transcendent personal God of traditional theology. But the mythical principle, which was in no way dependent upon the Hegelian philosophy, remained valid, and was, in fact, the only adequate explanation which could account for the formation of the Gospel narratives. The layout of the work was altered, the historical aspect discussed in more detail, but the mythical principle underlying the whole work remained essentially the same. 'As for me, I adhere to the position which I adopted from the beginning...'[3]

The new developments in the field of New Testament criticism between 1835 and 1864 may be divided into three main categories.

### *1. Attempts to discover the Jesus of History*

After the appearance of Strauss' first *Life of Jesus* there was a flurry of books and articles from every shade of theological viewpoint. Neander had written a conciliating book;[4] Ebrard one definitely hostile to Strauss';[5] and Bruno Bauer had even gone so far as to claim that the Christian faith was simply the fabrication of one ingenious poetical mind, that the Gospel of Mark had been created by a single poet, and that Jesus was merely – like King Lear or Faust – an invention of literary fiction which later authors had embellished and fancified.[6] The bombastic Göttingen Old Testament scholar Ewald had

---

[3] *Ibid.* III, p. xxv; ET, I, p. xiii.

[4] *Das Leben Jesu-Christi* (Hamburg, 1837).

[5] *Wissenschaftliche Kritik der Evangelischen Geschichte* (Frankfurt am Main, 1842). Joh. Heinrich Ebrard (1818–88) was professor of theology at Erlangen.

[6] *Kritik der evangelischen Geschichte der Synoptiker* (Leipzig, 1841–2).

also climbed on the biographical band-wagon with a rather unsupernatural Life of Jesus,[7] but the most important contribution in these years was the small volume of Theodor Keim,[8] which considered Jesus' human development, and especially the development of his messianic consciousness, according to the strictest laws of psychology and history. Finally, in 1863, appeared the romantically sentimental work – 'with its faults, but only one fundamental error' – by Renan,[9] which in popularity surpassed every Life of Jesus previously written. Strauss learnt from all these works and set out to present a clearer and more consequent historical representation than any of his predecessors.

## 2. The Literary Criticism of the New Testament

One of the chief criticisms levelled at the first Life of Jesus was that Strauss had paid little attention to the origin of the Gospel sources. The charge was certainly true in itself but took no account of the fact that Strauss' mythical principle was completely independent of the sources. It really made no difference at all, from this point of view, who had written the various books of the New Testament, and especially the Gospels. If the stories were miraculous then they were unhistorical and mythical, whoever had written them.

Nevertheless, the question was whether the sources could be shown to be historically trustworthy, or untrustworthy, and to this question Strauss saw himself obliged to devote a large section of the book. That was only necessary if he was to close the loop-hole to such criticism as had previously been mounted against him.

The most important investigation into the Gospel sources in the previous two decades had been carried on by Baur and the

[7] Georg Heinrich August Ewald, *Geschichte Christus' und seiner Zeit* (Göttingen, 1855).

[8] *Die menschliche Entwicklung Jesu Christi* (Zürich, 1861). Theodor Keim (1825–78), a pupil of Baur's, was professor of theology in Zürich (1860–73) and Giessen (1873–8).

[9] Ernest Renan, *La Vie de Jésus* (Paris, 1863). The one fundamental error, according to Strauss, was Renan's acceptance of the authenticity of the fourth Gospel.

Tübingen School. Baur held that Matthew was the earliest Gospel and the most historical; Luke stemmed from an early second century revision of a Pauline proto-Luke; Mark was the youngest of the Synoptics, a late second century epitome of Matthew and Luke; and John was also composed late in the second century by an unknown author in Asia Minor.

Strauss accepted these views and when his survey had been completed the result was as negative as it had been in 1835 – the Gospels as historical records were completely untrustworthy.

### 3. Conscious and Unconscious Mythologising

In 1835 Strauss had attributed all supernatural narratives in the New Testament to an unconscious mythologising process, but Baur had shown convincingly that this could not hold true in every case, and especially for the stories in John's Gospel. And so Strauss conceded the presence of a conscious mythologising, but accepted that both unconscious and conscious myths belonged in the same mythical category.

In this new edition of the *Life of Jesus* I have conceded far more room than previously – mainly as a consequence of Baur's investigations – for the acceptance of conscious and intentional mythologizing; but I have seen no reason to change the term itself. On the contrary, to the question whether conscious fabrications of an individual are also properly to be called myths, I must – even after all the previous discussion on this point – still always reply: absolutely, as soon as they have been believed and have passed into the history of a people or a religious sect; at the same time, this also shows that they were formed by their author, not merely according to his own fancies, but in close association with the consciousness of a majority. Every unhistorical narrative – however it may have originated – in which a religious community recognises a constituent part of its sacred origins as an absolute expression of its fundamental sentiments and ideas is a myth; and if Greek mythology is desirous of distinguishing a more limited concept of the myth, which excludes conscious fabrication, from this wider concept, critical theology, conversely, is desirous – over against the so-called believers – of including all those Gospel narratives to which it ascribes only an ideal significance, under the general concept of myth.[10]

[10] *GS*, III, p. 202; ET, I, pp. 213–14.

## THE CONTENT OF THE BOOK

The new *Life of Jesus* falls into three parts: an introduction deals with the investigation into the historicity of the Gospel sources; Book I, consists of Strauss' new attempt to write a historical account of Jesus' life, in so far as the sources will allow such an account to be written; Book II is simply an abridgment of the 1835 edition and recapitulates how the mythical stories in the New Testament were derived from the Old.

The layout of the book was criticised as being inferior to the form of the 1835 edition. This criticism is unjust. The layout could hardly have been other than it was, for Strauss wanted only to take account of the more recent historical developments, but to retain the mythical interpretation unaltered. The alternative to the form of the 1864 edition would have been merely a revised edition of the original; and that would have received even more criticism.

### I. THE PICTURE OF JESUS

The result of Strauss' investigation in 1864 could not have been expected to differ markedly from that of 1835, for the same presuppositions determined the outcome in advance: everything miraculous and supernatural in the Gospels was *ipso facto* pronounced mythical and the Gospel records themselves were declared untrustworthy and unhistorical sources.

The determining presupposition was the exclusion of the miraculous. The only positive fact which Strauss knew for certain was that 'Jesus was not supernatural and did nothing supernatural.'[11]

We are usually accustomed to regard the hero of a biography as, above all, completely and entirely human. A personality who, on the one side, was certainly a man, on the other side, however, a higher being, a son of the gods or a son of God, certainly born from a human mother but begotten by no human father – such a subject we will relinquish to fable and poetry but never seriously consider making it the object of an historical representation.[12]

In fact, not only does Strauss find it egoistic of Jesus to insist upon his divine nature, but he even concludes that had Jesus

[11] *GS*, III, p. 204; ET, I, p. 216.     [12] *Ibid.* III, pp. 3–4; ET, I, pp. 1–2.

really uttered such assertions, then he must have been out of
his mind.

But quite apart from any references to an alleged pre-existence,
Jesus' own utterances about himself in the fourth Gospel are of a
kind which makes it difficult to determine his own personal self-
consciousness from them.  Whether a God who had become man
would behave as the Johannine Jesus does, whether in his speeches
he would insist upon his divinity so strongly and incessantly, continually challenging the opposition of men to whom a divine 'I'
speaking out of human lips is intolerable, whether a God who had
become man would not find it wiser and more becoming to let his
divinity shine forth more indirectly through the radiance of his
humanity – about all this nothing definite can be said since the
presupposition belongs solely to the sphere of the imagination.  But
a man, whoever he may have been, could never have uttered the
speeches about himself, as are put into the mouth of Jesus in the
fourth Gospel – quite apart from those high-points which even pass
over into a pre-temporal, other-worldly realm – if his head and
heart were sound.[13]

But now, having settled his score with supranaturalism, the
question remained how to explain the relationship of the Jesus
of history with the Christ of faith; for Strauss was convinced
that such a Christ could never have arisen unless an actual and
historical figure lay behind the portrait painted by the evangelists.  What did Jesus think about himself?  Who did he claim
to be?  These were the vital questions which Strauss had to
answer.  The main difficulty lay in separating fact from fiction,
what Jesus himself had actually said and claimed, from what
his followers attributed to him afterwards.  On this point Strauss
was vague and it is clear that he could not make up his mind.
If Jesus had asserted his divine nature as the Son of God and
Messiah, in the sense in which orthodoxy had always used these
designations, then he must simply have been a deluded fanatic.
But if that was really the case, how was his remarkable working
in the world to be accounted for?  It was quite evident to Strauss
that Jesus had had an effect upon the human race surpassed by
no other man in world history.  Was it then really possible that
such an influence could originate from a mentally deficient, or,
at least, emotionally unstable character?

[13] *Ibid.* III, p. 255; ET, I, p. 272.

He who has given up the orthodox view is immediately confronted by the fanatic, but by such an arrant fanatic, that the longer one scrutinizes him, the harder it becomes to conceive how so much fanaticism can be united with so much intelligence. So it is not merely apologetical weakness when one finds oneself always tempted to transfer a part of the messianic-eschatological sayings in his speeches, to the Gospel writers, or, with Baur, to distinguish a general human side of Christ from the Jewish-nationalistic side. The error is simply that this is expressed too abstractly; one omits showing how just these two sides were combined, and worked through one another. I believe – just from the historical-philosophical standpoint – that in the long run it is impossible for such a solid, sterling working as Christianity and the rebirth of the world through it, to have originated from such a dissimilar cause as a Jewish-messianic fanatic and from the chance that through his death and the non-fulfilment of his prophesies the affair was thrown back violently into the inner consciousness and then gradually spiritualized.[14]

The crucial point concerned Jesus' statements about his second coming. Whereas his utterances about his pre-existence were to be found only in John's Gospel and could easily be explained away as words which the author had placed in Jesus' mouth, the statements about the second coming were not so easily disposed of since they appeared in all the Gospels, and especially in the more historically trustworthy Synoptics. If Jesus had really uttered statements about his return upon the clouds of heaven, then he deserved only scorn and pity.

For us, however, Jesus exists only as a human being, or not at all. The like of which he here prophesied about himself could not happen to a man. If he did prophesy it and actually expected it to happen, then he is for us nothing but a fanatic; if he expressed these things about himself without any personal conviction, then he was a braggart and a fraud. There is only a very slight difference here from the alleged sayings of Jesus about his pre-existence. He who thinks he remembers a former existence prior to his birth (not merely, like Plato, who considered certain ideas already existing in his mind to be recollections of a former state of existence) which no other human being remembers and which he himself does not really remember, is, in our opinion, nothing but a madman; he who expects to come again after his death in a manner by which no man has ever returned – such a man is, in our opinion, to be sure, not

14 To Käferle, 15.6.62; *AB*, p. 441.

quite a madman, because imagination is more possible in matters related to the future, but still an arrant fanatic.[15]

But whether Jesus had actually predicted his coming again was uncertain. He might, indeed, have understood his prediction in a different way, perhaps given his words another meaning which had been distorted by the disciples into the cruder literal and supernatural sense. On the other hand the possibility still remained open that Jesus had never uttered these predictions at all, that his whole appearance was to be given an ethical interpretation. Thus Strauss thought that it might be possible to understand Jesus as a religious reformer who had adopted the messianic conception only in a moral and ethical sense.

In Jesus the messianic idea was not the primary thing, but the impulse towards a better religion, towards the religious exaltation of his people generally – so then, if you desire, the prophetic impulse. It was initially from this point that he drew nearer to the messianic idea and came to believe that this idea – rightly conceived – contained nothing else but just that impulse. Now he himself was certainly the Messiah, but since he well knew that the usual conception of the Messiah was completely different from his own, he proceeded extremely cautiously, and when the disciples – whom he himself allowed to hit upon the idea – recognized him to be the Messiah, he immediately put a damper upon this recognition by proclaiming his suffering and death (Mat. 16, 13f., 21f.).[16]

In the end, however, Strauss made no clear decision one way or the other about the crucial issue and was content to fall back upon the old rationalist explanation of Jesus as an extraordinary religious personality. Jesus was a great ethical teacher, although neither the first nor the last of such exceptional characters who have appeared upon the stage of world history, and certainly not without his defects – he had little to say on family life, trade and the arts – which Strauss did not hesitate to point out.

None the less, however high the place which Jesus has among those who have provided humanity with a purer and clearer example of what man ought to be, he was still neither the first nor the last to do

---

[15] *GS*, III, pp. 299–300; ET, I, pp. 322–3.
[16] To Meyer, 9.11.62; *AB*, p. 449.

so. But just as he had predecessors in Israel and Greece, on the Ganges and the Oxus, so he has also not remained without successors. On the contrary, that model which he set has been further developed after him, perfected from every point of view, its different features brought into more complete harmony with each other.[17]

## II. THE RESURRECTION OF JESUS

The most important new feature in the whole book was Strauss' more detailed explanation of the resurrection. In his first *Life of Jesus* he had never satisfactorily elucidated what became of Jesus' earthly body after it had been taken down from the cross, nor how the disciples had come to believe that Jesus had been raised from the dead and had appeared to them personally. It may be that in 1835 Strauss felt his explanation was far too radical for the time and that it would be better omitted, but more probably, he had not yet attained to the clearer explanation which he put forward in 1864.

The rationalist theory that Jesus was only apparently dead never found any sympathy with Strauss, and in the 1835 edition he had vigorously ridiculed the hypothesis. Now, in 1864, he presents an even clearer portrayal of its absurdity.

It is impossible that a being who had crawled half-dead out of the tomb and slunk around weak and ill, needing medical treatment, bandaging, convalescence and tender care, and who finally succumbed to his sufferings, could have given his disciples the impression of being the Victor over death and the grave, the Prince of Life – an impression which formed the basis of their subsequent public testimony. Such a reanimation could have only weakened the impression which he had made upon them during his life and in his death, could have, at most, given it an elegiac voice, but by no possibility have transformed their sorrow into enthusiasm or elevated their respect into worship.[18]

The problem was to explain what had become of Jesus' body, for in a world governed by scientific laws, bodies could not simply vanish into thin air. There had to be an explanation to account for it's disappearance. Reimarus had put forward the unconvincing theory that the disciples had stolen the body from the tomb and then proclaimed Jesus as having been resurrected.

[17] *GS*, IV, pp. 388–9; ET, II, pp. 437–8.
[18] *Ibid.* III, p. 378; ET, I, p. 412.

Strauss' explanation, ingenious as it is simple, is that when the
body was taken down from the cross it was simply buried with
other condemned criminals in a dishonourable place, and that
since some weeks elapsed before the disciples began to proclaim that Jesus had been raised from the dead, it must have
been more difficult for their opponents to produce his corpse in
still recognisable condition which afforded any proof of its
original identity.[19] Moreover, continued Strauss, in view of
the horror which the Jews felt for dead bodies, this neglect to
look for the corpse was far from being so incredible as we might
imagine. The Gospel accounts which depict Jesus as being
buried in a tomb hewn out of rock, were, according to Strauss,
a later mythical invention derived from Is. 53, 9: 'They made
his grave with the wicked and with the rich man in his death.'
However since the first half of the verse – the association with
the wicked – had already been fulfilled in his crucifixion with
the two thieves, it was thought fitting that the sinless Son of God
should be buried in a rich man's tomb which had never been
defiled by any other human body. The reports that Jesus had
risen from the dead on the third day were invented – perhaps
with reference to the three days which Jonah spent in the
whale – and the prophesies of the resurrection were placed in
Jesus' mouth in order to lend credence to the newly invented
assertions.

The greatest problem which confronted Strauss, however,
was to explain how the disciples' sorrow had been changed into
enthusiasm, their respect into worship and their scepticism of
the resurrection into the belief that Jesus was indeed alive from
the dead. There was only one real possibility and Strauss did
not shrink from stating it: the disciples were the victims of
hallucinations. After the crucifixion they had returned to their
native Galilee and here, away from the tumult and turmoil
which had marked their last weeks, their faith began to revive;
here also, where no body lay in the grave to contradict their
flights into phantasy, they gradually conceived the idea of a
resurrection whose reality was to be attested by the disappearance of Jesus' body. And when such an idea had once taken
root in their minds, it was, indeed, but a short step to a vision
of the risen Christ.

<hr>

[19] *Ibid.* III, p. 396; ET, I, p. 432.

H

Now as regards the shortness of the time necessary for the development of a state of mind among the disciples, from which those
visions could proceed, this difficulty also is not insuperable. The
visionary process did not and could not take place in a strictly
logical fashion through the reception of clear thoughts, but the
revolution happened in the dark depths of the mind; there was a
violent burst, a flash of lightning in which the sultriness of the over-
loaded inner feelings unloaded itself. Such a burst does not wait
until everything is first ordered in the intellect; on the contrary, it
anticipates with the power of the imagination that which reflection
afterwards seeks to elucidate, represents as a fact with one stroke,
that which the understanding only afterwards receives for clarifi-
cation.[20]

The constant retelling of these visions brought about their
slow sublimation into an historical fact; and once this fact had
been accepted by the disciples, then under the aegis of apostolic
authority, its development into rigid dogma was henceforth
assured.

But not only did the company of simple believers experience
such visions; the fanatical persecutor of the new sect, the in-
tellectually-inclined Saul of Tarsus, also became convinced of
Jesus' resurrection, through an ecstatic experience, which Strauss
explains psychologically as follows:

If, on the one hand, he now saw the new sect extending its influence
wider and wider about it in spite of all persecutions – indeed, as a
result of them – and if, on the other hand, he felt the inward
tranquillity, which he as their persecutor had ample opportunity to
observe in the persecuted, diminishing within himself, then we cannot be surprised if in hours of despondency and inward unhappiness
he sometimes put to himself the question: 'Who is finally right, you,
or the crucified Galilean, about whom these men are so fanatic?'
And when, with his physical and mental peculiarities, he had once
got so far as this, an extasy easily resulted, in which the Christ whom
he had formerly so passionately persecuted appeared to him in all
the glory of which his adherents had spoken so much, showed him
the perversity and folly of his actions and called him to come over
into his service.[21]

By such emotional and psychological experiences, belief in
Jesus as the Resurrected One was born, and Strauss' historical

[20] *GS*, III, pp. 396–7; ET, I, pp. 432.   [21] *Ibid.* III, p. 385; ET, I, p. 420.

portrayal of Jesus' life ends with a recapitulation of how the traditional Christian faith evolved from such a grandiose illusion.

In this way the faith in Jesus as the Messiah, which through his violent death had suffered an apparently fatal blow, was again subjectively restored through the instrumentality of the mind, the power of the imagination, and nervous excitement. A living continuation was now ensured for all that new and profound religious life which had been present in Jesus and imparted by him to his followers through teaching and example. But the fanciful form of this restoration continued henceforth to be the measuring standard by which his image was contemplated, his words, acts and fate remembered. His whole life became veiled in a shining cloud, which continued to lift it ever higher above the human sphere, but also alienated it more and more from the sphere of natural and historical truth.[22]

We may conclude by briefly summarising the points of agreement and difference between the 1835 *Life of Jesus* and that of 1864.[23]

1. In 1835 Strauss demanded a presuppositionless investigation, i.e. an investigation not dominated by supernatural or miraculous presuppositions, but rather a non-supernatural and non-miraculous inquiry. In 1864 this demand was not in the slightest way toned down.

2. In 1835 Strauss declared the sources historically untrustworthy and did not concern himself with their origin. In 1864 he did investigate their authorship and found them just as untrustworthy.

3. In 1835 Strauss did not deny the presence of an historical core. In 1864 his acceptance of such a core was firmer, but with no real difference in the extent of that core.

4. In 1835 Strauss had simply shown what Jesus was not, but had made no attempt to portray what Jesus was. In 1864 he paid more consideration to Jesus' character, but could not pass through the veil which determines the final picture – viz. whether Jesus was or was not a deluded fanatic.

[22] *Ibid.* III, p. 403; ET, I, p. 440.
[23] We follow here the five points enunciated by Barth (*Die protestantische Theologie im 19. Jahrhundert*, 505f. ET: *From Rousseau to Ritschl*, p. 378f.) who, in general, failed to understand the antitheses correctly.

5. In 1835 Strauss made no pronouncement on Jesus' place among the world's leading men. He did not deny that Jesus held a high, if not the highest, place, but merely asserted that Jesus was no supernatural being, with a unique place on that account. In 1864 this same position was maintained: Jesus was one of the great religious geniuses, but neither the first, nor the last, nor incapable of being surpassed by other human beings who might live after him.

The book did not have the success which attended the first *Life of Jesus*. This was only to be expected, for many other works dealing with Jesus' life had appeared since 1835, and Strauss had said nothing fundamentally different from what he had written in the first edition. Moreover, it was still too academic and scholarly for the general public to appreciate and could never have become popular reading like Renan's biography. Even so, it was still, as Ziegler remarked,[24] one of the best Lives of Jesus, and the strictures passed on it by Schweitzer[25] were quite unwarranted. And now came an acrimonious and bitter clash with the author of another portrayal of Jesus – a portrayal which gave the appearance of possessing supernatural features, but which, in reality, was just as non-supernatural as the portrayal of Strauss.

[24] Ziegler, p. 618.          [25] *Von Reimarus zu Wrede*, p. 192f; ET, p. 193f.

# 19

# THE CLASH WITH SCHENKEL

In the summer of 1857 the King of Prussia, Frederick Wilhelm IV, suffered a stroke which left him helpless in body and mind, and unable to rule. The new Prince Regent, Wilhelm I, was in favour of a certain measure of reform, and in the succeeding four years a new freedom was again introduced into the government. However, this new reform programme met with stiff opposition from the conservative forces, and by 1862, when Bismarck took office as Prime Minister, the pendulum had swung back again to the right.

In Baden, where a strong conservative line had been the dominating power in Church affairs, this liberal interlude brought about a change in the ecclesiastical realm, and the formerly conservative governing body of the Church did a right-about-turn and became liberal. The man most of all responsible for this change was the Heidelberg professor of theology and Higher Consistorial Councillor, Schenkel.

Daniel Schenkel (b. 1813), the son of a Swiss pastor from Canton Zürich, bore arms for three years in the Basel war of 1831 as a member of the fusiliers. He was interested in studying law, but was so captivated by the lectures of de Wette that he became convinced of the necessity for critical research into the Bible, and decided for a theological career. In 1838 he habilitated in Basel with a dissertation on the church in Corinth and during the following three years he edited the *Baseler Zeitschrift*, which opposed the liberal and radical tendencies of the time. His talents did not remain unnoticed and he was soon called as First Preacher to Schaffhausen, where he gained much attention, not only on account of his preaching, but also because of his theological research into the Reformation. In 1851 he accepted a call to become professor of theology and head

213

of the theological seminary at Heidelberg, where he remained until his death in 1885.

In the first few years at Heidelberg he showed himself extremely conservative, opposing the ingress of the Jesuits, initiating charges of pantheism against Kuno Fischer, protesting against the introduction of a new liturgy which smacked suspiciously of Catholicism, and opposing the Concordat of the liberal Government. All this occurred before 1861; but soon after, Schenkel and his followers scented in which direction the winds were now blowing and alligned themselves accordingly. For although Schenkel had been ecclesiastically conservative, his theological views, influenced by de Wette, had long been liberal; what he and his party now strove for was a free constitution for the Church, which would allow greater theological freedom of thought and expression and put an end to the Church controlled by the Government. The orthodox, on the other hand, were resolutely opposed to any change in the status quo which would enable the liberal party to make radical innovations in Church doctrine and practice; moreover, they were just waiting for a suitable opportunity to arise, in order to mount an attack on Schenkel, as the leader of the new liberal party in the Church in Baden. This opportunity presented itself in 1864 with the publication of Schenkel's *Portrait of Jesus' Character*.[1] On 2 June 1864 an open protest fanned the smouldering dissatisfaction of the orthodox into flames:

Herr Dr. Schenkel denies the incarnation of the Son of God; he denies the supernatural birth, the sinlessness, the miracles and the reconciling power of Jesus; he no longer recognises Scripture as a divine revelation; Herr Dr. Schenkel, through his destructive and erroneous teaching, has given offence to the Church and has disqualified himself from holding office in it, especially the task of preparing the future clergy for their ministry.

and the petition closed with the request that Herr Dr Schenkel may be 'relieved of his position as Director of the seminary'.[2]

The petition was signed by 117 clergymen from Baden, but was coldly rejected by the Baden Higher Consistory. At this point in the drama Strauss appeared on the scene with an

---

[1] *Das Charakterbild Jesu* (Wiesbaden, 1864).
[2] Herzog's *Realencyklopädie*, 3rd edn., XVII, p. 557; Hausrath, II, p. 318.

article which appeared in the *National-Zeitung* on 21 September 1864.[3] This small critique of only eleven pages caused great consternation and anger among the liberals in Baden, for Schenkel's book was torn to pieces by Strauss' ruthless and penetrating analysis.

After some introductory remarks on the current situation, Strauss cited a statement by the president of the Durlach Conference,[4] that Schenkel had always stood firmly for a positive Christianity. This was certainly the case some years previously, replied Strauss, when Schenkel had been instrumental in securing the dismissal of Kuno Fischer from his position as lecturer in philosophy, when 'he who is now accused of heresy was then the grand inquisitor'; but that, he continued, was no longer so, and Schenkel's book was not only in opposition to the teaching of the Church, but simply a rehash of what others had already written.

What was new in the book, which called forth such violent opposition, was, at most, the form: half lecture for the educated, half sermon, spiced in places with that sarcastic tone one usually hears when labourers are spoken to. Among the conclusions of the book which one took offence at there is scarcely one which is new or original – almost all have long ago been proposed by other German theologians. One could even, in fact, say that they had been carried down the Neckar from Tübingen to Heidelberg, where they were fished out onto the land by Herr Schenkel and – certainly in a rather debilitated and sodden condition – incorporated in his building.[5]

Schenkel's view of miracles could be summed up as a cautious affirmation and a cautious denial of their reality. The narratives of Jesus' birth were abandoned as fictitious and a consideration of the divinity of Christ was omitted. Schenkel had excused this omission on the ground that he was concerned only with the human side of Christ's nature; to which Strauss replied:

But faith asks: where is the conception by the Holy Spirit? where at all in the book is the divine nature of Christ? 'In attempting to

[3] *Der Schenkelsche Handel in Baden.* The article was reprinted in 1865 as an appendix to Strauss' long study on Schleiermacher's *Life of Jesus*, and republished in *GS*, v, pp. 137–47.

[4] The Liberal Conference in Durlach on 3 August 1863. Among those present were Schenkel, Rothe, Hitzig, Steitz, Ewald, Schwarz and Baumgarten. Hausrath, II, pp. 314–15.          [5] *GS*, v, p. 140.

sketch a portrait of the Saviour's character', answers the author, 'I was, by the very nature of the subject, directed to drawing his human side'. (Preface, p. vi). As if, alongside of this human side, there was, for the author, also a divine side, and that this could be portrayed other than in and with the human side![6]

What aroused Strauss' anger was not that Schenkel, like himself, had denied the miracles in the Bible as supernatural events, but that he had sought to hide his rationalism under vague and biblical phraseology. Thus the healing miracles were attributed to psychological causes, others were discretely described as exaggerations, and when Schenkel asserted that the leper who came to Jesus was already in an advanced stage of healing, to which Jesus merely contributed a noticeable acceleration towards fuller health, Strauss asked what at all extraordinary was to be found here. Were not all the miraculous events, which were with one hand acknowledged, simply juggled away with the other under Schenkel's magician's cloth?

Those who signed the 'Protest' also reproached Herr Schenkel with denying the miracles of Jesus. In actuality, Jesus' gift of miracles is, for him, not 'the outflowing of his indwelling omnipotent power', not 'the emanation of his divine nature', but 'a human gift of nature – even if it is significantly elevated in him'. There, once again, we have Schenkel's whole ambiguous position. The so-called miraculous power is a natural gift – and criticism must be satisfied with this; it can make no objection to an elevation, i.e. to the acceptance of various grades of a natural gift, while the indeterminateness of the measure of this elevation is supposed to pacify faith and dazzle it with the possibility of still winning an exceptional position for Christ, above all other men. But this time faith and criticism remain in complete agreement, that there can be no intermediate stage between natural and supernatural, and beyond this, the elevation of the natural gifts has very definite limits.[7]

Strauss also accused Schenkel of playing with words, of using orthodox terminology with a hidden and completely different meaning:

It is just the same with the word Redeemer, or Saviour, which Herr Schenkel (certainly with so many other like-minded theologians of our time) unceasingly employs, while with him it has lost its usual meaning. Redeemer, in the true and honest sense of the word

<hr />

[6] *GS*, v, p. 141.                    [7] *Ibid.* pp. 143-4.

can only refer to the God-man who sacrifices himself for the sins of the world; to call a man – however exemplary his life and however vital and full of blessing his continuing influence – Redeemer, is a deceptive play with words which creates the impression – and not just on the over-pious – of a sacrilege in the holy place.[8]

And as for the resurrection of Christ:

Herr Schenkel speaks out clearly in a surprising – and, compared with his usual restraint, one could almost say imprudent – manner as regards the main miracle of the Gospel story – the resurrection of Jesus. Here, in unambiguous terms, he rejects both the miracle of the resurrection and the apparent death – thus any real coming-back-to-life of the Crucified One – and conceives the event as being a purely psychological process in the minds of the disciples; this has an outward cause only in the grave which was found empty, and in visions which first manifested themselves in extremely excited women. When, therefore, the supporters of the 'Protest' accused the author of the *Charakterbild* of denying the resurrection of Jesus, then one would think that the charge, before God and man, was just.[9]

It was hardly surprising that after this analysis of Schenkel's book, Strauss took the part of the 117 orthodox pastors, and after some further caustic remarks about Schenkel's half-way-ness and ambiguity – so congenial to his followers – Strauss concluded the article with the following words:

But half-wayness is an imprecise expression: Herr Schenkel I should say, is three-quarters on the side of the critics, but he still finds it advisable to concede a quarter to the believers; and this is also just to his followers, who are generally the enlightened middle-class (I would say the philistines were it not impolite). People no longer want to be limited by the restrictions of the strict Church creed, but desire a comfortable amount of room for their duly acquired intellectual education. Yet, on the other hand, they do not want to shake the existing Church order; they do not want to lose their Sunday sermon on the Gospel, their Christian calendar and holy communion; they hope to gain both these things by the hand of a man like Schenkel. But one should not be deceived. If everything in the Gospel history which the author of the *Charak-terbild* surrenders is not true, then there is a lot more which is even less true; if Christ is no longer the God-man, but only a God-like

---

[8] *Ibid.* p. 143.          [9] *Ibid.* p. 145.

man, he can no longer be the object of our worship, no longer the centre of the religious ceremonies; and if everyone in the Church adopted the views set forth in the *Charakterbild*, then a crash which would terrify the gentleman of Durlach would necessarily follow in the Church and its institutions. Only the fact that the mass of the people still stand – even naively and half unconsciously – on the standpoint of the 117, still holds the church together in its present state; these men know this and act accordingly, and this clear knowledge and definite resolve sets them above those others, who partly do not know what they want, but also, partly, do not want what they know.

'Freedom and the kingdom of heaven', sings the old Ernst Moritz Arndt, 'are not won by the advocates of half-wayness'. But they possess the earthly kingdom and whoever writes on behalf of half-wayness – especially in religious matters – is certain to find numerous followers who will flock around him like keen warriors whenever the whole-hearted of the one or the other side want to find something against him. It is said of the seven Swabians that they went out heavily armed, and with great fear, against a monster which finally turned out to be a hare: and in the future it will be said of the seven hundred men at Durlach that they fought gallantly so that the banner – which in reality was only a worn-out floor cloth – should not fall into enemy hands.[10]

The article caused a furore among the liberal clergy: Strauss had fallen upon them from behind at just the worst moment and that was nothing less than treachery. Why then did Strauss decide to write the article when he must have known that it would greatly injure the liberal cause?

The first reason was undoubtedly his personal dislike of Schenkel and his contempt for the man who, some years earlier, had initiated the action depriving Kuno Fischer of his position. During the years which Strauss resided in Heidelberg he must have become well acquainted with all the details of Fischer's dismissal, and his antipathy towards the then leader of the conservative faction is quite understandable. For what was Strauss to think when he heard that the formerly so conservative and orthodox leader had become a liberal, and that Bluntschli, one of his leading supporters, was the same Bluntschli who had been one of his (Strauss') bitterest opponents in Zürich during the controversy over the professorship in 1839? Was it any

---

[10] *GS*, v, pp. 146–7.

wonder that Strauss had developed a deep aversion for the Heidelberg theologian, whom he regarded as a turncoat?

The second reason lay in the fact that Strauss had an extremely low opinion of Schenkel's colourless and insipid book, and it was especially annoying to him when people began comparing it with his own. Worst of all was the sham with which Schenkel attempted to cover up the fact that he no longer believed in the supernatural character of Jesus. Strauss had openly declared his unbelief and had been dismissed from his position; Schenkel carefully concealed his heterodoxy and remained as professor of theology, University Preacher and Higher Consistorial Councillor. That was the injustice which grated on Strauss.

Schenkel replied to the attack with a rather weak article[11] in the *Allgemeine Kirchliche Zeitschrift*, of which he was the editor. He had not, he declared, made any open denunciation against Kuno Fischer, and Strauss' accusation that he had denounced Fischer to the Church authorities as a pernicious member of the University was a monstrous untruth.

It is true that in a casual *private conversation* with a member of the Baden Higher Consistory I expressed my grave doubts about Fischer's lectures, which at that time had just appeared in print, and also the wish *that an eminent teacher of philosophy might be called to the University as a counterbalance to Fischer's commanding influence*. That means then, according to Herr Strauss, to denounce a lecturer to the Higher Consistorial Authorities and bring about his removal from the lecture room.[12]

The right of freedom to teach, he maintained, had always been supported by him.

That the Higher Consistorial Authorities directed – and, moreover, as a result of a wholly independent examination of those printed lectures – that Fischer should be removed from his position as lecturer, *was not only absolutely none of my doing, but was done against my express disapproval and to my deepest regret...* Without doubt, after twelve years experience, my judgment on the then-assailed book would now be different; at that time it seemed to me harmful and destructive, not on account of its unchristian content, but – as I felt compelled to believe – on account of its atheistic content. Even a man like Gervinus speaks of the 'devouring worm of atheism

[11] 'Das Christenthum und die Humanitätsreligion des Herrn Dr. D. F. Strauss,' *AKZ*, VI (1865), pp. 225–36.  [12] *Ibid.* pp. 229–30.

which is obnoxiously gaining ground', and only against this atheism did I at that time emphatically speak out. On the other hand, in my official vote I openly acknowledged and defended *the right of freedom to teach*. The orthodox party among the Baden clergy has never forgiven me for this vote and since that time its hatred has surrounded me.[13]

Schenkel now turned to the question of miracles. He did not deny that miracles could happen, only, for him, the meaning of the word 'miracle' possessed a natural rather than a supernatural sense:

For me, each individual account of miracles in the Gospel story falls to pieces on the inexorable judgment of criticism; in each individual case it is not faith which decides, but only the strictest tests of reason. Over all appearances and facts of the finite world rules the eternal holy cause of all that is and happens. I do not fully comprehend this cause because my understanding is limited, but I believe in it for just this reason, and believing, I worship it as the living Deity. Deity itself is for me the miracle of miracles; God is for me the Spirit of spirits; the life of the spirit is for me something wonderful, already in the first stutterings of the child, and how much more in the heroic figures of spiritual might and moral courage, in the holy battles fought on paths soaked in sweat and blood which lead to the redemption of mankind from sin, slavery and torture.[14]

and he regretted that Strauss had quite misunderstood his views about the resurrection of Jesus.

I can only regret that my critics have misunderstood me on this point. I certainly reject the apparent death and the miraculous revival of the earthly body of Jesus; but I do not deny the miracle of the resurrection – the personal transfiguration of the Crucified One after his death into a higher, real existence – nor the influence of his transfigured personality upon the company of the disciples. This spiritually communicated influence of the transfigured, risen person is, for me, no more miraculous in itself than the effects of the spirit everywhere.[15]

Schenkel's reply presented Strauss with the opportunity of writing the most blistering and devastating polemic of his whole

---

[13] 'Das Christenthum und die Humanitätsreligion des Herrn Dr. D. F. Strauss', *AKZ*, VI (1865), p. 230.

[14] *Ibid.* pp. 234–5.          [15] *Ibid.* p. 235.

career. Schenkel was methodically torn to shreds, not only theologically, but also personally. Strauss had perceived, however, that were he to write solely against Schenkel, he might be accused of being in league with the orthodox, and so to show his complete independence of any party he composed his polemic in two parts – the first against Schenkel and the second against Hengstenberg. The second part, however, in comparison with the first, is quite dull. It consists in a discussion of three questions – Quirinius and the census reported in Luke's Gospel, the historicity of Lazarus, and the discrepancies of the resurrection narratives. After the brilliance of the first part it was, indeed, a real anticlimax and one of Strauss' dryest and most uninspired pieces of writing, a further discussion of which may be spared to the reader.

Strauss wrote his *The Halves and the Wholes*[16] during the spring of 1865 and it fell like a bomb into the liberal camp. There was a short introduction in which Strauss discussed the relation between Schenkel's Life of Jesus and his own; then turning to the personal issue, he began to demolish Schenkel's assertions that he had been an almost innocent party to the dismissal of Kuno Fischer.

Firstly, he says he did not denounce the lecturer in question to the Church Authorities. He only 'shared his views about Fischer's lectures ('A History of Recent Philosophy', which had just been published), with a friend who he had met by chance', and 'nobody will say it is wrong for friends to have shared their views about the matter with one another'. How innocent! how detestable to make a denunciation out of such a harmless conversation between two friends. But who then was this friend to whom Herr Schenkel poured out his troubled heart and where was the chance meeting when he did it? This friend – as we learn in another place from Schenkel himself – was 'a member of the Baden Higher Consistorial Council' and the chance meeting was 'a minister's conference at Durlach in October 1852'. Herr Schenkel knew very well that he was speaking not merely to a friend but to a higher Consistorial Councillor, and he did not want merely to speak to the former, but at the same time to the latter. For he himself, for his part, spoke not merely as a friend, but 'as University Chaplain and Director

[16] *Die Halben und die Ganzen. Eine Streitschrift gegen die HH. DD. Schenkel und Hengstenberg* (Berlin, 1865). *GS*, v. I. Gegen Schenkel (pp. 152–90); II. Gegen Hengstenberg (pp. 191–228).

of the seminary for ministers, in which position he had been invited
to the conference'.

The occasion on which he spoke thus meant that much was suggested in confidential form which was afterwards to be officially
set in motion. In such a position and on such an occasion, Herr
Schenkel – as he himself relates – drew the attention of the befriended
Higher Consistorial Councillor to the 'influence of Fischer, which
seemed to him detrimental, indeed, even destructive', and 'force-
fully expressed the need for a strong counterbalance, for the calling of
a convinced Christian-minded philosopher to Heidelberg', – a need
'motivated by the pantheistic tones of Fischer's published lectures'.

So far we have only inquired after the official position of the
'befriended man' and found him to be a member of the Higher
Consistorial Council; we will now permit ourselves to go one step
further and inquire about the identity of the man. On doing so we
learn as a 'notorious' fact that the man was the 'Ministerial Councillor Bähr', and it is further notoriously known about this gentleman,
that he was nothing less than an opponent of the objectionable or,
more generally, freer direction in the Church and in scientific,
criticism. If Herr Schenkel wanted to set something in motion
against the representative of that tendency which seemed to him so
harmful, then he certainly went to the right address; he could be
certain that the carefully planted grain of wheat would not lie
dead, but would soon sprout up in corresponding official disciplinary measures. At all events, Herr Schenkel was the first to denounce
the philosophy lecturer; he denounced him before proceedings had
been initiated against him from any other direction.[17]

Yet the action taken by the Higher Consistorial Authorities
against Kuno Fischer is supposed to have proceeded 'as a result of
a wholly independent examination of his printed lectures'. That may
be; but this examination ensued only after Herr Schenkel had
drawn attention to the book, after he had set the man in a bad
light, and after he had designated the points to which special consideration was to be paid. That was enough to start the avalanche
which was to overwhelm a capable man; it was Herr Schenkel who
set the first ball in motion and he did this not at all innocently and
unintentionally, but consciously, and with the intention of trig-
gering off an avalanche.[18]

Schenkel insisted that he had always sought to preserve freedom of teaching and Strauss quoted with approval the follow-

[17] *GS*, v, pp. 158–9.    [18] *Ibid.* p. 164.

ing words, which Schenkel had written in 1846, i.e. before his denunciation of Fischer.

Philosophy should be free to move in its own circles with no external limitations and restrictions! Only it should not presume to suppress theology; there should be unconditional freedom for both![19]

But now, asked Strauss, if Schenkel had really been sincere in writing such words, why had he then denounced Fischer – a lecturer not in theology, but in philosophy? Schenkel had attempted to find various excuses. He had, he claimed, never wanted to see Fischer dismissed, but solely that his influence among the students should be counteracted; alternatively, he pleaded that he had

at that time held Dr. Fischer for a young man who had been led astray, but who might perhaps still find the right way were he to experience a severe shaking of his conscience.[20]

a statement on which Strauss poured out his scorn:

There we hear the real clerical drivel, which stamps him who once used it, for all time, among the clerics, even if he should later find it expedient to have his clerical dress dyed red. A university lecturer – still young, to be sure, but proven through the most searching tests to be intellectually mature and brillant – is to be taken to task like a schoolboy and convicted in his conscience, not on account of any action, but – mark you – on account of his teaching, and because, according to Herr Schenkel's conviction, he is going astray.[21]

and with reference to Schenkel's statement, that after twelve years his opinion of Fischer's book would be somewhat different, Strauss continued:

Nevertheless, he gives us to understand that he no longer holds his former judgment about Fischer's philosophical standpoint to be correct. But his opposition to Fischer was the consequence of his judgment at that time, and this opposition resulted in Fischer's removal from his academic position. This removal with all the consequences connected with it – both for Fischer and for the

[19] Schenkel, *Die protestantische Geistlichkeit und die Deutschkatholiken* (2nd ed.; Zürich, 1846) p. 7.
[20] Schenkel, *Abfertigung für Herrn Kuno Fischer in Heidelberg* (Heidelberg, 1854) p. 9.         [21] *GS*, v, p. 166.

University from which he was removed (for the second, as is well known, stagnation of philosophical study for many years) – all these consequences are dependent upon the former error of Herr Schenkel. He wants to hide himself in the cloak of his conviction, of his sincere belief: in our eyes an open word of regret admitting an error which had such disastrous consequences would not so much have diminished the reputation of the Higher Councillor, as raised that of the man.

Instead of this Herr Schenkel prides himself with the assurance that in his open vote he 'openly acknowledged and defended the right of freedom to teach'. We have not seen this official vote, but have no fear of being unjust to its originator when we keep to that which he himself tells us about it. In the most detailed report which he himself gives about the matter there is nothing to be found which refers to the defence of freedom to teach. No matter; it could have been contained in the vote itself. On the other hand we read his confession: 'In cases where Christianity in its basic essentials is attacked in public lectures, I recommended (in that vote) the right of the Higher Consistory to call for the intervention of the civil authorities'. A fine freedom of teaching, that![22]

In the second section which dealt with the dogmatic questions Schenkel fared little better, and Strauss' opening description of Schenkel's book set the tone for the rest of the discussion.

I have said: it is a divine comedy that he who is now supposed to be a martyr, is the same man who a few years ago was the grand inquisitor. Herr Schenkel has tried to deny that he was the latter; I believe that in the foregoing part I have convincingly shown that this was in fact the case.

Now I also said further that it is also a divine comedy that the progressive party in Baden must accept a book written by Schenkel in order to preserve freedom of teaching. A book whose author is attended by two equally zealous parties, the one trying to secure his dismissal, the other seeking to retain him, is usually at least a book of decisiveness and character. But Schenkel's *Charakterbild Jesu* is a woolly, opportunist, compromising book of no character.[23]

With regard to the resurrection of Jesus, Schenkel had denied any raising of the natural body and insisted that the resurrection consisted in the 'personal transfiguration of the Crucified One after his death into a higher real existence'. What he meant was that the personality of Jesus lived on after his death

[22] *GS*, v, p. 167–8.     [23] *Ibid.* p. 175.

in the minds of his followers. The visions which the disciples experienced after Jesus' death were not simply unrelated to any real historical facts, but were indeed the result of Jesus' personality upon them.

Yet we are going a little too fast; we have not yet heard everything Herr Schenkel wants to say. Not only does he allow his Christ to possess a higher real existence after death, but he also speaks of 'an influence of his transfigured personality upon the company of the disciples', an influence which he further on designates as 'spiritually communicated' and, moreover, finds no more miraculous than the effects of the spirit everywhere. Whether now this is supposed to be something special which distinguishes Christ from all other men depends on whether or not Herr Schenkel also accepts an influence of the departed upon those they have left behind, and the appearances and effects of spirits. He could possibly also refer back to the sentence in which he denied only the reanimation 'of the earthly body of Jesus'. This can also be so interpreted: the body of Jesus with flesh and bones was certainly not reanimated as an earthly body, but as a celestrial, with that 'transfigured, newly-organized corporeality' which was brought back again onto the track by Keim, just at the right time; and the mediation of this corporeality has now enabled the celestial body of Jesus to influence those whom he left behind, in a way which is not permitted to other departed souls.

In one of the most recent articles[24] which I have just seen, Herr Schenkel has adopted this way out. After rejecting both alternatives – the visions-hypothesis and the hypothesis of a miraculous or natural reanimation of the real or merely apparently dead earthly body of Jesus – he declares that he stands by the third possibility, which is his own: that the appearances of the Resurrected One were 'real manifestations of his living and transfigured personality which had issued out of his death'. Jesus' corpse remained in the grave, or was removed from it in a natural way, which is no longer ascertainable; only the soul proceeded out living and clothed itself with a new corporeality appropriate to its present state, 'because the human person necessarily requires an organ to manifest itself'. Even so, Jesus would always only stand on the same standpoint as all other human souls; and if he now made himself known to his disciples in this new corporeality, then it would be what we usually call an apparition, whereby one likewise often talks about a higher corporeality, a more delicate organ of the

[24] 'Die Auferstehung Jesu als Geschichtstatsache und Heilstatsache', *AKZ* (1865) pp. 289–304.

soul. No! says Herr Schenkel, there can be no apparitions of ghosts, for ghosts are creations of phantasy; but 'a real, mysterious self-revelation of the living and imperishable personality of Jesus Christ which proceeded out of death,' and which – however little we are able more closely to describe it – was still, under all circumstances, of such a nature 'that the disciples received the impression of actually seeing Jesus, and being vouchsafed a strengthening and renewing communication of his personal life'. But if all human souls, without distinction, after laying aside their earthly bodies, require a corporeality appropriate to their new state, which they then also receive, then there seems to be no reason why they themselves should not be able, by means of their new corporeality, to make themselves known to those they have left behind, especially where there is no lack of 'spiritual communication' i.e. according to Schenkel's statement, no lack of faith. But one fears making a fool of oneself by the concession of apparitions and since, on the other hand, something special is supposed to remain to Jesus, then as a substitute for so much taken away from him, the prerogative is saved for him – that for a time he may be permitted to haunt.

Against my view of the resurrection of Jesus, Schenkel writes: to explain the origin of the Christian Church by means of hallucinations 'runs counter to the higher-organized historical feeling'. What a higher-organized historical feeling is is just as little known to me as a transfigured higher-organised corporeality; but this I do know, that shams, like these shams of Schenkel, are an abomination even to the lowest-organised historical and moral feeling.[25]

Strauss concluded his whole polemic with an account of his reasons for taking up arms against his adversary.

Herr Schenkel is looking around everywhere for causes in order to explain my attack on him and his theology. One reason, he thinks, is that his *Charakterbild* irritated me because it came athwart my *Life of Jesus*; another supposition is that I am peeved because he immediately sent out his winged Tom-cats into his and other journals to snarl against my book. Can then a writer have only personal, only selfish reasons when he steps out in opposition to another? My antipathy – which is thoroughly grounded in the matter itself – towards the kind of theology which Herr Schenkel advocates is well known to him from of old; recently one of his own shield-bearers bitterly criticised me for this antipathy. When I now saw the man and his latest book cheated through the menace and resistance of martyrdom into a position, of which I could not

25 *GS*, v, pp. 187–9.

esteem them worthy – neither in the good nor in the bad sense – I seized my pen and held it for a duty inherent in my calling to take up my pen.

Yes Herr Councillor, one may have a calling and hold it as a matter of conscience to fulfil this calling even if one is not a professor of theology, not Director of a seminary and First Preacher in the University. This calling of mine, let me inform you, is directed against counterfeiting. That just at this present time there is much counterfeiting in the theological fashions, perhaps even you will not deny; and I would further maintain – even if you would like to know nothing about it – that the very party to which you belong lives almost exclusively from counterfeiting. To commission someone to expose such mischief has long been overdue; but because it is so widespread, nothing happens; there are too many involved and among these many too influential. Never mind, I'm not waiting till someone commisions me; here I am, I need no external cause, I follow my inner calling. I cannot be everywhere; but I do what I can. When I cross the market place, when I pass by a money bag, I keep my eyes pealed. I am not concerned about the small coins – that would simply cause endless worry; but when someone puts down copper coins or promissory notes instead of gold sovereigns then he must reckon with me, and he will not be free of me until he has paid the full price. Certainly I gain no popularity thereby; I gain no thanks except from truth whom I serve. Did he receive thanks, who once drove the traders and money-changers from the temple? 'Zeal for thy house consumes me' is a fine motto and such a sacrifice is certainly a more fragrant savour to the Lord than bulls and goats.[26]

Schenkel had no answer to Strauss' pulverising attack. In a 'statement' in the *Allgemeine Kirchliche Zeitung*[27] he simply denounced Strauss' attack to defame his character and declared that he would not attempt to answer such base libels. The liberals were all enraged; Hengstenberg, on the other hand, was delighted, and saw Strauss as fulfilling a 'divine mission'; Vischer was also in sympathy, but Zeller had no intention of becoming involved, as the following passage from Strauss' letter to Vischer reveals:

Dear Friend,
  Your kind letter of 28th July arrived here just at the right time and I was especially pleased about the friendly judgment which you passed on my polemic against Schenkel. That almost all the liberal

---

[26] *Ibid.* pp. 189–90.          [27] 'Erklärung', *AKZ* (1865) pp. 507–9.

newspapers would assail me is something I had to expect; stranger
is that our Zeller wants to know nothing about my war against
Schenkel – I could not help noticing this when I was in Heidelberg;
this may be because he himself was present at the Durlach conference in July last year, or because he is of the opinion that a man
who in general belongs to those pursuing the freer line must be
spared, or because (and I don't know whether it is true) he has to
thank Schenkel for his appointment at Heidelberg. This, in fact, is
the case with Hitzig and he therefore stands completely on Schenkel's
side.[28]

When we look back upon the whole controversy it becomes
apparent that the vital issue at stake was, fundamentally, a
question of Schenkel's sincerity; for the orthodox alleged that
Schenkel no longer accepted the essentials of the Christian faith,
but hid his unbelief behind orthodox phraseology and ambiguity. Schenkel and his friends protested, and claimed the immunity of freedom to teach. They refused to be forced into the
strait-jacket of an outmoded orthodoxy, but asserted their right
to think freely, to revise the old and express new ideas. This
assertion was the initial ground for Strauss' attack: for why
should Schenkel be able to appeal to the right of freedom to
teach when he himself had previously been responsible for the
dismissal of Kuno Fischer – at that time not even a member of
the theological faculty? Was that not double dealing?

But of even more importance was the fact that Schenkel
attempted to conceal his disbelief of the orthodox Church
doctrine. That was what Strauss found so intolerable! Better
Hengstenberg who at least believed the Bible and the orthodox
doctrine – even if it was false, than the counterfeit Christianity
of Schenkel, who merely pretended to do so. Hengstenberg's
views were at least logical and clear, but Schenkel's shams were
intolerable, and this counterfeit Christianity so grated upon
Strauss that he cut through all party divisions in the cause of
truth.

One last passage is of interest to us. In 1872 Zeller was
called to the chair of philosophy in Berlin, and Fischer was
appointed to succeed him in Heidelberg. Both Fischer and
Schenkel were naturally uneasy about the appointment and
Zeller attempted to bring about better relations between them.

---

[28] To Vischer, 9.8.65; *SVBr*, ii, p. 200.

In a letter to Fischer he described the outcome of a conversation between himself and Schenkel, in which he had communicated to Schenkel Fischer's desire to let bygones be bygones:

He (Schenkel) was very pleased and relieved, and asked me to tell you that it is also his most sincere wish to forget the old feud and be permitted to enter into full, friendly and cordial relations with you. I believe that he is completely in earnest about it. For so vain as he is, even he cannot hide it from himself, that 18 years ago he was on a false track; and he also did not try to hide from me, that he is no longer the same man as he formerly was.[29]

[29] Zeller to Kuno Fischer, 2.5.72. The letter lies in the Heidelberg university library under the signature Hd. Hs. 2618.

# 20

## THE WAR YEARS (1866–71)

In 1864 Fritz completed his secondary schooling in Heilbronn and having decided to become a doctor, enrolled in the medical faculty at Tübingen. In the same year Georgine became engaged to Konrad Heusler, a mining assessor from Deutz, and the marriage took place in November. Since both his children were no longer so dependent upon him, and recognising the need for a change of environment, Strauss decided to leave Heilbronn. But where was he to go? He resolved first to visit Berlin where he remained several weeks, enjoying the company of Vatke and Auerbach. Early in 1865 he returned to Heidelberg, but on account of his first article against Schenkel and the accompanying ill-feeling which it had caused, he found the society there an embarrassment and was glad to leave. At Baden he composed *The Halves and the Wholes* and after a short stay in Munich we find him at the end of 1865 in Darmstadt, where he lived for the next five years. And here in Darmstadt romance once more began to bloom, blossoming into love and then withering away.

Shortly after he had taken up residence in the town, he came into frequent contact with Marie Locher, the widow of Dr Locher who had studied under Vischer at Tübingen and had been director of the theatre in Meiningen. The first mention of her in Strauss' letters is found in November 1865.

Here, everything is going well, as usual. I am also gradually making acquaintances; certainly I have no close friends – but in fact, I scarcely seek any. I could become more friendly with Frau Locher if our hours fitted in better, since she is a woman who espouses the same standpoint as ourselves with a certain ardour. But just at the time when I gladly make a visit (after my walk), she sits drinking coffee with her children.[1]

[1] To Vischer, 22.11.65; *SVBr*, II, p. 205.

Gradually the relationship became more intimate. They used to meet twice in the week at her house to read literature; she would play the piano to him and together they visited the theatre and the concerts and made walks in the woods. The mutual interests which they shared soon brought the lonely pair closer and the companionship turned to passionate love, as the following poem by Strauss reveals.

*Pleasure*

When our hands together greeting
Press in gath'ring twilight dim;
When our eyes in rapture meeting
Pierce the soul with blissful hymn;
When, your passionate kiss entreating,
My cheek close to yours now slips,
With our hearts so quickly beating
Finally, you yield your lips.[2]

Once before his hopes of remarrying had been dashed by his wife's refusal to grant him a divorce and in 1867 also, they foundered once more on the same rock. For although Agnese knew that he no longer belonged to her, she was determined that as long as she lived, he would belong to no one else. Thus the relationship between the two lovers suffered under the constant strain of uncertainty and hopelessness. They became objects of local gossip and with Strauss' highly-strung and irritable temperament it was inevitable that frictions would arise and that both should come to doubt whether a marriage would be successful even if he were free. Strauss finally decided that a break had to be made and fled to Munich in the autumn of 1867, from whence he wrote to Vischer:

But how does all that help me now? Our relationship is, at the most, consigned to a mere exchange of letters. And hope in a future, with which my lady-friend wants to console me, is nonsense. One year lost means ten at our age, and in just the two months which I have been here, I have grown older by ten years. I believe that we shall never see each other again, and in the mood in which I am now, I do not even desire it.[3]

He returned to Darmstadt in March 1868, but the relationship had obviously cooled, and in May Marie shifted from

[2] Ziegler, p. 672. The poem was not published in Strauss' collected works.          [3] To Vischer, 30.11.67; *SVBr*, II, p. 253.

Darmstadt to nearby Forst, where her father was living. Both she and Strauss must have finally realised the impossibility of any permanent relationship and even the death of Agnese, on 22 December 1870, did nothing to alter the situation. In fact, Strauss' last words about Agnese were that 'if he had anything to thank her for, it was that she had not at that time given him a divorce, and so hindered this marriage'.[4]

Also of interest are the accounts of Strauss' acquaintance with two prominent English women – Mary Ann Evans, better known as the novelist George Eliot, and Princess Alice, daughter of Queen Victoria.

Strauss first met Miss Evans, whose English translation of his *Life of Jesus* had appeared in 1846, while she was travelling on the continent in 1854 with her friend George Henry Lewes. Dr Brabant, a mutual friend of both Strauss and Miss Evans, brought Strauss to the hotel in Cologne, where Lewes and Miss Evans were breakfasting on the morning of 30 July.

Last Sunday I met the English translator of my *Life of Jesus*, Miss Evans. She made arrangements through my old friend Brabant, who has again popped up after four years, for a visit, which I then paid to her in the hotel. She may be in her middle thirties, a very intellectual face; but she speaks no German and our conversation quickly came to an end, which I concluded with the expressive performance of kissing the hand with which she writes.[5]

Miss Evans on her part wrote from Weimar to Charles Bray:

On the way to Cologne we were joined in our railway carriage by Dr Brabant, who kindly exerted himself to procure me an interview with Strauss. It was rather melancholy. Strauss looks so strange and cast down, and my deficient German prevented us from learning more of each other than our exterior which in the case of both would have been better left to imagination.[6]

A second meeting in Munich four years later, in 1858, was described by Strauss in a letter to Rapp:

[4] Ziegler, p. 675.

[5] *SVBr*, II, p. 163. The passage, a postscript, is misplaced and has presumably been severed from Strauss' letter to Vischer dated 3.8.54; *SVBr*, II, pp. 64–6.

[6] To Charles Bray, 16.8.54; *The George Eliot Letters* (ed. G. H. Haight; London, 1954) II, p. 171.

I had a very pleasant meeting here also with the translator of my *Life of Jesus*, who is now the wife of Mr. Lewes, who has written a biography of Goethe. When they heard that I was here they both wanted to visit me, but I wasn't in. When I visited them on the following morning I met only her. I had already seen her once, as Miss Evans, in Cologne, but at that time she could speak scarcely any German. Now she is much better. She is in her 30s, not pretty, but with an almost transparent face, full of expression, with even more feeling than spirit. Between a man and a lady who is his translator there always exists a mystical marriage. As I left the good lady said: 'How you came in, I was so thrilled, that I not at all could speak'.[7, 8]

and George Eliot wrote:

You will be interested to hear that I saw Strauss in Munich. He came for a week's visit before we left. I had a quarter of an hour's chat with him alone, and was very agreeably impressed by him. He looked much more serene, and his face had a far sweeter expression than when I saw him in that dumb way at Cologne. He speaks with very choice words, like a man strictly truthful in the use of language.[9]

Dr Brabant will be pleased to hear that Strauss looks much more placid and healthy than he did four years ago – not happy, perhaps, but as if he were contented to bear sorrow.[10]

Since his *The Halves and the Wholes* Strauss had written practically nothing of importance except a few small monographs and dialogues on various social and political topics. Now he sought a new subject to occupy himself, something of a biographical nature. While staying at Munich during the winter of 1867–8 he had begun reading the letters which Voltaire had written to Frederick the Great, and the plan evolved in his mind for a series of sketches on Voltaire. But somehow the inspiration was lacking; he needed, as he himself relates,[11] someone to write for, and this someone he found in the Princess Alice (1843–78), the second daughter of Queen Victoria and her German consort Prince Albert. The two elder daughters of this marriage had received an extremely broad education from their German father, who had introduced them to the rationalistic explanations of religion. The

[7] Strauss is illustrating the grammatical errors in George Eliot's German.
[8] To Rapp, 16.7.58; *AB*, p. 395.
[9] To Sara Hennell, 28.7.58; *The George Eliot Letters*, II, p. 472.
[10] To Mrs Call, 4.8.58; *Ibid.* II, p. 475.          [11] *GS*, I, pp. 69–70.

Princess, now married to Prince Ludwig of Hesse-Darmstadt, learning that Strauss was also residing in the same town, expressed her desire to meet him and sent her secretary to arrange a visit. Strauss was not enthusiastic, as he related to his friend Fischer in Öhringen.

Absolutely unbelieving that the higher dignitaries had a real interest for people like us, I resisted for $\frac{3}{4}$ hour and wouldn't even then have yielded if it had been a prince; but towards a lady, the continued refusal appeared like rusticity, which I could not allow to be charged to the German scholars' account. I went therefore at the appointed time in my ordinary suit and found myself most touched. She possesses the most natural and open manner over against which one immediately finds oneself in a genial atmosphere. The father himself had given religious instruction to her and her elder sister (the present German Crown-princess) from a popular textbook of the blessed Bretschneider and led them to thinking and doubting. She and her sister in Berlin thereby attained a completely free standpoint, of which Frau Mama is not allowed to know anything.[12]

In consequence of this first meeting Strauss visited the Princess regularly and read to her various literary works under a soft green light which she had provided in order to protect his eyes. Thus the stimulus for the lectures on Voltaire came from the Princess, and on their completion he read them through to her during January 1870. Her Highness was delighted and at the conclusion of the readings expressed the pleasure which she had derived from his visits. Strauss on his part took the opportunity of declaring that the book would never have been completed without her sympathetic encouragement, whereupon the Princess replied:

     It would be lovely if you dedicated it to me.

I:     To request that, your royal Highness, was originally my intention; however, I thought about the offence which the book will certainly cause, and I would not like to involve your royal Highness in it.

She:   I do not worry about offence which has no grounds; my sister does and she doesn't gain anything by it.

I:     Well let us at least not decide anything before your Highness has spoken about the matter with your husband.

She:   You are right, I will do that.[13]

[12] Ziegler, p. 653.          [13] Ziegler, p. 655.

The Prince was agreed and apart from the posthumous dedication to his brother of the 1864 *Life of Jesus*, this was the only book that Strauss ever dedicated.

The years 1866–71 were the war years and Strauss was intensely interested in the political issues of the times. Although born and bred a Swabian, through his visits to Berlin and his friendship with various Prussians, he had a far more open outlook than most of his fellow countrymen and he saw Prussia with her well-developed culture as the only power fitted to take over the leadership of a united Germany. Austria he had always disliked and the idea of a unified Germany under Austrian hegemony was abhorrent to him; he expressed these views in a letter to Vischer.

Since you yourself give up the federal relationship as inadequate, it is then a question of headship, and there you are quite correct when you say that Prussian headship would make the resistance of Austrians, Bavarians and Swabians impossible. But when you also call the Prussian state incapable in and for itself of providing this headship, then I believe that you do it an injustice. This may be conceded as regards the present and all the former Prussian regimes – but the people just at this present time show themselves so capable that even proud England is forced to pay respect and it is the people which – as regards political capability – actually sets Prussia at the head of Germany. Where in Austria, Bavaria, Württemberg, is the material for such a government as in Prussia? That you describe the Prussian people as a mixture of Slavs, French and Jews made me really annoyed. So then, *at present* Prussia is not suitable because the government is not competent and because a part of the other lands won't have it; but I do not see how it will *ever* succeed with Austria so long as it 1. has these predominantly external-German appendages,[14] and 2. is Catholic. A Catholic state can never stand at the head of Germany, for it does not represent what is the best in Germany.[15]

When Bismarck took over the office of Prime Minister in 1862, Strauss, like most of the other liberals, remained aloof and suspicious; however, he decided to wait and see. The war in Schleswig-Holstein[16] was also difficult for him to understand

[14] The non-German-speaking lands (Hungary, Bohemia and the slavic countries) which were at that time under Austrian rule.

[15] To Vischer, 17.6.63; *AB*, p. 462.

[16] Denmark was defeated by a combined Prussian and Austrian force in 1864.

in all its significance, but after the province had come under Prussian control he began more and more to perceive Bismarck's political ability, and with the defeat of Austria in November, his former views about Bismarck were so completely changed that he could write:

It would not cost me anything to apologise to Count Bismarck in the public market place for every word which I have spoken or written against him, in the best opinion, but with defective knowledge of the facts.[17]

Certainly, as he conceded to Vischer, who was a fanatical opponent of Prussia, it was grim when Germans were fighting against Germans, but once the war against Austria had broken out, he gave it his fullest support.

To me also this war appears an abomination; however, now that it has broken out, I set myself with my wishes completely on the side to which I have always belonged, convinced that a victory for our side can, to be sure, bring us little good, but that a victory for the other side can bring only bad. Or, more precisely, I mean that a victory for Prussia would at the moment bring us also bad, but gives at least some hope of good in the future, while from Austria (the middle states[18] I can never consider as anything but =0 [=nil]) now and in the future, only bad can come to us.[19]

In a letter to Rapp a few days later he briefly summed up his political views in the following words:

I can summarize my political confession of faith short and to the point as follows:
1. Germany's whole constitution is so desperate that on the path to the right it cannot be further helped, but only through force.
2. This force can come from above or from below.
3. It was attempted from below in 1848 and it did not succeed.
4. Prussia is attempting it now from above and it has half succeeded.
5. In order to succeed completely, the action from above must have been combined with that from below, or yet (if possible) must be combined.
    I can express this differently so:
      I hate Austria,
      I despise the middle states and their politics,

[17] To Frau Lewald, 27.10.66; Ziegler, p. 648.
[18] The smaller German states – Bavaria, Baden, Württemberg, Hesse-Darmstadt etc.       [19] To Vischer, 3.7.66; *AB*, p. 483.

I have respect for Prussia, love I have not yet attained; but my hope for Germany rests on Prussia. Germany is either to be helped through Prussia or not at all.[20]

Finally in 1870–1 came the war against France. Following the publication of his book on Voltaire, Strauss sent a copy to Ernest Renan who replied with a friendly and cordial letter of thanks. The letter dated 31 July 1870 was written two weeks after hostilities had commenced, and in his letter Renan expressed his regret that the two countries should be at war. So far as was possible he wanted to be a quite impartial on-looker, and judged that both sides were equally to blame.

Strauss replied in a letter dated 12 August and recounted the history of the German nation since the beginning of the century. He saw Germany's fundamental problem as one of unification of the various independent states and he accused France of wanting to hinder that process on account of her selfish desire to remain the leading power in Europe.

Renan, somewhat piqued by this unexpected reply, counter-argued that the French were a peace-loving people and that Germany, driven by territorial designs on Alsace and Lorraine, had provoked the war in order to annex these two lands.

In his final letter, written on 29 September, Strauss laid the blame for the war fairly and squarely on France, and poured out a jubilant and patriotic praise of Prussia, which so vexed Renan, that the personal relationship between them came to an end from this time forth.

Who had the more right is a matter for historians to debate, but the two letters, printed along with the second letter of Renan, aroused great sentiment and jubilation throughout Germany, so that their publication was the most enthusiastically-greeted work which Strauss ever wrote. But it was, as Ziegler expressed it, the last view of the setting sun which he was to have; for now came his last book, *The Old Faith and the New* which received a totally different reception. 'After the "hosanna" followed in rapid reversal the cry of "crucify".'[21]

[20] To Rapp, 12.7.66; *AB*, p. 484.                    [21] Ziegler, p. 666.

# 21

## THE OLD FAITH AND THE NEW

Up! Up! old warrior, hush your fears,
And gird your loins for strife!
Fierce storms were yours in early years,
And storm shall close your life.[1]

'I would give a finger of my right hand', wrote Biedermann to Vatke, 'if it could have prevented Strauss writing the ominous book.'[2] This ominous book which appeared in the autumn of 1872 was *The Old Faith and the New*.

Since 1866 Strauss had been studying Schopenhauer's *The World as Will and Representation*, 'with an interest which I have not had for a long time in a book of systematic philosophy',[3] and after the completion of the book on Voltaire, his interest centred upon the problem of discovering a consistent and rational explanation for the phenomenon of the world. Along with Schopenhauer, he read the treatises of Lotze – which he did not appreciate – and while finding the philosophy of the unconscious, as expounded by Eduard von Hartmann, possessed certain worthy features, he criticised the crudities contained in it and turned for his new ideas to the evolutionary investigations of natural science, as presented by Darwin and Haeckel. He began writing the book at the end of 1871 and after a break of 3 months, during which inspiration failed him, the work was taken up again in May 1872 so that it was ready for publication by October. It was a last proclamation of his belief – a final reckoning with both theology and philosophy.

In addition there is also a personal motive for speaking out. I have now laboured for almost 40 years in the literary field with always

---

[1] *GS*, XII, p. 181.   [2] Cited Ziegler, p. 722.
[3] To Zeller, 20.5.68; *AB*, p. 482.

238

the same purpose. I have continually fought for that which appeared to me as true, perhaps even more against that which appeared to me as false; and in the pursuit of these aims I have attained, nay, overstepped the threshold of old age. Then it is that every earnest-minded man hears the whisper of the inner voice: 'Give an account of your stewardship, for you can no longer be steward.'

Now I am not conscious of having been an unjust steward. An unskilful steward at times and certainly also an inactive one – heaven only knows; but on the whole, I did what strength and desire enabled me to do, and did it without looking to the right or to the left, without trying to curry anyone's favour or being afraid of anyone's displeasure. But what is it that I did? One has, doubtless, in one's own mind, a certain unified conception, although this always finds only fragmentary expression; but do these fragments cohere and harmonize among themselves? We are often eager to shatter much of what is old, but have we something new in readiness which we can set in its place.

This reproach, especially, of merely destroying without rebuilding, is repeatedly made against those who have pursued such aims. In a certain sense I will not defend myself against this accusation for I do not acknowledge it as a reproach. I have already said that I had not the slightest intention, certainly at the present time, of constructing anything external, because I do not believe the right time has yet arrived. We can only concern ourselves with inner preparation – preparation in those who are no longer satisfied by the old, no longer appeased by half-measures. I did not, and do not want to disturb anyone's contentment or faith; only where these have already been shattered will I point out the direction where, according to my conviction, a more solid ground is to be discovered.

This ground, in my opinion, can be nothing other than that which we call the modern world-view, the laboriously attained result of continued scientific and historical research, in contrast with that of Christian theology.[4]

Interest in the work was certainly not lacking and the book went through six large editions in as many months – a success which had never before attended any theological or philosophical work in Germany. But after the warm reception of his *Voltaire*, and the *Letters to Renan*, the completely negative

---

[4] *GS*, VI, pp. 5–6; ET: *The Old Faith and the New* (2nd ed.; London, 1873) pp. 8–9.

reaction was all the more apparent. Even his friends either remained silent or came out against him and the only one to write in his favour was the young and comparatively unknown Theobald Ziegler. What was it, then, in the content of the book which caused so much vexation among friend and foe alike?

The work itself falls into six sections, the first four being a discussion of four questions: Are we still Christians? Have we still religion? How are we to understand the universe? and, How do we order our life? Two long appendices on literature and music form the concluding sections.

### *1. Are we still Christians?*

The first question which naturally arises is what is meant by the word Christian. Strauss here uses the word as meaning someone who still believes in the historic Christian faith as contained in the creeds and the traditional orthodox belief of the Protestant Church. The subsequent discussion of these cardinal beliefs was even more radical than previously. The trinity, the fall, original sin, the resurrection, immortality – Strauss simply bundled everything together and threw the lot into the rubbish bin. Not even the Person of Christ was this time spared, for whereas, formerly, Strauss had been willing to allow that Jesus had been a great religious personality whose ethics deserved a certain respect, now he declared that Jesus was a fanatic, a deluded Jew who expected a miraculous intervention by God which would confirm him as the Jewish Messiah.

May he have designated his kingdom only for Jews or also for Gentiles; may he have ascribed much or little importance in it to the Mosaic law and the temple worship; may he have foreseen his death, or been surprised by it; either there is no historical basis to be found anywhere in the Gospels, or Jesus expected to appear in the immediate future on the clouds of heaven to inaugurate the messianic kingdom which he had proclaimed. Now were he the Son of God or some other kind of higher supernatural being, there would be nothing to object to – except that the event did not occur and therefore he who prophesied it could not have been a divine being. But if he was not such a being, if he was only a mere man, who still cherished that expectation, then there is no alternative: according to our definitions he was a fanatic [Schwärmer]. This word long ago ceased to have the disparaging and derisive connotation which it had in the last century: there have been noble and ingenious fanatics; a fanatic can stimulate, can improve things; the results of his actions can often be quite long-lasting; but we would not choose such a man to be our guide in life. He would lead us astray if we did not set his influence under the control of our reason.[5]

In consequence of Jesus' unexpected death, his disciples were thrown into bewilderment; but having experienced certain hallucinations, they began to proclaim that their Master had been raised from the dead – a proclamation which, according to Strauss, can only be designated as an historical humbug of world significance.

Are we then still Christians? No! because we cannot believe all this absurd nonsense.

So then, my conviction is: if we would not look for means of evasion, if we would not try to twist and explain away the facts, if we want our yes to remain yes and our no to remain no – in short, if we would speak as honest, upright men, then we must confess: we are no longer Christians.[6]

## 2. Have we still Religion?

The answer which Strauss gave was: 'Yes or no, according as to how we understand the question.'[7] In the old theistic sense in which religion is equated with belief in a personal God and immortality, the answer is no, but if religion is understood as some form of feeling then the question may be answered in the affirmative. But exactly what this feeling is and how it should be defined is unclear; the feeling of absolute dependence, perhaps – as Schleiermacher expressed it – but dependence upon what? Upon 'the All'. But what is this 'All', this 'Universum' which Strauss preferred to the concept 'God'? Was there really an unseen moral and spiritual power lying behind the universe? That was the vital question which leads to the third section.

---

[5] *GS*, vi, pp. 52–3; ET, pp. 91–2.
[6] *Ibid.* p. 61; ET p. 107.    [7] *Ibid.* p. 97; ET p. 168.

I

*3. How are we to understand the Universe?*

The problem which Strauss faced was how to explain the universe if there were no personal God who had created the natural world, in all its amazing intricacy. How did the world originate? Was the material always there and if so, how had living organic matter arisen out of dead inorganic material? And what was the final purpose of it all? These were certainly the right questions to ask and what Strauss sought was a view of the world which would provide a logical and rational explanation for the existence of the universe, and especially of man himself.

The old metaphysical explanations had long since ceased to satisfy him. Hegel had posited the existence of an Infinite Spirit which dirempted itself into nature and, after coming to consciousness of itself, was finally subsumed back into the Godhead as the Absolute Spirit. But that was no longer credible; Feuerbach's criticism had dealt Hegel's philosophy its death blow, and Strauss had long since broken with the speculative metaphysics. But what was now to be substituted? Schopenhauer had declared that everything was to be derived from an unconscious primeval Will, which evolved through consciousness and intelligence and thence through the plant and animal world to man himself as the highest manifestation of the Will. Eduard von Hartmann developed these ideas further and asserted that everything must have originated from the Unconscious, since were God conscious and aware of what he was doing when he created the world, then his creation would be an enormous and inexpiable crime. Strauss was fascinated by these solutions, and although he did not accept all of Schopenhauer's ideas and was extremely critical of Hartmann, he saw in the evolutionary process the key for which he was looking in order to unlock the riddle of creation. In the natural scientists, Darwin and Haeckel, he found the confirmation he was seeking.

The origin of the world was certainly obscure, but the assertion that man was the pinnacle of a long process of evolution provided Strauss with a satisfying and liberating hypothesis. Here at last was a rational and scientific explanation which absolved him from the necessity of accepting the mythical creation narrative contained in the first chapters of Genesis. Science was at last beginning to vindicate the critical viewpoint.

But two problems still remained. Could a living organism issue out of dead inorganic matter, and could it really be shown that man was descended from the apes? As regards the first question there was little evidence in favour of the possibility that life could arise out of inert matter. Kant believed that one could say: 'Give me material and I will show how the world could originate out of it', but not: 'Give me material and I will show how a microbe (or better, a living cell) could be produced.' Nevertheless Strauss was convinced that not only was such a process feasible, but, indeed, must have taken place. Whether or not man had actually evolved from the apes was again unproved, for the 'missing link' had not been discovered; even so, Darwin's theory of natural selection and Moriz Wagner's laws of migration made the possibility so credible that Strauss found no problem in accepting such ideas, and he was certain that the truth of the evolutionary viewpoint would be decisively vindicated in the future.

*4. How do we order our Life?*

Strauss believed that there was a moral basis for life and that the development of moral consciousness was a gradual process in society. The essence of this moral development was to be found in the self-determination of each individual in accordance with the idea of the species, i.e. the moral standards are not determined for individuals but, fundamentally, in the community and for the human race as a whole.

As regards the practical problems of the day Strauss showed himself extremely conservative. He preferred the monarchy to the republic, had little time for social-democratic ideas, thought that the aristocracy should be retained and that inherited property was a good basis for family life; he was against the abolition of the death penalty and regarded strikes as anarchical acts against the state, which deserved severe punishment. In the question of marriage his views were liberal, for he had learnt from bitter experience the vexations faced by an incompatible couple; he therefore urged easier laws for divorce, and a civil marriage, which would free those no longer wishing to remain in the Church from the then obligatory Church ceremony. As for the Church itself, Strauss regarded it as a worthless institution for those who had once been enlightened, and although he admitted that the majority of the people were unable to get along without it, he thought that those who no longer stood in need of the orthodox religion were better to ignore the Church completely and to refrain from substituting insipid and rationalistic services such as those instituted by the 'Friends of Light'.

The most consistent of all are the so-called Free Congregations, which take their stand outside the dogmatic tradition on the ground of rational thought, natural science and history. This ground is, at any rate, solid, but no basis for a religious society. I attended many services of the Free Congregation in Berlin and found them dreadfully dry and uninspiring. I really longed for an allusion to the biblical legend or to the Christian calendar in order to receive just something for the imagination and the heart; but the refreshment I desired was not offered me. No, this is not the way either. After the edifice of the Church has been demolished, to hold a devotional hour on the bare, roughly-levelled site is horribly depressing.[8]

But if the Church and the old Christian faith were no longer necessary, what did Strauss intend to substitute in their place? What did the world have to offer for happiness and contentment apart from the Church? Literature and music, answered Strauss, and the two long appendices are devoted to a discussion of the works of Goethe and Schiller, and the music of Bach, Handel, Haydn, Mozart and Beethoven. In literature and music Strauss found his solace, and herein also lay his tranquilliser – if not his panacea – for the woes of humanity.

Strauss had no grounds for being disconsolate with the financial success of his book, but the almost completely negative verdict passed upon it – even by his friends – cast a shadow over the remaining months of his life.

The reception which my new book is finding is not able to lift me over the isolation which I feel here in Ludwigsburg. It is eagerly bought and read, but with just as much ardour rejected. I expected

[8] *GS*, vi, p. 197; ET, pp. 340–1.

hefty opposition from many sides, but not the almost complete absence of open and public agreement. I know that in the main I have spoken out frankly, but even if this statement of my views has been very imperfect, I believe it still merited thanks. 'Where are your "we"?' they will ask me, and I would almost rather remain silent, than answer what I shall have to answer.[9]

The fact was that every party, both inside and outside the Church, had felt the lash of Strauss' criticisms. The orthodox had certainly expected little different from what they found in the book and they, perhaps, were the most contented with it, in that Strauss had taken the last logical step and decried Jesus as a fanatic and the resurrection as humbug. What else, they asked, could one expect from a man who denied the existence of God? But even those who held the same radical views as Strauss himself were also offended by his materialism. His friends, Vischer, Zeller and Kuno Fischer could not accept that the whole moral, intellectual and spiritual world was merely derived from the brain – from matter! That was the bone of contention among his friends: Strauss had gone too far! To assert that everything was derived from matter and that there was no unseen spiritual basis lying behind the world was quite unacceptable to those holding a pantheistic or immanent-ist view of nature. There was more to life than just matter, and the emotions, thinking and feeling were much more than mere material manifestations. But here was the root of the misunder-standing, for even Strauss himself was hesitant about making such a claim, and on this point he remained uncertain. He did not wish to deny that such a spiritual ground or basis for the world existed – but only maintained that the old Hegelian process, where the Infinite Spirit objectifies itself in nature, could no longer be accepted. But this, in fact, was merely a matter of definition: it was not a case of either/or, but of both/ and.

If one here finds the pure crass materialism expressed, I will not at all dispute it. In fact I have always, in my own private opinions, viewed the opposition – which is often asserted with so much noise – between materialism and idealism (or by whatever term one may designate the view opposed to the former) as a mere dispute about

[9] To Kuno Fischer, 3.12.72; *AB*, p. 541.

words.  Both have a common foe in the dualism which has dominated man's view of the world throughout the whole Christian era, and separated man into body and soul, his existence into time and eternity, and opposed an eternal Creator-God to a created and perishable universe.  In contrast with this dualistic view of the world, materialism and idealism behave as monism, i.e. they seek to explain the totality of the phenomenal world from a single principle, to fashion world and life out of the same piece.  In this process one theory starts from above, the other from below; the latter constructs the universe from atoms and atom-forces, the former from ideas and idealistic forces.  But if they would fulfil their tasks, the one must lead us down from its heights to the lowest circles of nature, and to this end allow itself to be controlled by careful observation; while the other must deal with the higher intellectual and ethical problems and provide a solution to them.[10]

Strauss believed that both idealism and materialism could be reconciled in monism, although he was unsure as to how this was to be achieved.  What Strauss denied was the system of Hegel and not the fact that a spiritual ground lay behind the world.  Thus to a large degree it was a question of words and, in the last analysis, the only difference between himself and Vischer, who held that nature and spirit were one, concerned the origin of the non-material world.  Vischer gave no explanation and simply accepted the fact; Strauss remained a monist and viewed everything as evolutionising out of matter.

If Strauss' materialism was found somewhat repulsive by his more philosophically inclined readers, it was his political views which caused the greatest indignation among the radicals. Strauss supported the monarchy, respected the king and wanted to retain the aristocracy.  That was too much, and the radicals poured out their scorn upon him as an apostate from the cause of the people.  Nor were the liberals any less annoyed at the strictures which Strauss had passed upon their plans for the creation of a Free Church, where more enlightened and rationalistic teaching should prevail.  And not only Strauss' theological, political and ecclesiastical views were in bad odour, but even his musical taste.  For the great musical controversy of the times centred around the music of Richard Wagner, towards which Strauss had a strong aversion.  His hostility to the great

[10] *GS*, vi, p. 140; ET, pp. 241-2.

opera composer was well known – he had even contemplated writing a brochure against the new noise which threatened to deprive the world of his beloved Haydn and Mozart. The fact that Wagner was not even mentioned among 'our great musicians' only exacerbated the hostility of the enthusiastic Wagnerians. True, Strauss had spoken about 'room for other great composers', but he was thinking here of Schubert or Mendelssohn, and certainly not of Wagner.

And so almost no one was satisfied; if one section was acceptable another was odious. But now today, one hundred years later, how shall his book be estimated? Was the belief which he expressed in his final words: 'The time of vindication will come, as it came for the *Life of Jesus*: only this time I shall not live to see it.'[11] merely an empty hope, or can it be said that time has shown him to be in the right?

It may be confidently claimed that present-day opinion would be overwhelmingly in Strauss' favour in so far as a transcendent personal God is left out of the reckoning. If there is no Creator, in the traditional Christian understanding of the word, then the scientific and evolutionary explanations which Strauss championed are the only possible alternatives. Scientists no longer bother with complex metaphysical systems such as those of Hegel and Schelling, but explain the world by facts obtained through scientific investigation. Astronomy and physics provide us with theories for an expanding universe and the hypothesis that the universe originated from an enormous explosion. The possibility of life being created from inorganic material is no longer remote and many scientists now believe that life may be produced by a synthesis of inert elements into nucleic acids, which form the basis of the living cells. This has, it is true, not yet been accomplished, but what Strauss believed possible is now accepted by many scientists as being on the verge of attainment. The views which Strauss advocated a century ago, today find support[12] – a far different cry from 1872 when they received only scorn and ridicule.

And evolution? One needs only to browse through school and university textbooks on biology to see that the evolutionary

[11] 'Ein Nachwort als Vorwort', *ibid.* p. 278; ET, 3rd ed.; II, p. 263.
[12] One could even argue that Teilhard de Chardin is Strauss' logical successor.

hypothesis has found general acceptance in present-day scientific circles. And for holding such evolutionary views, Strauss was denounced and damned. For although Schelling and Schopenhauer had trodden a similar path before him, both had died before the results of Darwin's investigations had been available to them, and it can therefore be said that Strauss was the first theologian to champion the evolutionary theory. That also redounds to Strauss' credit. He perceived what all his critics did not, or would not, see – that if there is no God, then the universe must be explained by an evolutionary process. There had to be an explanation for the existence of the world and Strauss perceived that the scientific theories were logical and consequent. And if at the time not everything could be scientifically proved, there was no good reason for doubting that such proof would not be forthcoming in the future, as man's knowledge of the world and science progressed.

Even so, the theory of evolution is doubtless still very imperfect; it leaves an unlimited number of things unexplained and, moreover, not merely details, but really essential and cardinal questions; it points more to possible future solutions, rather than giving them already in the present. But be that as it may, it contains something which exerts an irresistible attraction on spirits athirst for truth and freedom. It resembles a railway whose track has just been marked out. What abysses will still require to be filled in or bridged over, what mountains to be tunnelled through, how many a year will pass by before the train, full of eager travellers, will glide swiftly and smoothly to its destination! Nevertheless, we see the direction it will take: thither it shall and must go, there where the flags are fluttering merrily in the breeze.[13]

Strauss did not live to see his vindication, but it came, just as he had prophesied.[14] However, one must also add that it

---

[13] *Ibid.* p. 119; ET, p. 205.

[14] And, one must add, in spite of the widespread depreciatory criticism which originated with Nietzsche, Hausrath and Schweitzer. Barth too seems to have simply followed the general, adverse opinion in his unjust description of the book as an 'incoherent journalistic conglomeration of a little Darwin, a little Goethe, a little Lessing, a little consideration of the arts, and a great deal of indescribably flat bourgeois morality' (Karl Barth, *Die protestantische Theologie*, p. 493, ET, p. 366). Such criticism is quite unfair and fails to take account of Strauss' aims and objects in writing the book. *The Old Faith and the New* is certainly no deep theological work, but neither is it incoherent. It must be said that Barth's unsympathetic

was only a partial vindication – a vindication which lies only within the non-theistic circle. Whether there might in fact be a God who had created the world (and perhaps employed evolution in the process), was a possibility which Strauss had long previously excluded.

---

attitude towards Strauss is marked in many places by his failure to present Strauss' views truly, and a tendency to dismiss him all too lightly.

# 22

## THE END

*The Old Faith and the New* had been written in Darmstadt and after its completion Strauss no longer desired to remain there. His daughter Georgine was living in Bonn, his son Fritz in Stuttgart, where his old friend Rapp was also now residing. But instead of either of these two towns his choice fell on his birthplace, the smaller and quieter town of Ludwigsburg, whither he shifted in November 1872.

Since the middle of November I have been living in our old Ludwigsburg and believe I can now say that I have found the right town to dwell in. The older I grow, the more I require solitude, and one can find that here.[1]

'For living', wrote Theodore Ziegler, 'Ludwigsburg would have been too lonely; for dying it was just right.'[2]

The event which cast a shadow over the last year of his life was the final break with Vischer after a friendship of 60 years. The friendship, certainly, had always been rather brittle: in the early 30s they had fallen out with one another; in the 40s relations had been somewhat strained owing to their opposed political views, and by 1872 it had again cooled on account of their disagreement during the war years on political and literary questions. By the autumn of that year Vischer was 'basically fed-up' with Strauss, who on his part declared in a letter to his friend Fischer in Öhringen, that Vischer, for him, had become only 'a pathological object'.[3]

And now came *The Old Faith and the New*. It had been the custom for Strauss and Vischer to review each other's books, but this time Vischer remained silent since he could not agree

---

[1] To Emil Kauffmann, 8.2.73; Hausrath, II, p. 376.
[2] Ziegler, p. 731.    [3] *SVBr*, II, p. 293.

with the ideas contained in it, declaring that Strauss had 'laid no solid foundation for the religion which remains to us'.[4]

What is treated quite inaccurately, with perceptible contradictions, is the concept of the inward appropriateness, of the development, and the question of materialism and idealism. He gives no reason on the questions of where the trust in reason in the universe is supposed to come from... In the ethical-political part are many sentences which I would have strongly attacked – indeed, even with scorn – had the book not come from a friend.[4]

Strauss learnt through Rapp that Vischer wanted to write a criticism of the book, and was decidedly displeased. Finally, he resolved to send Vischer the following frank and explicit letter setting forth his view of the matter.

My dear friend,
    I hear from various sides that you are about to write against me, i.e. against my latest book. So surprising as such a report would have been to me even a quarter of a year ago, it is now less surprising, since you have for so long been silent about the book. Thus I concluded that you must have something against it, and therefore found it rather unfriendly that you did not say anything to me by letter. For you must certainly grant me, that in my literary productions I have never been inaccessible to the objections of my friends, but, on the contrary, sought to use them as much as possible in order to make improvements. Certainly the present book was already printed; but it has repeatedly appeared in new editions and wherever I perceived an error I was concerned to correct it in them. Why then did you not, in a friendly spirit, make your criticisms available to me, so that I could use them for the subsequent improvement of my work?
    According to your mode of answering, which I have come to know, you will say: 'There was nothing to improve; it is a question of two views of the world, of which one excludes the other. Over against a view which conceives the world, and mankind especially, in a purely realistic, indeed materialistic fashion, I will and must maintain the ideal Moment.' But do I then exclude this view? Do I not declare that the opposition between the two views is simply a mere dispute over words, i.e. each of the two is necessary for comprehending the matter from the one side, which shall be complimented through a corresponding representation of the

[4] Vischer to Biedermann in an undated letter; *SVBr*, ii, p. 295.

matter from the other side. If I, in my representation, have kept predominantly to the realistic side, because the accomplishments of this direction which lay before me were more comprehensible than the ideal construction, e.g. the Hegelian, which has for a long time been foreign to me, I could have certainly and thankfully used it to supplement my work. I would have then been placed in a position where I could not merely assure, but actually show that one standpoint does not exclude the other.

Yet you deprived me of this contribution for improving my work, and now the form in which it has remained appears so offensive to you, that you – as I have heard – hold it for your duty to oppose it publicly. As I understand it, you believe that my book is bringing the free philosophical direction into bad odour and that it is summoning the true friend of this direction, in the name of philosophy, to break with philosophy. On this point I am certainly convinced that the task of philosophy at the present time can only consist in its going hand in hand with the materialistic natural science and not in opposing it. No one sees better than I that both these directions are not sufficiently enough worked in together; but the attempt had to be at least made – even if only in sketchy fashion – to trace the basic principles for a view of the world without the miraculous, and constructed from the principle of evolution.

You intend – so I hear – to set yourself on the basis of monism, likewise over against me, not even coming to meet my criticism of dogma. But the mere announcement of a dissension which has broken out between two so old comrades in arms – however the battle be conducted – will immediately raise shouts of jubilation in the enemy camp and actually put the enemy on the advantage.

The obligation to a principle precedes that to a friendship; I will therefore, finally, say just a few personal words. In a fight where I have been so sorely attacked from every side, when a friend appears in the ranks of my adversaries instead of standing in defence by my side, then he himself will have previously declared that with his act he cuts in two the long-tied bond of an old friendship.

I hope that you will accept these lines in a friendly spirit and greet you as always as

your   D. F. Strauss.[5]

After further indirect communications between them carried on through Rapp, Vischer wrote Strauss a personal critique of the book and sent it with a covering letter enclosed in the same packet.

[5] Strauss to Vischer, 11.2.73; *Ibid.* II, pp. 296–7.

Rapp tells me that you are too tired out from the babble of voices which are crying at you, to read such a manuscript. If this is still your disposition then put the pages peacefully back until you have a desire to read them; my actual object will then have been attained when you see from the writing-down and sending to you of my views, that I have not acted indifferently and unfriendly, nor unfaithfully, but that I have been faithful in this matter.[6]

Strauss refused to open the packet and asked Rapp to inform Vischer why he had not read Vischer's letter.

I would certainly have read the letter from Vischer if it had come by itself; but he stuck it in the packet whose seal I cannot open so as not to release spirits which at present I cannot use. Tell Vischer that is idiosyncrasy, but that I am a sick man who is allowed to have idiosyncrasies.[7]

Vischer allowed the matter to drop for two months, and then resolved to pay Strauss a personal visit, the outcome of which he described in a letter to Biedermann.

Since his condition grew continually worse, I informed him that I wanted to visit him. He rejected the idea: that would either lead to a mere visit or to a discussion which he could not endure. However I went to him a week ago today. It was, unfortunately, an unpleasant, dismal meeting. I could not simply remain silent; he claimed that as a sick man he had the right to lock my packet in a trunk with everything else that has to do with his book. Neither could I remain completely silent on the points in question in his book. He wouldn't go into the matter any further and became silent; after a short conversation on this and that, I, inwardly annoyed that one should think oneself permitted to derive such rights from an illness, went my way, separating unreconciled from my oldest friend, and, in all probability, never more to see him again.[8]

In August Vischer's criticism appeared in his *Kritische Gänge*[9] – a rather mild criticism which dealt mainly with the relationship between idealism and materialism and left the important political and moral issues untouched. Nor were the orthodox

[6] Vischer to Strauss, 14.3.73; *Ibid.* II, p. 299.
[7] Strauss to Rapp, 24.4.73; *Ibid.* II, p. 300.
[8] Vischer to Biedermann, 1.7.73; *Ibid.* II, p. 300.
[9] 'Der alte und neue Glaube. Ein Bekenntnis von D. F. Strauss', *Kritische Gänge* N.F. VI, pp. 203–27.

able to derive much satisfaction from seeing the two friends at loggerheads, since Vischer had vented his disgust with the traditional doctrine even more strongly than Strauss had done. But the publication of Vischer's criticism was the last nail in the coffin of their friendship and Strauss never more mentioned him in his letters. At Strauss' funeral Vischer did not – could not – speak, but ten years later when the memorial tablet on the house in which Strauss had been born was unveiled, Vischer, at the request of Strauss' family, gave the address and once again spoke warmly of Strauss and what he had accomplished.

In the autumn of 1873 appeared the first book of Nietzsche's *Unzeitgemässe Betrachtungen*[10] in which Strauss was attacked as the representative of the traditional 'classical' education in Germany and also as one of the best known writers of modern German prose. Strauss was not particularly concerned since he regarded Nietzsche's polemic as having little or no ground, and in a letter to Rapp he treated the whole affair in a rather light-hearted mood.

Nietzsche has indeed absolutely bewitched the people. I was treated here as it runs in the Abduction:
First beheaded and then hung...
Certainly, if he succeeded in hanging a person already beheaded, then the sensation that he made was not unmerited. You will see, by the way, how in vain are your efforts to reanimate a person who has been twice killed. It would also scarcely be desirable; for in the Abduction it runs further:
Then impaled on hot stakes –
which must be even more painful than hanging and beheading. What is remarkable to me in the fellow is the psychological problem, how a man can fly into such a rage against a man who has never encroached on his territory – in short, I cannot understand the actual motive for his passionate hate.[11]

The reasons for this attack were of a personal nature. Nietzsche thought of himself as the greatest prose writer in Germany and was furious that many awarded the crown to Strauss. Secondly, his friendship with Wagner and his passionate admiration for Wagner's music stirred up his hatred against

---

[10] *David Strauss der Bekenner und Schriftsteller* (Leipzig, 1873).
[11] To Rapp, 19.12.73; *AB*, p. 570.

the anti-Wagnerian Strauss. And thirdly, Nietzsche was influenced by the theologian Overbeck, who was extremely critical of Strauss' theological views. Thus Nietzsche perceived the opportunity of attacking his rival and the resulting excess of exaggerated and rude criticism did him little credit.

Strauss lay dying and he knew there was no hope of recovery: nor had he any wish to live; only to die with as little pain as possible. His son Fritz came regularly to attend him and his old friend Rapp wrote to him almost daily; but his life continued to drain away and at the end of 1873 he composed the charming poem which expresses his quiet resignation in the face of death.

> He to whom my plaint is
> Knows I shed no tear;
> She to whom I say this
> Feels I have no fear.
>
> Time has come for fading,
> Like a glimmering ray,
> Or a sense evading
> Strain that floats away.
>
> May, though fainter, dimmer,
> Only, clear and pure,
> To the last the glimmer,
> And the strain endure.[12]

The end came in February, a few days after his sixty-sixth birthday. When Fritz arrived on the morning of the 8th he found his father unconscious, and in the early afternoon Strauss breathed his last. The funeral on the 11th was described by Theodor Ziegler.

It was a cold, fine Winter's day: bright and clear shone the sun as if it wanted to show that here a man was being buried who had sought, like her, to shine lucidly. It was a stately procession that wound its way through the more than usually animated streets of his home town to the cemetery; and while my heart was so sad, yet I rejoiced that today so many acknowledged him – be it only

[12] *GS*, xii, p. 226. The two persons referred to in the first verse are Strauss' son, and Rapp's daughter Frida, to whom the poem was dedicated. The translation by Montgomery is contained in Schweitzer's *The Quest of the Historical Jesus*, p. 77.

with the head or also with the heart. At the same time I felt myself – and many others with me also felt themselves – lifted up by the glimpse which had previously been ours. We had seen once more the deceased, once more the forehead of the thinker, which rose above the closed eyes so free and firm, once more the mouth which testified of suffering and yet expressed friendliness and peace. So he lay, in the midst of his books, in the most beautiful greenery: it was a glimpse into all simplicity, beautiful and great, the like of which I had never seen.[13]

To this description may be appended the words of Wilhelm Lang:

Whoever on that Winter's day when his body was delivered to the earth of his home town, whoever entered into the house where the deceased lay in the open coffin surrounded by greenery, while around the sides of the coffin were the books which were finally the only world of the lonely man, stood deeply moved by the nobleness of these rigid features. Long rested the gaze on the scholarly expression cut by the noble, finely-traced lines. Only about the mouth was a hard, harsh trait noticeable, which reminded one that he who lay here in quiet peace was a man of battle with a character which had been steeled in the storm. A kind of promethean defiance still lay on the cold, tightly-closed lips which seemed to say: What I have written, I have lived.[14]

Strauss had expressly forbidden a Church funeral.[15] No church bells were to be rung, no prayers to be said, and no clergyman was to speak – not even his old friend Rapp. He had wanted words which he himself had composed, to be sung to the tune *O Isis and Osiris*, but the words were mislaid and instead the mourners sang a hymn.

It had been hoped that the funeral address might have been given by Zeller, but he, unfortunately, was not in good health and the long train journey from Berlin to Ludwigsburg in the middle of winter was too much to undertake. Kuno Fischer excused himself with the plea that his lectures prevented him from coming, for which cause he was in bad grace with Strauss' children; and Vischer dared not say anything. In these circum-

---

[13] Ziegler, pp. 741–2.

[14] *David Friedrich Strauss* (Leipzig, 1874), pp. 59–60.

[15] Strauss' Last Will and Testimony with regard to his burial is to be found among his letters to Kuno Fischer in the Heidelberg University Library. It is printed, for the first time, at the end of this chapter.

stances his old friend Gustav Binder offered to speak and even this last scene in Strauss' life was to cause a new outburst of indignation. For Binder, who in his address had declared, 'Your people will remember you and the youth of your people will not forget you,'[16] was the Director of the Board of Education, which had the oversight of the theological seminary. A statement with 214 signatures appeared the following month protesting that the Director had chosen to honour a confessed atheist – the orthodox thereby hoping to effect the resignation of a man who had been a thorn in their flesh. However, Strauss' old friends sprang to the attack and after strong denunciations of the statement from Vischer, Zeller and others, the affair slowly died down with the orthodox failing to achieve their objective.

But of all this Strauss knew nothing. The storm, the strife and the bitterness which he had so often experienced passed over him; he could no longer be touched.

### LAST WILL AND TESTIMONY WITH REGARD TO MY BURIAL

1. The burial must be simple, without any pomp.

2. In order that this may not be seen as stinginess, but as the conviction that pomp is not appropriate for a corpse, 100 fl. shall on the day of my burial be placed at the disposal of the local authorities to be given to the poor in the district.

3. Most important of all, the Church shall be excluded from all participation in the burial service. For this decision I am responsible and my children are responsible to me for carrying this out; all the less responsibility falls on them when definite instructions from me stand behind them.

4. So then, no church bells, no music from the Church tower, no cross on the pall, but a simple black covering, or even none at all.

5. But above all, no minister shall take part; there shall be no speech, no prayer, neither at the grave, nor in the house. I should most of all prefer complete silence during the act; yet I was also extremely taken with what I recently read about the instructions which Sainte Beuve gave for his own burial: The retinue only of friends and other participants; then after the coffin had been lowered, one of the friends stepped up to the grave with the words:

[16] Ziegler, p. 744.

'Adieu Sainte Beuve, adieu cher ami.' Following this came a few words of thanks to the retinue. 'Messieurs la solennité est finie.' Something like that will be necessary so that no unauthorised person speaks and afterwards gives cause for gossip.

6. Also in regard to the later erection of a gravestone, will my children keep within the limits of the simplest kind.

22nd June 1873                                         D. F. Strauss

# 23

⟺

# THE ORIGIN OF STRAUSS' MYTHICAL INTERPRETATION

We have seen how Strauss, in his letter to the Director of Studies in 1835, asserted that he had done nothing more than bring to light principles long previously enunciated by others, which had hitherto remained hidden in obscurity. The substance of his statement was also repeated some years later by Baur, who attempted to belittle the importance of the *Life of Jesus* with the charge that nothing really original was to be found there. What we must now determine is how far these statements accord with the truth and whether there might not be more originality in the *Life of Jesus* than has generally been recognised. To what extent did Strauss derive his mythical[1] interpretation from his predecessors and how far was he indebted to them? To provide an answer to this question it will be necessary to make a survey of eighteenth- and early nineteenth-century views of the mythical interpretation of the Bible.[2]

The mythical principle has its roots in the eighteenth century and especially in connection with the old classical literature. It was the philologist Christian Gottlob Heyne[3]

[1] The words 'myth' and 'mythical' as they are used here, refer to any single story which is unhistorical – regardless of its inner significance. 'Mythology' denotes a body of myths, and its cognate adjective 'mythological' also possesses this wider meaning, which includes within itself the term 'mythical'. Thus where 'mythical' and 'mythological' refer to a single event or story, they are roughly synonymous and interchangeable. The verb 'mythologise' refers to the process in which myths are formed and to 'demythologise' is to analyse a mythical narrative in order to lay bare the myth and its underlying basis.

[2] The only comprehensive investigation in this field is by C. Hartlichs and W. Sachs, *Der Ursprung des Mythosbegriffes in der modernen Bibelwissenschaft* (Tübingen, 1952).

[3] Heyne (1729–1812) was a professor and director of the philological department in Göttingen.

259

who brought to light a decisively new and important conception of the essence of the myth. Confronted with the problem of the relation between poetry and myth in the ancient world, he defined a myth as a mode of conception and expression found in the primitive stages of the human race. Myth, for Heyne, was a necessary and universally primitive form of poetry.

He classified myths into two groups: first, historical myths (saga), where an actual historical event lies behind the stories, and secondly, philosophical myths, which are invented for ethical or educational reasons, or as explanations of natural events (theogonies, cosmogonies, geogonies etc.).[4] He also added a third category, the poetical myth, which may be either historical or philosophical and which simply expresses the aesthetic feelings of the author in poetic form.

Heyne may be regarded as the founder of the 'mythical school', but the first to apply his ideas to the Bible was Johann Gottfried Eichhorn[5] whose anonymous *Urgeschichte* first appeared in 1779. However, not until a new edition of the work, with an introduction and commentary by Johann Philipp Gabler,[6] was published in 1790–3, did his views begin to influence the course of biblical scholarship. Through the mythological researches of Heyne, Eichhorn's field of vision had been considerably enlarged, and he came to the conclusion that divine interventions must be alike admitted, or alike rejected, in the primitive histories of all peoples. Hebrew history, therefore, was to be treated in the same manner as pagan history: if celestial beings could appear among the Hebrews then they could also appear among other nations, but if they could not make themselves known to the heathen, then what ground was there for supposing that the assumed revelations to the Jewish people had any real foundation. If these ostensible revelations had no historical reality, were they not then to be ascribed to deceit and falsehood? This, indeed, had been the view of Reimarus, but Eichhorn held that such an idea could only arise where the ancient records were not interpreted in accord with the spirit

---

[4] Theories about the origin of gods, the universe and the world (i.e. the earth).

[5] Eichhorn (1752–1827) was professor of oriental languages at Jena (1775–88) and professor of philosophy at Göttingen (1788–1827).

[6] Gabler (1753–1826) was professor of philosophy at Jena (1804–26).

of the age in which they had been written. Myths were the spontaneous and natural attempts of primitive peoples to express their comprehension of unseen realities in the thought-forms and conceptions of the time.

Myths, generally speaking, are sagas of the ancient world expressed in the sensual way of thinking and speaking of that time. In myths, one may not expect an event to be presented just as it actually happened, but just as it must have appeared to the ancient world which thought and drew conclusions in its sensual way and in the pictorial, visual and dramatic speech and presentation in which an event at that time *could only* be related. All stories from the ancient world and those relating the origin of each people *must then necessarily be myths*; and the older a book is, the more myths it must contain. These ancient myths, or folk-lore, which contain the oldest history and philosophy have, however, received many modifications, invented additions, amplifications, artificial combinations and pleasant embellishments, according to the taste of the age, through the length of time, through poetic fiction and artistic genius, indeed, even through philosophical speculation. And from just these sources flowed completely new fables, which, on account of the similarity of content and recitation with the oldest myths, also came to be called myths, even if they were the later product of human poetry and not the old folk-lore.[7]

*Myths are not fables*, as they were customarily viewed, whereby their true nature was completely confused until a Heyne arose, who developed and determined the true nature and intention of myths more correctly. According to these admirable elucidations of Heyne, myths are not fables or fairy-tales, but ancient sagas; and mythology is not teaching contained in fables but in and for itself *the oldest history and the oldest philosophy*, the embodiment of the old sagas of peoples and families *in the uncultured and sensual speech of the ancient world*; it hands down to us, then, the oldest modes of comprehension and the thoughts of the people.[8]

Here, certainly, was progression along the mythological road and yet, for the most part, Eichhorn still attempted to explain the Old Testament events in a natural (rationalistic) manner: the flame and smoke which ascended from Mount Sinai at the giving of the law were merely the result of a fire which Moses kindled in order to make a deeper impression upon the imagina-

---

[7] *Urgeschichte*, ii, pp. 482–3; cited Hartlich and Sachs, p. 30.
[8] *Ibid.* ii, p. 260; cited *ibid.* p. 31.

tion of the people, together with an accidental thunderstorm which arose at that particular moment; the shining of his face was the natural effect of being overheated, etc. etc.

At first Eichhorn and Gabler only applied their views to the Old Testament but later they turned to the New Testament and began to consider the Gospel narratives in the light of the principles which they had applied to the Old Testament. The problem was to distinguish what was factual from that which was merely a clothing of the facts in mythical forms – angels, miracles, etc. – a distinction, according to Gabler, of which the primitive Jewish mind was completely unconscious.

At the time of Jesus angels belonged to the *theological machinery of the Jews*: according to Jewish thought God worked everywhere through angels; these were the agents of his general and special providence; every favourable piece of luck, every happy thought came from an angel, every unexpected phenomenon, every incomprehensible event, every unexpected sudden help must have been the work of an angel, just in the same way as we call it God's providence. This was certainly the belief of the older Jews and this belief further developed during and from the time of the exile. *Where we think of an indirect providence of God, the Jews thought of angels.*[9]

The views of Heyne formed the basis of Eichhorn's initial investigation of the biblical narratives, and Gabler had given Eichhorn's ideas a more thorough grounding, but it was left to Georg Lorenz Bauer[10] to consolidate the mythical position and to furnish the clearest exposition of the mythical view of history. In his book, *Entwurf einer Hermeneutik des alten und neuen Testaments* (1799), Bauer presented a short summary of the meaning of the word 'myth':

Generally we understand myths to be old stories about the origin of the world, the human race, or the future state after death, or the origin of peoples and their earliest history, which have been handed down by tradition, symbolically related and embellished with the miraculous. From this it follows that there are three kinds of myths: 1. Philosophical myths – stories about the origin of things and the physical causes. Here belong the cosmogonies and geogonies, the first crude attempts to reflect upon the cause of things. 2. Historical myths – stories from the oldest histories of the peoples,

---

⁹ Gabler, *Neuestes theologisches Journal*, 1 (1798) p. 241; cited *ibid.* pp. 66–7.
¹⁰ Bauer (1755–1806) was a professor in Altdorf and Heidelberg.

their founders and their fate, the oldest benefactors of nations, and inventors of useful things. 3. Poetical myths – either newly-invented stories of the poets, or those first stories of the poets embellished, enriched with additions, and given a more miraculous content.[11]

and then explained how these different myths were to be recognised.

The criteria by which a myth is to be recognised and differentiated from a true story are as follows. 1. When the origin of the universe and the earth, for which there was no witness, is narrated. 2. When instead of the natural causes through which events have happened, everything is traced back to the activity of gods, or heavenly beings, who appear personally and act in a direct way. 3. When everything is presented in a sensual way, when men speak and act where they only thought. 4. When the matter related either does not now happen, or, in accordance with the orderly province of nature, cannot happen, but exceeds all belief.

The criteria, however, by which the myths are differentiated from one another, must be derived from *the inner nature of the myths*. The myth in which the causes of things, of the world, and of physical events, are explained, are philosophical. Those in which stories about the oldest families of the human race and the founders of peoples are retold in miraculously embellished sagas are historical. Both kinds may have been worked over poetically, receiving many additions.[12]

Bauer's whole standpoint was basically rationalistic and anything incapable of a scientific proof was labelled mythical – a designation which included all narratives making weak attempts to explain the origin of the world, the origin of evil, the appearance of heavenly beings upon the earth, and certain poetic myths such as the abode of the dead and the myth of the Messiah. Thus after the particular type of myth has been determined, the appropriate origins may be established, and Bauer went even further, suggesting certain rules by which the mythical narratives should be interpreted: for example, with philosophical myths one enquires after the intention which lies behind the myth; with historical myths the historical event is to be separated from the mythical (fabulous) accretions, and with poetical myths the successive embellishments are to be carefully noted.

The *Entwurf einer Hermeneutik* laid the ground for his later

[11] *Entwurf*, pp. 155–6.         [12] *Ibid.* p. 156.

exposition of the mythical problem, and in his *Hebräische Mytho-logie des alten und neuen Testaments* (1802), he compared many of the biblical accounts with myths from Persia, India, China and other lands. But if there were myths in the Old Testament – and for Bauer this was beyond dispute – then there was no ground for maintaining that myths were not to be found in the New Testament. For if angels were mythical in the Old Testament, they could not be historical simply because they were found in the New Testament. And if angels were mythical in the New Testament then so were demons, theophanies, and the like.

What is related about the angels cannot be historical for it concerns the super-sensory world of which we can have no experience. The conception of angels is originally the remains of polytheism: The Elohim were certainly first gods and then became subordinate gods subject to Jehovah...The theophanies also belong to the realm of myths. Where appearances of God take place, there is myth. Where a theophany or angelophany occurs, where heavenly beings appear and converse with mortals, there is myth. Where God appears on earth, there is no true history, but a myth.[13]

Bauer had to be, and was, particularly careful about listing the mythical narratives in the New Testament, but the following are regarded as belonging to the mythical category: all narratives where angels (and demons) are present, the virgin birth of Christ and the transfiguration. Doubtless Bauer would have gone further and characterised all supernatural narratives in the same category had not prudence warned him that such a procedure was too drastic for an age not yet ready to receive such views. He therefore contented himself with mythical explanations so far as was prudent, and for the rest, he simply followed the rationalistic explanations of the Enlightenment.

A further development is to be seen in the writings of de Wette,[14] who held that myths usually have no historical basis and are mostly derived from the poetic feelings of the author; they are expressions of the religious life, of the human spirit, and whether the historical events related in the story possess an element of historical truth or are completely false is neither

[13] Summarised from different passages of the *Hebräische Mythologie* by Hartlich and Sachs, pp. 82–3.

[14] W. M. L. de Wette (1780–1849) was professor of theology in Berlin (1810–19) and Basel (1822–49).

here nor there. Thus de Wette disputed the findings of the 'Mythical School' and opposed the usual separation between the historical and philosophical myth. For him, the Pentateuch was merely the product of the patriotic religious feelings of the Israelites and as an historical source was absolutely useless, except as a document which illuminates our knowledge of Hebrew poetry and the religious character of the poets themselves. He did not dispute that there were historical facts lying behind the poetry, but only the possibility of recovering these facts. And what could not be ascertained with certainty as being historical, had therefore to be considered mythical.

Up to this point there is nothing to suggest that Strauss' own exposition of the mythical principle was derived from any of the above-named theologians; it is in fact quite distinct. For the mythical school of Heyne and his successors was concerned with individual myths (where myths are equated with fables) and not, as was Strauss, with the mythical principle. Strauss' theory differs significantly from all previous mythical interpretations in that the mythical principle which he employed derived the Gospel stories from the Old Testament narratives by means of an unconscious mythologising process. Were we to go only as far as Hartlich and Sachs, we should be forced to conclude that far from being a mere follower of his predecessors, Strauss had in fact developed a most original mythical principle which he had in turn applied to the Gospel narratives with the most extraordinary results.

That is, however, not the case and when we delve deeper into the sources than Hartlich and Sachs have done, we find that Strauss' mythical principle was, for the most part, derived from four little-known writings.[15] This is not to say that no other writings were important; Strauss read widely on the

---

[15] It is rather astonishing that a discussion of the following literature dealing with the mythical interpretation is completely neglected by Hartlich and Sachs and also by J. F. Sandberger, *David Friedrich Strauss als Theologischer Hegelianer* (Göttingen, 1972). There are two major defects in Sandberger's otherwise excellent book: 1. Like almost every other interpreter of Strauss, Sandberger fails to perceive that Strauss' mythical interpretation of the New Testament is not simply a matter of accepting the New Testament narratives as mythical. Because of this misunderstanding Sandberger relies upon the older (incorrect) interpretations of Strauss (p. 14), and makes no attempt to trace the origin of Strauss' mythical

subject and separated out the wheat from the chaff, but of the literature on the mythical interpretation which appeared during the late eighteenth and early nineteenth century, four authors in particular advocated the mythical viewpoint – if only in a still undeveloped form.

In 1796 an article dealing with the first two chapters in Matthew and in Luke[16] was printed in Henke's *Magazin* under the signature 'E.F.'. Here we find the first beginnings of the mythical principle which Strauss finally adopted. The article itself deals only with the narratives of Jesus' birth, but it points the way to the mythical interpretation in principle when the author asserts that the story of the virgin birth was derived from Is. 7, 14 because it was the common belief in the time of Jesus that the Messiah would be born of a virgin. 'So then, this text also must refer to Jesus; if he were the Messiah, then he must have been born of a virgin.'[17]

More important was an anonymous work entitled *Revelation and Mythology* which appeared in 1799.[18] Various suggestions were put forward as to its authorship and for a time it was attributed to Schleiermacher who in 1806, however, wrote an open letter to the Jena *Literatur-Zeitung* denying the rumours. The book was in all probability written by J. C. A. Grohmann (1769–1847), professor of philosophy at Wittenberg.[19]

Jesus as he really was, maintained Grohmann, was in fact quite different from the Jesus presented in the Gospels. 'His life and deeds, his death and resurrection were portrayed completely according to an opinion common to the people. But Christ as he really lived was completely different to the Christ

---

principle. 2. Sandberger omits any discussion of the one presupposition which governs not only the whole of Strauss' thinking, but also of Hegel's – the existence, or rather non-existence, of a transcendent personal God. But the existence or non-existence of such a God is the crucial presupposition which determines not merely the validity of the Hegelian philosophy, but also of the mythical interpretation itself and any discussion of Strauss' philosophical views must first deal with this fundamental question.

[16] 'Beyträge zur Aufklärung über die beyden ersten Kapitel im Matthäus und Lucas'. *Magazin für Religionsphilosophie, Exegese und Kirchengeschichte,* v (1796) pp. 146–81.          [17] *Ibid.* p. 153.

[18] *Ueber Offenbarung und Mythologie* (Berlin, 1799).

[19] See *ADB* ix, pp. 709–11; Elliot van N. Diller, *Revelation and Mythology* (1948).

who, according to the stories of this superstitious, mentally-limited, hoping and waiting people, was supposed to have lived. Only when the event was over was his life embellished with fables, with stories either half-true or completely false...'[20] But the idea of what the Messiah should be, asserted Grohmann, was in fact actually present before Jesus appeared. The hopes, desires and longings of the poor, the suffering, the blind and the lame stretched out towards the arrival of their deliverer and his appearance could not be otherwise than the picture painted in the stories which preceded him. 'A helper will come out of Judah: the exact portrayal of this helper was sketched before he came.'[21]

And, so, continued the author, it was only natural that the people should fashion the Messiah whom they so desired.

This man had to be the Christ, and, moreover, *the* Christ for whom they had yearned and dreamed, the Christ whom they had imagined, whom they had previously seen in the Old Testament prophecies. He must and would do everything that they wanted him to do.[22]

This view was the basis of Strauss' mythical interpretation: the picture of the Messiah painted after Christ's death was based on the Old Testament portrayal already accepted by the people.

In the early years of the nineteenth century a new interest in the mythical interpretation of the New Testament arose. Bauer's *Hebräische Mythologie* (1802) gave the initial impetus and a number of articles followed in which the whole question was discussed. In 1803 an article written by Wilhelm Krug[23] appeared in H. P. K. Henke's *Museum für Religionswissenschaft* – a journal advocating the most liberal theological viewpoint. Krug distinguished between the genetic and formal explanations of miracles; the latter was simply another name for the natural or rationalistic explanation while the genetic explanation investigated not the miracle itself, but the way in which such stories arose. Those who first invented the stories, maintained Krug, had no intention of deceiving, and the stories

[20] *Ueber Offenbarung und Mythologie*, p. 105.
[21] *Ibid.* p. 98.        [22] *Ibid.* p. 103.
[23] 'Versuch über die genetische oder formelle Erklärungsart der Wunder'. *Museum für Religionswissenschaft*, 1 (1803) pp. 395–413.

gradually grew with the new mythical accretions until they were finally written down by the evangelists. In this same issue appeared an article on the first two chapters of Luke[24] by G. K. Horst who treated the Lucan narratives as a work of fiction and constantly referred to the author as 'the poet'. In the following issue of the same journal J. C. Greiling wrote an article[25] disagreeing with the views of Krug and advocating that the New Testament narratives should all be psychologically treated. Gabler too, in his review of Bauer's *Hebräische Mythologie*[26] supported the mythical interpretation as the best means of extirpating the old rationalistic explanations, and he recommended the distinction of myths into historical and philosophical categories.

But the most significant work, and probably the most important single factor in finally convincing Strauss that the mythical interpretation was the only feasible possibility, was a short anonymous article entitled 'The different aspects in which and for which the biographer of Jesus can work',[27] which appeared in 1816. All mythical ideas which hitherto had been only cautiously expressed were now given full reign. The natural explanation was pronounced untenable; nor would the author have anything to do with the middle way proposed by Gabler, whose mythical distinction was considered to be quite unnecessary; the anonymous author wished rather to abstain from all speculation as to how the myths originated. What he did demand, however, was a consistent carrying through of the mythical interpretation in the New Testament, and in a most important passage he declared that since the Gospel stories are so similar to the ancient myths of heathendom and Judaism, then one was surely justified in assuming that the Gospel narratives also belonged to the mythical category. To illustrate this assertion he then drew parallels between the stories in the Old Testament and those in the Gospels.

[24] 'Über die beyden ersten Kapitel im Evangelium Lukas'. *Ibid.* pp. 446–538; 685–758.

[25] 'Psychologischer Versuch über die psychische Kur des tobsüchtigen Gergaseners'. *Ibid.* pp. 620–54.

[26] *Journal für auserlesene theologische Literatur*, ii (1805) pp. 39–59.

[27] 'Die verschiedenen Rücksichten in welchen und für welche der Biograph Jesu arbeiten kann'. *Kritisches Journal der neuesten theologischen Literatur* (ed. Berthold) v (1816) pp. 225–45.

The Old Testament prophets may be compared to Jesus in many respects; they are true types which the Gospel history has copied. Many conspicuous similarities are especially to be found in a comparison of Jesus with Elisha, and if stories about Elisha are mythical then the same must also hold true for the stories about Jesus. Elisha raises the Sunamite woman's son from the dead (2 Kings 4); Jesus the young man of Nain, Jairus' daughter and Lazarus. Elisha feeds 100 men with a small amount of bread and multiplies the widow's oil; Jesus feeds 5000 men (2 Kings 4; cf. Jn. 6; Mk. 8). Elisha and Jesus both cure leprosy; both go through the water (2 Kings 2; cf. Mt. 14, 25); both know how to strike blind those sent against them (2 Kings 6, 18; cf. Jn. 18, 6); both have a great host of invisible protectors (2 Kings 6, 17; cf. Mt. 26, 53; 4, 11; Lk. 22, 43). Another prophet, Elijah, is taken up living to heaven; Elisha watches him go; likewise with Jesus and his apostles (2 Kings 2, 12; cf. Acts 1, 9–10). Who can fail to perceive the same spirit? Jesus shall not be inferior to the wonder-working prophets in the Old Testament.[28]

Similar ideas were expressed by Leonard Usteri in his article dealing with the narrative of Jesus' temptation.[29] The whole story, in his opinion, is best explained by the hypothesis that it was written to present Jesus as the Messiah. The forty days which Moses spent on Mount Sinai provided the example for Jesus' time in the wilderness, and the angel which ministered to him when the devil departed, was traced back to the story of the angel feeding Elijah in the desert.

Usteri confined himself to the story of the temptation but he was not slow to see other parallels between the stories in the Gospels and those in the Old Testament: the slaughter of the Israelite children in Egypt and Herod's massacre of the children in Bethlehem; the gifts which the Queen of Sheba brought to Solomon and those brought to Jesus by the wise men; the giving of the law on Mount Sinai and the Sermon on the Mount; the passage of the Israelites through the Red Sea and Jesus' stilling of the storm; the shining of Moses face when he descended from Mount Sinai and the transfiguration of Jesus.

Unlike the anonymous author of the article in Berthold's Journal, Usteri did not advocate a mythical interpretation of

---

[28] *Ibid.* pp. 237–8.

[29] 'Beitrag zur Erklärung der Versuchungsgeschichte'. *TSK* (1832) 3: pp. 768–91. Usteri (1799–1833) was a professor in Bern.

all the Gospel stories, but confined the mythical element to a relatively pre-historical period, the time before Jesus began his public ministry. Nevertheless, one can hardly fail to notice that only prudence prevented him from going further. Myths, he argued, were not fairy-tales but poetical productions whose content consisted of religious or philosophical ideas expressed in historical forms. The stories in the Gospels did not originate with someone sitting down at a table and consciously inventing them, like a poet composing poetry; rather, their origin is shrouded in darkness and no longer ascertainable; the myths arose slowly and were finally written down by the evangelists some thirty years after Jesus' death. This time, according to Usteri, was sufficient for the supernatural embellishments of the underlying historical facts to creep in and be accepted as true history.

It must have been in the constant engagement with this literature that Strauss became convinced that the mythical principle was the key to unlock all difficulties in the biblical narratives. And if he was not the actual originator of the mythical interpretation, he was at least the first to lift it out of obscurity and use it in a systematic exegesis of the New Testament. He saw what many others failed to perceive – that the best and simplest non-supernatural solution to the New Testament problems is the mythical interpretation.

Three points may finally be noted. The first is that there is no evidence that Ferdinand Christian Baur exercised any significant influence upon the development of Strauss' mythical viewpoint. It is true that Baur lectured on mythology while Strauss was a student in the Blaubeuren lower seminary, but when we examine Baur's *Symbolik und Mythologie* (1824–5) we see that it is concerned almost entirely with classical and non-biblical mythology; further, it was predominantly dependent upon the work of Creuzer and made no mention of Eichhorn, Gabler, G. L. Bauer and the articles in Henke's journal. Moreover, as we have seen, there is no hint that the mythical principle played any part in Strauss' thinking before 1832.

Secondly, and more important, the mythical principle is entirely independent of Hegelian philosophy.[30] It is true that

[30] Cf. the conclusion of Hartlich and Sachs: 'The hermeneutical principles and criteria by means of which Strauss ascertains the mythical element in the Gospels are free from specific speculative presuppositions.

in 1835 Strauss thought of the myth in Hegelian terms as one of the forms in which the Idea expresses itself in the world, but this view plays no part in the critical section of the book. Strauss was not concerned with the philosophical explanation for the origin of myths in general, but with the historical process by which the myths in the Gospels arose. Only in the concluding section of the book, when the critical analysis of the Gospels has been completed, are the Hegelian views employed in order to explain the unity of God and man in the God-man. In the 1864 *Life of Jesus* the mythical principle remains substantially unchanged while the Hegelian viewpoint is abandoned. When therefore the *Life of Jesus* is described as being a product of the Hegelian philosophy, then this description is misleading.[31] The mythical principle and the Hegelian philosophy are related only in that both are ultimately dependent upon the same underlying presupposition – the denial of a transcendent personal God.

Thirdly, we should note that Strauss' explanation of how the mythical stories in the Gospels originated was neglected and ignored by his contemporaries (Baur especially was to blame here) and was soon no longer understood. The central issues with which Strauss had dealt were slurred over and later generations did not understand the ingenuity and simplicity of the mythical principle which Strauss had so adroitly explicated and employed. His formulation was forgotten, never again advocated by later theologians, and allowed to sink back into the

---

What lies at the bottom of his critical presuppositions was exactly fixed by himself, as has been shown, and bears a purely empirical-rational character. His presuppositions are not those of a particular philosophical standpoint, but those which exhibit a scientific character in the particular realm of historical science'. *Der Ursprung des Mythosbegriffes in der modernen Bibelwissenschaft*, p. 147. Similarly Sandberger: 'Historical criticism, according to Strauss' conception, is in no way dependent on the speculative philosophy, but is a rational consideration of history which works in accordance with its own specific laws'. *David Friedrich Strauss als theologischer Hegelianer*, p. 87.

[31] Cf. Heinrich Weinel: 'It was often believed that Strauss could easily be refuted with the reproach that he had written his book from an Hegelian point of view. That is completely false if one thinks that such a reproach has any bearing on the main part of the book. Only in the short concluding section does Hegel come into view'. *Jesus im neunzehnten Jahrhundert* (Tübingen and Leipzig, 1903) p. 27.

oblivion from where it had been salvaged. Even the later demythologising programme simply assumed the presence of myths and was not concerned with their origin.

In this respect it is interesting to compare Strauss and Bultmann. Strauss regarded the Gospels as a hopeless conglomeration of mythical stories from which no trustworthy picture of Jesus could ever be won. Bultmann too is of the same opinion and renounces all attempts to penetrate behind the sources to the historical Jesus.[32] Both Strauss and Bultmann, in the last analysis, have the same view of myth, in that everything supernatural or other-worldly is regarded as unhistorical and therefore mythical.[33] 'Mythology is the way in which the non-worldly and divine are represented as worldly and human, in which the other-worldly appears as this-worldly, as when, for example, God's other-worldliness is thought of in terms of spatial separation.'[34] Such primitive conceptions, according to Bultmann, are today incredible because twentieth-century man has a modern and scientific view of the world in which other-worldly conceptions can have no place. Strauss' objection was essentially the same although his starting point was rather the premiss that miracles are impossible in the natural world. But behind this premiss, as we have seen, lies the really determining presupposition that there is no transcendent personal God, and the question must be asked whether this is not the one presupposition which also, ultimately, governs the theological views of Bultmann.

In contrast to Strauss, Bultmann never attempts to ascertain how the myths in the Gospels arose, while for Strauss, this was the key to the whole understanding of the Christian faith. Once this had been demonstrated then the origin of Christianity no longer required to be explained in terms of the miraculous and supernatural. And having accomplished this explanation Strauss washed his hands of theology and departed from the field

[32] 'I am of the opinion that we can know practically nothing about the life and personality of Jesus'. *Jesus* (Tübingen, 1926) p. 12; ET: *Jesus and the Word* (London, 1953) p. 8.

[33] Gunther Backhaus, *Kerygma und Mythos bei David Friedrich Strauss und Rudolf Bultmann* (Hamburg-Bergstedt, 1956) pp. 41–50.

[34] Rudolf Bultmann, 'Neues Testament und Mythologie' (1941). Reprinted in *Kerygma und Mythos* I (ed. H.-W. Bartsch; Hamburg, 1948) p. 23, footnote 2; ET: *Kerygma and Myth* (London, 1953) p. 10, footnote 2.

of action.  There was, in his opinion, essentially nothing more that needed to be said or was worth saying.  The Christian faith as traditionally understood was all nonsense and there was no sense in attempting compromise solutions.  Bultmann, on the other hand, attempts to interpret the New Testament in existential categories.  In Jesus Christ, he declares, God challenges man to authentic existence.  But who and what Jesus was, what kind of a God it is who challenges (certainly not a transcendent, other-worldly, personal God) – these questions and many others are deemed, in the last resort, to be indeterminable.

# 24

# STRAUSS' INFLUENCE UPON THEOLOGY

In the nineteenth century Strauss was 'probably the best known and most significant theologian in non-theological and non-Church circles'.[1] His *Life of Jesus* made him notorious at once and for many years to come. No one of any reputation supported his views and he was ostracised in all Church circles. For the next quarter century theology remained solidly entrenched in the old orthodox framework, and the most influential figures of the time – Neander, Ullmann, Tholuck, Hengstenberg, Nitzsch, Rothe Harless and Müller – were all of an orthodox or pietist persuasion.

And yet from 1835 onwards the critical movement, which Strauss had set in motion, began to shoot forth blossom. In that same year the apostolic authorship of the Pastoral Epistles was rejected by Baur and the radical criticism of Vatke opened up a new chapter in the investigation of the Old Testament. In the following year Baur published his long study of the Epistle to the Romans and consolidated a new interpretation of early Church history, the seeds of which were to be found some five years earlier in his article on the Corinthian church. By the beginning of the 1840s the debate over the problem of the historical Jesus and the authenticity of the Gospels was well under way, and Bruno Bauer's radical criticism of the Gospels coupled with Feuerbach's proclamation that God was simply a magnified projection of man's own self brought the new criticism into even greater disrepute. The middle years of this decade saw the Tübingen School in its full bloom. Works dealing with every important aspect of the New Testament flowed from the pens of Baur and his younger disciples, and the orthodox theology was compelled to engage in combat with the new critical

[1] Barth, *Die protestantische Theologie im 19. Jahrhundert*, p. 491; ET, p. 363.

views. It was in this crucible that the methods were forged which were to determine New Testament criticism for the next half century. The new ideas began to spread like a river which, having broken its banks, begins to flood out over the surrounding countryside. The effect caused by Strauss' *Life of Jesus* may be likened to the breaching of the river-bank.

And yet theological opinion has never regarded Strauss as a great theologian. 'He possessed a sharp critical acumen', wrote Hausrath, 'but he was not a great thinker'.[2] This unfavourable judgment has often been echoed down through the years to our own time. 'He was not a thinker',[3] declared Barth, and 'no great theologian'.[4]

Such statements as they stand are misleading and present only a part of the true picture. They are misleading because they are ambiguous and too general. Only when we make a clearer delineation of the words 'theologian' and 'great' are we able to attain to a more accurate estimate of Strauss' greatness in the theological world.

The word 'theologian' possesses a wider and a narrower meaning. In the nineteenth century, when the present-day theological disciplines were not so separated, a course of theological study involved competence in the four major fields of Old Testament, New Testament, Systematic Theology and Church History, and the word 'theologian' in the broadest sense was used of those who had studied theology in preparation for the ministry. Within this broader usage there were naturally gradations between the academic theologians appointed to university posts and the pastors, but by and large the word had a fairly general meaning and theologians were those ordained to the ministry, in contrast to the laity.[5] In a more specialised sense the theologian was especially involved in the theological issues of the day, usually by writing journal articles or books. If the word 'great' is understood as 'important', 'influential' or 'famous', then in this wider sense of the word we may indeed say that Strauss *was* a great theologian.

[2] Hausrath, ii, p. 395.
[3] Barth, *Die protestantische Theologie im 19. Jahrhundert*, p. 494; ET, p. 366.
[4] *Ibid.* p. 513; ET, p. 387.
[5] The distinction is still made in Germany when representatives for the General Assembly of the Church in each district are chosen.

With the separation of theology into more specialised disciplines the word 'theologian' came to acquire a narrower meaning – the specialist in Systematic Theology or Dogmatics in contrast to the specialist in the other disciplines – and only in this narrower sense can it be said that Strauss was not a great theologian. He was not a theologian of the same stature as Schleiermacher or Baur, Ritschl or Kähler – in fact, there was something of an anti-theologian about him. What he lacked, however, was not theological ability, but the desire to engage in deep theological thinking. And almost certainly this lack of desire sprang from his opinion that all biblical theology was futile, that the most one could do was to expose its errors. This attitude is especially noticable during the 1840s, from the time of the writing of the *Glaubenslehre*. He withdrew from the theological debate because he believed there was nothing more to say. That is why he cannot be reckoned among the theologians in the narrower sense of the word. His *Dogmatics* is simply a negative criticism of the Christian doctrines, the work of a critical philosopher, of a sceptic, rather than of a theologian who intends to formulate a constructive theological exposition of the Christian faith.[6]

We must also be extremely careful in saying that Strauss was not a thinker, that he was only interested in destroying, and that he 'lacked the "thinker's" ability to build up consecutively, to construct, to synthesize'.[7] For Strauss believed that no worthwhile theological construction of the Christian faith was possible. If Jesus was not the Son of God, then in Strauss' opinion it was pointless attempting to construct a system of scholastic subtleties with a mere man in the guise of a supernatural divine Christ. Strauss had no time for such half-way solutions. Nor is it wholly true to say that his criticism was purely destructive, for he believed that one could build constructively only after the old antiquated supernatural structure had been pulled down and the rubble cleared away. He went to the heart of the matter. He refused to accept the supernatural

---

[6] Cf. Gotthold Müller: 'Strauss *never* actually became and was a "theologian" in the full meaning of the word, but simply sought to apply his "philosophical" presuppositions to theological questions'. *Identität und Immanenz*, p. 261.

[7] Barth, *Die protestantische Theologie im 19. Jahrhundert*, p. 493; ET, p. 365.

presuppositions of traditional orthodoxy and began instead with those of Hegelian philosophy, where a personal God was replaced by an impersonal Idea, the corollary of which was an Enlightenment cosmology in which the world was regarded as a closed system of natural laws allowing of no supernatural intervention from an other-worldly source. From this denial of a personal God, Strauss proceeded in perfectly consequent and logical steps. If there was no God, then Jesus could not be the Son of God, and the world could not have been created by God. This being so, then three further questions arose:

(i) Who was the Jesus whose influence brought the Christian Church into being?
(ii) How did he come to be portrayed as a supernatural divine personage?
(iii) How did the world and its inhabitants originate?

To these questions Strauss set out to provide *positive* answers. Jesus was either a religious genius, a great ethical teacher or a deluded fanatic. In 1872 Strauss inclined to the latter solution but any final verdict was precluded by the unhistorical and untrustworthy nature of the sources. In answer to the second question Strauss formulated and employed his mythical interpretation, and no more logical and realistic non-supernatural solution to the problem was ever produced. If scholars after Strauss had only understood his solution they might not have wasted so much time with lesser and inferior explanations. Finally, to account for the origin of the world Strauss turned to the latest scientific discoveries. And if one were not prepared to accept the existence of a divine Creator, what other solution was there except that to which Strauss pointed? – unless one was prepared to simply sweep the whole problem under the carpet.

Strauss was a thinker, but in his own way. He was not a thinker like Kant and Hegel who remorselessly pursued the most abstract philosophical problems deep into their innermost recesses. Strauss was more a practical thinker; he thought logically rather than in a deeply reflective way. He did not lack the ability to think – to master Hegel was no mean achievement – but he had little interest in complex epistemological problems which had little relevance for his life. His thoughts moved in other directions. That is why the deeper philosophical and theological issues remained like a blind-spot in his eye. His mind gradually became set in an anti-theological direction so that he was unable – or rather, unwilling – to see the other side of the picture. For this reason – even in the clearest and most well-reasoned passages – a certain superficiality is often found to pervade his writings where religious issues are involved. He had the mind of a thinker, but neither the desire nor the determination to become what he was.

It is not easy to estimate Strauss' influence in the theological world of the nineteenth century. He held no university post or pulpit like Schleiermacher; no disciples gathered around him as they did around Baur; he had no pupils in professorial chairs like Ritschl. Yet his importance for theology is perhaps greater than any of these three theologians.

Schleiermacher's influence waned quickly after his death; the basic principles on which he had built his system were attacked with trenchant criticisms by Baur and Strauss, by Schenkel and Ritschl. Moreover, his influence was not as great as it has often been made out to be. His system, to be sure, was universally admired, but it was never really accepted as a legitimate solution to the crucial problems of theology and the sharper minds perceived its invalidity in terms of practical reality.

Whereas Schleiermacher always remained in the old traditional framework, Baur began to push forward with his historical investigations into the New Testament. These critical investigations aroused a great deal of annoyance among the orthodox theologians, and during his lifetime Baur was treated with coldness and disdain. Certainly he was regarded as an extremely able scholar, but his views and conclusions were almost everywhere rejected by the overwhelming majority of theologians – both orthodox and liberal. Apart from his small circle of disciples, almost no one supported him. After Schwegler had departed from the theological field in 1846 and Zeller was forced to accept a chair of philosophy at Marburg in 1849, the Tübingen School began to decline and Baur became even more isolated. His influence in the theological world of his day was small; only a century after his death was it really possible to assess its full extent.

In the last quarter of the nineteenth century theology was dominated by Ritschl and his school; but Ritschl stood very much on the shoulders of his predecessors and his importance can in no wise be said to be as wide or epoch-making as that of Strauss.  The enormous influence which the *Life of Jesus* exerted on the theological world of the nineteenth century is incalculable.  There was hardly a single sphere which was not in some way, directly or indirectly, affected, for it was Strauss' book which opened up the whole critical investigation of the Bible in a manner which had not been possible earlier.  When we survey the whole century and the ever-widening ripples caused by the stone which Strauss had thrown into the pond, then it is perhaps not too much to describe him as the most important theological figure of the nineteenth century.

We may briefly sum up Strauss' influence in three different spheres.

1. It was Strauss who set in motion the whole 'Quest' for the historical Jesus.[8]  The hundreds – indeed thousands – of books about Jesus, which flooded the rest of the nineteenth century and spilled over into the twentieth were the direct result of his.  It was Strauss who was responsible for formulating the problem which was to occupy theology from that time forth: Who was Jesus of Nazareth?  Was he really and actually God incarnate in human flesh, as the traditional theology had always accepted, or was he simply a man like all other men, different only in degree but not in kind?  Was he a religious genius, a great ethical and social reformer, a political revolutionary, an existentialist, or merely a deluded fanatic and blandiloquent egoist?  Was there only a quantitative difference between himself and

[8] By the term *historical Jesus* is meant *Jesus as he actually was* and quite irrespective of what we know or do not know about him.  This is the traditional nineteenth century usage of the term and it is only in recent years that some have sought to change it.  It is utterly impracticable to change this meaning, so that Jesus thereby becomes equated with the picture obtained by the so-called scientific methods of historical research.  For we should then have to ask: Whose picture?  Käsemann's or Jeremias', Bornkamm's or Braun's?  There must be a measuring stick and this can only be *Jesus as he actually was*.  Whether the Jesus portrayed in the Bible – the Biblical Christ (Kähler) – or the Jesus of historical research (the lowest common denominator of the pictures obtained by the more recent scientific historical method) approaches more closely to the historical Jesus, is still an open question.

other men or was there a qualitative difference of such an order that it set him apart as absolutely unique, and not as first among equals? Or did he never actually live – except as a figment of man's imagination? Those were the choices with which the historical investigation was – and still is – confronted. And whatever the so-called newer methods of historiography and biographical representation, the interpretation of Jesus' Person can only be made on the basis of a knowledge of the historical facts about his life. Interpretation is only as firm as the historical basis on which it rests. That is why the true representation of the kerygmatic Christ will always be dependent upon the veracity of the picture of the historical Jesus.

2. The *Life of Jesus* precipitated the great critical examination of the biblical sources. For Strauss had declared the Gospel narratives to be non-apostolic and almost entirely unhistorical; thereupon commenced the great operation to prove or disprove the authenticity of the New Testament writings. At first it was the Gospels which were the main object of the critical investigation, but once the ball had been set rolling, it was only a matter of time before all the books of the New Testament were systematically investigated by Baur and his disciples. More than any other, it was Baur who laid the foundation of present day critical research; but without Strauss' book his work would have been delayed by many years. Only slowly would the historical criticism have been able to develop and emancipate itself from the traditional framework. Strauss' book effected this emancipation with one stroke.

It was because Strauss and Baur had rendered the New Testament sources so uncertain that theology sought to flee from history and take refuge in ethical or existential categories. For if the historicity of the Gospels was so precarious, then – so it was reasoned – faith could not be made dependent upon history; for if the historical facts should be proved to be untrue, then faith would necessarily crumble. And so, in the late nineteenth century there was a move away from the traditional picture of Jesus, and an emphasis on Jesus as the bearer of divine truth, or of truths about God. If Jesus himself should disappear into historical obscurity, the truths which he proclaimed – so it was reasoned – would still remain eternal and imperishable.

This reasoning, as we now see, was a false path. The Christian faith is rooted and grounded in history and dependent for its validity on the actuality of certain historical events. Therefore theology cannot and must not flee from history; rather, it must investigate the historicity of the events which underlie the Christian faith, but with a more conscious awareness of the philosophical presuppositions on which historical criticism is based.

3. Strauss was also instrumental in influencing the course of Old Testament studies for the *Life of Jesus* opened up a new interest in the Jewish background to the New Testament. To understand the development of Jesus' religious consciousness it was necessary to study the historical, political, social, cultural and religious background of his time, and hand in hand with this study went a lively concern to determine the date and origin of the Old Testament writings. Here the investigation of the New Testament by Baur and the Tübingen School provided the methodological example. Strauss himself had no *direct* influence upon the course of this Old Testament research – although we should not forget that Wellhausen, who gave the JEDP theory its most 'classical' exposition, was greatly influenced by the critical work of Strauss' friend Vatke – but his *Life of Jesus* created a climate in which these investigations could proceed.[9] To be sure, the mythical principle which Strauss had elaborated was ignored and forgotten, but what remained was a general acceptance of a mythical element in the Bible. Further, the acceptance of the view that the Jewish religion was not to be placed on a different plane from the other great religions of the world, and that the Old Testament was permeated by myths related to or derived from neighbouring lands provided a foundation for the work of Gunkel and the history of religions school. Finally we should remember that Strauss was in fact the precursor of the later demythologising programme. Demythologising did not begin with Bultmann. Strauss was the first to carry out a consistent demythologisation of the Gospels.

Strauss' *Life of Jesus* was the most intellectually reasoned attack

[9] There could have been few Old Testament scholars in the later nineteenth century who had not read his *Life of Jesus*. Gunkel, for example, regarded Strauss as one of his forefathers and his picture hung on the wall of Gunkel's study.

which has ever been mounted against Christianity. There have been other assaults more radical and bitter, others expressed in more vituperative language – one needs only to think of Voltaire, Bruno Bauer and Feuerbach, Kalthoff and Drews,[10] Nietzsche and Overbeck, or on the more absurd explanations proposed in our own day, which are usually written either in the hope of gaining public attention, or alternatively, money – but no one since Strauss has so acutely concentrated on the crucial cardinal issues which must be dealt with. Strauss confronted theology with an either/or: either show that the Christian faith is historically and intellectually credible, or admit that it is based on myth and delusion. That was the alternative. Nothing less was and is at stake than the whole historical and intellectual basis of Christianity. If Strauss cannot be convincingly answered, then it would appear that Christianity must slowly but surely collapse.

That was the radical challenge which Strauss threw down and it can only be met by an equally radical defence which goes right to the heart of the problem. Stephen Neill has pointed out that a great theological work such as Strauss' *Life of Jesus* can only be answered by a thorough investigation of the premisses and principles on which it is built.

In what sense is it ever possible to *answer* a great work of the intellect? It is possible to go through it point by point, indicating inaccuracies or errors in detail. Such demonstration is usually highly tedious; and for the most part it is ineffective, because it leaves the main structure unshaken. A principle may still be valid, even though the working out in detail of its applications may leave much to be desired. In dealing with such a work as that of Strauss, there are only two possibilities. Either it must be shown that the method adopted is inappropriate to the material to be considered, or, granted that the method is not illegitimate, it must be shown that the application of the method has been vitiated from the start by concealed presuppositions and prejudices...[11]

The method which Strauss employed was certainly not inappropriate to the material and, as we have seen, he proceeded in the most logical and consequent manner. What is,

---

[10] Albert Kalthoff (1850–1906) and Arthur Drews (1865–1935) denied that Jesus had ever lived.

[11] *The Interpretation of the New Testament 1861–1961* (London, 1964) p. 17.

however, in question, is the whole presupposition from which he started. All Strauss' historical judgments were determined in advance by the philosophical presupposition that miracles do not and cannot occur, which in turn was derived from the prior presupposition that there is no transcendent personal[12] God. This assumption of Strauss was not necessarily wrong, but it was only one of two possibilities. Either there is such a God (as has always been held by the traditional Christian faith), or there is not. If not, then any supernatural intervention of God in the world is also impossible. Jesus cannot be the Son of God (in the traditional understanding of the phrase) and cannot have been raised from the dead; and then the apostles and the early Christian Church laboured under a great misunderstanding – indeed a delusion – of the Person of Jesus. In short, granted this initial presupposition, then the Bible is necessarily permeated through and through with unhistorical and mythical elements and must, consequently, be demythologised, desupernaturalised and demiracleised. Historical investigation will then, necessarily, proceed along much the same path as Strauss pursued and must finally end in an evolutionary theory for the origin of the world and the phenomenon of man. Whether the existence of the world would then be viewed as pure chance, or whether some mysterious and unknowable force such as Schopenhauer's unconscious Will might lie behind the universe – that question would have to be left to scientists and philosophers to debate. What may be criticised in Strauss' methodology is that the presupposition that there is no God was simply taken for granted as proved and not held tentatively as one of two valid possibilities.

This same presupposition determined Strauss' mythical interpretation of the New Testament, for if what is unhistorical is also mythical, then wherever supernatural elements occur, there is also myth. Now no one will deny that the ancient classical literature and the extra-biblical writings abound in myths, but there are great differences between the stories of the gods in Homer, in Egyptian and Mesopotamian folk-lore, or in other eastern religions, and the biblical passages which purport to be a revelation of the one true God. Similarly, the miracle stories reported in Herodotus are on a distinctly different

---

[12] That is, a God possessing personality in himself.

level from the accounts of Jesus' miracles contained in the Gospels. To cast everything supernatural and miraculous into the mythical category was certainly a valid procedure on the assumption that there was no supernatural realm; but then it was also possible that there might be a Creator God who was the supreme ruler of both the natural and the supernatural worlds. If that were so, then not all supernatural and miraculous events would necessarily be mythical, and new criteria would accordingly have to be formulated in order to separate the mythical from the non-mythical elements.

Strauss intended that his investigation should be without presuppositions but as we have seen, he simply replaced one presupposition by its direct antithesis, and the question arises whether a presuppositionless investigation is possible at all. In the last analysis we all have presuppositions of some kind, even if we are not always conscious of them; they are formed in our thinking during the course of our mental and cultural development and we cannot simply pretend that they do not exist. Instead, we should have a constant awareness and a frank and open acknowledgment of the presuppositions with which we work. A methodology which does not take this fact into consideration is an unscientific procedure. In the last resort all theological issues finally run up into the question of the concept and existence of God. Theology must be radical and honest enough to acknowledge that there are two possibilities here: either there is a transcendent personal God, or there is not. If God is dead, or if he never existed, then Strauss' arguments must be conceded. But if there is a personal God who created the universe, then his power to break into history and to suspend his physical laws for the sake of higher spiritual laws must likewise be conceded. And then it is a question of whether a better and more convincing explanation than Strauss' might not yet be provided for the problems which he sought to answer. That indeed would have to happen if Strauss is to be 'overcome'. For given his presuppositions then his essential conclusions follow clearly and logically. Either one must say yes to his solution or provide new and better answers to the problems which he so lucidly exhibited. For this reason theology cannot pass him by. Every solution which is not to be labelled 'half-way' must give account of itself before him.

# BIBLIOGRAPHY

## I LETTERS

### A ORIGINALS

The greatest number of Strauss' extant letters are to be found in the Schiller-Museum, Marbach, and others lie in various libraries throughout Germany. Many letters, e.g. those to Strauss' brother Wilhelm and to Agnese, along with many of a more personal and confidential nature, were destroyed; nevertheless there is an extremely rich selection of over 2000 letters from Strauss himself as well as another 1500 written by his intimate friends, either to him or among themselves. The following list is by no means complete and is intended only to provide a reference to the most important letters. The locations where the letters are to be found are abbreviated as follows:

SMM   Schiller-Museum Marbach
UBH   Universitätsbibliothek Heidelberg
UBT   Universitätsbibliothek Tübingen
WLS   Württembergische Landesbibliothek Stuttgart

(i) Letters from Strauss to:

| | | | | |
|---|---|---|---|---|
| Auerbach, B | 33 | letter(s) | 1862–74 | SMM |
| Baur, F. C. | 20 | ,, | 1836–60 | UBT |
| Binder, G. | 36 | ,, | 1827–72 | WLS |
| Boger, Ernst and Frida | 86 | ,, | 1857–73 | SMM |
| Daub, K. | 1 | ,, | 1832 | SMM |
| Fischer, Adolf | 208 | ,, | 1840–74 | SMM |
| Fischer, Kuno | 108 | ,, | 1855–74 | UBH |
| Hartlaub, W. | 4 | ,, | 1827–8 | SMM |
| Käferle, C. | 70 | ,, | 1836–73 | SMM |
| Kauffmann, Ernst | 62 | ,, | 1837–55 | SMM |
| Kern, Heinrich | 12 | ,, | 1836–55 | SMM |
| Kerner, J. | 3 | ,, | 1838, 41, 61 | SMM |
| Künzel, C. | 75 | ,, | 1843–72 | SMM |
| Mährlen, J. | 6 | ,, | 1838–46 | SMM |
| Märklin, C. | 92 | ,, | 1830–49 | SMM |
| Meyer, J. | 129 | ,, | 1856–73 | SMM |
| Mörike, E. | 15 | ,, | 1827–70 | SMM |
| Paulus, H. E. G. | 1 | ,, | 1835 | UBH |
| Rapp, E. | 655 | ,, | 1836–74 | SMM |
| Ruge, A. | 4 | ,, | 1839, 41 | SMM |
| Schnitzer, K. F. | 49 | ,, | 1839–61 | SMM |
| Schwegler, A. | 10 | ,, | 1846–8 | UBT |
| Sigel, Emilie | 183 | ,, | 1837–56 | SMM |
| Strauss, Agnese | 2 | ,, | 1846, 60 | SMM |

285

| Strauss, Fritz | 42 letter(s) | 1854–8 | SMM |
|---|---|---|---|
| Vatke, W. | 42 ,, | 1832–73 | SMM |
| Vischer, F. | 238 ,, | 1836–73 | SMM |
| Zeller, Eduard | 201 ,, | 1837–73 | UBT |
| Zeller, Hermann | 6 ,, | 1829–31 | WLS |

(ii) Letters to Strauss from:

| Fischer, Kuno | 31 letter(s) | 1855–73 | UBH |
|---|---|---|---|
| Märklin, C. | 64 ,, | 1830–49 | SMM |
| Paulus, H. E. G. | 1 ,, | 1835 | UBH |
| Rapp, E. | 330 ,, | 1840–74 | SMM |
| Sigel, Emilie | 230 ,, | 1837–61 | SMM |
| Vischer, F. | 170 ,, | 1836–73 | SMM |
| Zeller, E. | 42 ,, | 1837–73 | UBT |

(iii) Letters to and from Strauss' friends:

| Baur to Märklin | 13 letter(s) | 1837–47 | SMM |
|---|---|---|---|
| Fischer, Kuno to Zeller | 52 ,, | 1855–1904 | UBH |
| Kauffmann, Marie to Emilie Sigel | 53 ,, | 1828–52 | WLS |
| Märklin to Kerner | 7 ,, | 1842–9 | SMM |
| Märklin to Rapp | 144 ,, | 1836–49 | SMM |
| Rapp to Märklin | 77 ,, | 1830–49 | SMM |
| Rapp to Vischer | 104 ,, | 1844–71 | SMM |
| Strauss, Agnese to Kerner | 4 ,, | 1842–50 | SMM |
| Strauss, Agnese to Mörike | 1 ,, | 1846 | SMM |
| Strauss, Agnese to Fr. Strauss | 60 ,, | 1854–9 | SMM |
| Strauss, Agnese to Unknown | 9 ,, | 1842–70 | SMM |
| Vischer to Märklin | 107 ,, | 1830–49 | SMM |
| Vischer to Rapp | 150 ,, | 1836–73 | SMM |
| Zeller to Kuno Fischer | 71 ,, | 1855–1904 | UBT |

### B PUBLISHED LETTERS

The *Ausgewählte Briefe* edited by Eduard Zeller in 1895 contains the fullest selection of Strauss' letters; other letters printed in whole or in part are also to be found in the following sources (the letters are here listed alphabetically under the names of the recipients).

Baur, F. C., 20 letters from Strauss to Baur (1836–60); 3 from Baur to Strauss (1837–42). The whole extant correspondence was edited with footnotes by E. Barnikol, *ZKG*, 73 (1962), pp. 74–125.

Binder, G., Extracts from 46 letters to Binder (1827–72) were published, by Ziegler in the *Deutsche Revue* 30 (1905) II, pp. 196–208, 342–51; III, pp. 99–108.

Georgii, L., Extracts from the letters to Georgii were edited by H. Maier and published in the *Tübinger Universitätsschrift* (Tübingen, 1912).

Märklin, C., Letters to Märklin from 1830–7 are printed in J. F. Sandberger, *David Friedrich Strauss als theologischer Hegelianer* (Göttingen, 1972).

Mörike, E., Letters to Mörike were edited by H. Maync and printed in the *Deutsche Rundschau*, April–June 1903, pp. 49–72.

Ritter, C., Letters to Chr. Ritter selected and edited by W. Nestle were published by the Historischer Verein, Heilbronn: *Briefe von D. Fr. Strauss an Chr. Ritter* (Heilbronn, 1919). The originals were destroyed during the war.

Schwegler, A., Letters to Schwegler, edited by E. Ackerknecht, were published in the *Literarische Beilage des Staats-Anzeigers für Württemberg* (1903) pp. 238–44.

Strauss, Georgine, Extracts from the letters to Georgine along with letters from Strauss' mother to himself. *Briefe an seine Tochter (1854–74). Nebst Briefen seiner Mutter an ihn selbst* (1921). The originals are in the Strauss-*Nachlass* Dillenburg.

Vatke, W., Extracts from the letters to Vatke were published in H. Benecke's biography of Wilhelm Vatke (Berlin, 1883).

Vischer, F. T., Correspondence between Strauss and Vischer was edited and published by Adolf Rapp, *Briefwechsel zwischen David Friedrich Strauss und Friedrich Theodor Vischer* (2 vols.; Stuttgart, 1952–3).

## II  STRAUSS' PUBLISHED WRITINGS

The following is a complete list of all Strauss' published works. With some additions, it follows that given by Adolf Rapp in his edition of the Strauss–Vischer correspondence, II, pp. 340–4. Abbreviations not included in the main list on p. xv are as follows:

| | |
|---|---|
| *AZ* | *Allgemeine Zeitung* |
| *CK* | *Charakteristiken und Kritiken* (1839) |
| *DJPL* | *Deutsche Jahrbücher für Politik und Literatur* |
| *HJ* | *Hallische Jahrbücher* |
| *JG* | *Jahrbücher der Gegenwart* |
| *KS* | *Kleine Schriften* (1862) |
| *KS* (1866) | *Kleine Schriften* (Neue Folge) 1866 |
| *SM* | *Schwäbische Mercur* |
| *SMSK* | *Schwäbische Mercur, Schwäbische Kronik* |
| *UhH* | *Unterhaltungen am häuslichen Herd* (ed. Gutzkow) |

1830 'Die Seherin von Prevorst', *Morgenblatt für gebildete Stände*, Nr. 219, 13 September 1830. Reprinted by Gotthold Müller, *Identität und Immanenz*, pp. 271–3.

Sermon: 24 June 1830, in: *Feier des dritten Säkularfestes der Uebergabe der Augsburgischen Confession auf der Universität Tübingen* (Tübingen, 1830) pp. 78-86.

'Kritik der verschiedenen Ansichten über die Geister-Erscheinungen der Seherin von Prevorst', *Hesperus. Encyclopädische Zeitschrift für gebildete Leser* (1830) Nrs. 100-4; *CK*, XI.

1832 Review: Rosenkranz, *Encyclopädie der theologischen Wissenschaften*, *JWK*, May 1832, pp. 729–48; *CK*, II.

1833 Review: Umbreit, *System der Logik*, *JWK*, October 1833, pp. 588–96.

1834  Review: Marheineke, *Geschichte der teutschen Reformation*, *JWK*, March 1834, pp. 321–51.

Review: 'Schriften über den Ursprung des ersten kanonischen Evangeliums', *JWK*, November 1834, pp. 761–808; *CK*, III.

1835  *Das Leben Jesu. Kritisch bearbeitet* (2 vols.; Tübingen, 1835; vol. 2 bears the date 1836). New photo-mechanical reprint (Darmstadt, 1969). ET see under 4th edition, 1840.

Intimation of the first volume of the Life of Jesus, *SMSK*, 6 June 1835, p. 682.

Review: Böhmer, *Theologische Auslegung des paulinischen Sendschreibens an die Kolosser*, *JWK*, July 1835, pp. 37–40; *CK*, V.

Review: Mayerhoff, *Einleitung in die petrinischen Schriften*, *JWK*, August 1835, pp. 301–4; *CK*, IV.

1836  Review: Kerner, *Geschichten Besessener neuerer Zeit*, *JWK*, June 1836, pp. 812–40; *CK*, VI.

Review: Wirth, *Theorie des Somnambulismus...*, *JWK*, December 1836, pp. 880–94.

Review: Kerner, *Eine Erscheinung aus dem Gebiet der Natur*, *JWK*, December 1836, pp. 894–904; *CK*, VII.

'Über das Verhältnis der theologischen Kritik und Spekulation zur Kirche', *Allgemeine Kirchenzeitung*, 1836, Nr. 39; Ziegler, pp. 183–90.

1837  *Das Leben Jesu*, 2nd revised edition.

Review: de Wette, *Exegetisches Handbuch zum N.T.* I, part 1, *JWK*, January 1837, pp. 1–19.

*Streitschriften zur Verteidigung meiner Schrift über das Leben Jesu und zur Charakteristik der gegenwärtigen Theologie* (Tübingen, 1837). Part 1: Doctor Steudel; oder: Die Selbsttäuschung des verständigen Supranaturalismus unserer Tage; part 2: Die Herrn Eschenmayer und Menzel; part 3: Die Evangelische Kirchenzeitung, die Jahrbücher für wissenschaftliche Kritik und die Theologischen Studien und Kritiken in ihrer Stellung zu meiner Kritischen Bearbeitung des Lebens Jesu.

Anonymous reviews of Agnese Schebest, *Deutsche Courier*, 25 October, 9 and 16 November 1837.

1838  Pseudonymous poem on Agnese Schebest, *Ibid.* 28 February 1838. See *SVBr*, I, pp. 290–2.

'Justinus Kerner', *HJ*, I (1838), Nr. 1–7; reprinted in *Zwei friedliche Blätter* (1839) and *GS*, I.

Review: de Wette, *Exegetisches Handbuch zum N.T.* I, part 2, *JWK*, January 1838, pp. 110–39.

Review: Passavant, *Untersuchungen über den Lebensmagnetismus und das Hellsehen*, *JWK*, February 1838, pp. 228–43; *CK*, VIII.

Review: Eschenmayer, *Conflict zwischen Himmel und Hölle*, *JWK*, February 1838, pp. 243–64; *CK*, IX.

'Über Vergängliches und Bleibendes im Christenthum'. Printed in the third issue of the Hamburg quarterly magazine *Freihafen*. Reprinted in *Zwei friedliche Blätter* (1839). ET: *Soliloquies on the Christian Religion* (London, 1845).

Review: Auerbach, *Spinoza*, *JWK*, September 1838, pp. 470–72; *CK*, XIII.

Intimation: Vischer, *Über das Erhabene und Komische*, *Allgemeine Literatur-Zeitung*, September 1838 (anonymous).

'Über Bettina' (von Arnim), *Panorama de l'Allemagne* (Paris, 1838). See *SVBr* I, pp. 66–8.

Review: Hinrichs, *Schiller's Leben* and Hoffmeister, *Schiller's Dichtungen*, *JWK*, December 1838, pp. 917–55; *CK*, XII.

Review: Hirzel, *Die Klassiker in den niederen Gelehrtenschulen*, *CK*, XIV.

*Das Leben Jesu* (3rd, revised edition, 1838–9).

1839 Review: Wiener, *Selma, die jüdische Seherin*, *CK*, X.

'Schleiermacher und Daub in ihrer Bedeutung für die Theologie', *HJ*, February–March 1839; *CK*, I.

*Zwei friedliche Blätter* (Altona, 1839). Part I: Enlarged and revised edition of 'Justinus Kerner'; part II: 'Über Vergängliches und Bleibendes im Christenthum'.

*Sendschreiben an Bürgermeister Hirzel, Prof. Orelli und Prof. Hitzig in Zürich, nebst einer Zuschrift an das Züricher Volk* (Zürich, 1839). ET: *The Opinions of D. F. Strauss, as embodied in his Letter, with an Address to the people of Zurich, by Professor Orelli* (London, 1844).

*Charakteristiken und Kritiken. Eine Sammlung zerstreuter Aufsätze aus den Gebieten der Theologie, Anthropologie und Aesthetik* (Leipzig, 1839). Contains the above-mentioned numbers I–XIV.

1840 *Die christliche Glaubenslehre in ihrer geschichtlichen Entwicklung und im Kampfe mit der modernen Wissenschaft dargestellt* (2 vols.; Stuttgart, 1840–1).

*Das Leben Jesu*, 4th edition. ET: *The Life of Jesus critically examined* (3 vols.; London, 1846); reprinted in one volume, with an introduction by Otto Pfleiderer, in 1892 and 1898.

'Introduction' to the German translation of C. Hennell's book on the origin of Christianity (Stuttgart, 1840).

1841 'Riemer über Goethe', *AZ* (Beilage), 6–7 July 1841.

Review: Riemer, *Mitteilungen über Goethe*, *HJ*, 30 July 1841.

' "Warnung" against a Summary of his *Die christliche Glaubenslehre, allgemein fasslich dargestellt von Philalethus*", *HJ*, 22–3 October 1841.

Anonymous poems in the Stuttgart *Beobachter*, 1 December 1841.

1843 'Xenien' (satyric verses). *Einundzwanzig Bogen aus der Schweiz* (ed. Herwegh; 1843), pp. 250–2.

1845 'Zur Verständigung in der Angelegenheit des Professors Vischer. Von einem zur Ruhe gesetzten Denker', *Beobachter*, 17 January 1845.
'Prof. Vischer und seine Ankläger nach dem Erscheinen seiner Rede', *Ibid.* 27 January 1845 (anonymous).

1846 Foreword (written in Latin) to the English Translation of the *Life of Jesus*. Also printed in the *Theologische Jahrbücher* (1846) pp. 449–51.
'Das Hauptwerk von H. S. Reimarus noch immer ungedruckt', *JG*, March 1846, pp. 286–9.

1847 'Aesthetische Grillen, erster Fang', *JG*, April 1847, pp. 379–85.
'Eine Berichtigung Lessings betreffend', *JG*, May 1847, pp. 437–41.
'Ludwig Bauer', *JG*, June 1847, pp. 489–508; *KS*, VI; *GS*, II.
'Schubartiana', *Morgenblatt* (Cotta), 14–17 July 1847.
'Zwei deutsche Märtyrer' (E. M. Arndt and F. List), *JG*, August 1847, pp. 689–714.
*Der Romantiker auf dem Throne der Cäsaren, oder: Julian der Abtrünnige* (Mannheim, 1847); *GS*, I.

1848 'Aesthetische Grillen, zweiter Fang', *JG*, February 1848, pp. 61–9.
'Die Affaire Leotade. Auch eine Szene aus dem Kampf der Gegenwart zwischen Staat und Kirche', *JG*, March 1848, pp. 93–5.
'The King cannot do wrong. Eine theologisch-politische Parallele', *JG*, Nr. 25, pp. 97–8.
'Judenverfolgung und Judenemanzipation', *JG*, April 1848, pp. 117–119.
*Der politische und der theologische Liberalismus* (Halle, 1848). Five articles on political themes appeared in the *SMSK* between 6 April and 11 May 1848. See *SVBr*, II, p. 329.
*Sechs theologisch-politische Volksreden* (Stuttgart, 1848); *GS*, I.
'Erklärung' (Defence of his speech in Parliament on the 16 November), *SM*, 22 November 1848.
'An den Vaterländischen Verein in Ludwigsburg', *SM*, 28 November 1848.
'An meine Mitbürger in Ludwigsburg' (Resignation from Parliament), *SM*, 28 December 1848.

1849 Review: Diderot, *Soirées de Grandval*, *Morgenblatt*, 9–18 May 1849 (anonymous); *GS*, II.
Review: Vischer, *Aesthetik*, part II, *AZ*, 13 April 1849.
'A. W. Schlegel', *Die Gegenwart* (1849) 3, p. 74; *KS*, IV.
'Karl Immermann', *Ibid.* (1849) 3, p. 486; *KS*, V.
*Christian Daniel Friedrich Schubarts Leben in seinen Briefen* (2 vols.; Berlin, 1849); *GS* VIII–IX.
'Christian Märklin' (obituary), *SMSK*, 31 October 1849 (signed 'St').

1850 'Aus der Glyptothek' (epigrams), *Morgenblatt* 4, 7, 12 January 1850; *GS*, xii.

*Christian Märklin. Ein Charakterbild aus der Gegenwart* (Mannheim, 1850; the title page bears the date 1851); *GS*, x.

1851 Review: Vischer, *Aesthetik*, iii, 1, *AZ* (Beilage), 25 May 1851.

1853 'Musicalische Briefe von einem beschränkten Kopfe, 1', *AZ* (Beilage), 5 September 1853; revised and reprinted in *KS*, x: 4, with the title: 'Beethovens Neunte Symphonie und ihre Bewunderer'; *GS*, ii.

'Der verstorbene Freiherr K. F. E. von Uexküll und seine Gemälde-sammlung', *AZ* (Beilage), 27 and 31 October 1853 (anonymous); *KS*, vii; *GS*, ii.

Review: Vischer, *Aesthetik* iii, 3, *AZ* (Beilage), 20 November 1853.

1854 'Zur Erinnerung an den Maler Eberhard Wächter', *AZ* (Beilage), 1 January 1854 (anonymous); *KS*, ix; *GS*, ii.

'Gedanken über ältere und neuere deutsche Malerei. Aus einem hinterlassenen Manuskripte des Malers Joseph Koch. Mitgeteilt von D. Fr. Strauss', in Prutz' *Deutsches Museum*, February 1854; *KS*, vii.

'Zur Lebensgeschichte des Malers Gottlieb Schick', *AZ* (Beilage), 1–2 April 1854 (anonymous); *KS*, ix; *GS*, ii.

'Die Asteroiden und die Philosophen', *KS*, x: 2; *GS*, ii.

Review: Vischer, *Aesthetik*, iii, 4, *AZ* (Beilage), 15 July 1854.

'Frischlins Ende', *UhH* (1854), pp. 657f.

1855 'Ein patriotisches Lustspiel aus dem 16. Jahrhundert' (Julius redivivus by Nikodemus Frischlin). *UhH* (1855), Nr. 1.

*Leben und Schriften des Dichters und Philosophen Nikodemus Frischlin. Ein Beitrag zur deutschen Kulturgeschichte in der 2. Hälfte des 16. Jahrhunderts* (Frankfurt am Main, 1855; the title page bears the date 1856).

1856 'Kernsprüche der Pfalzgräfin Elizabeth Charlotte', *Wochenblatt für die Pfalz*, 3 May 1856.

'Nachruf für Ernst Friedrich Kauffmann', *SMSK*, 11 May 1856.

'Über Liederkompositionen und Lieder von E. F. Kauffmann', *UhH* (1856), Nr. 50.

'Der Papierreisende', first printed in *KS* (N.F.), 1866; *GS*, ii; separately reprinted (Weimar, 1907).

1857 *Des Nikodemus Frischlin Dichtungen übersetzt* (Tübingen, 1857).

Review: Vischer, *Aesthetik* (concluding part), *Blätter für literarische Unterhaltung*, 9 July 1857.

'Barbara Streicherin von Aalen', *KS* (1866), x; *GS*, ii.

'Der Bildhauer Isopi und die Wappentiere vor dem Stuttgarter Schlosse', *KS*, x: 1; *GS*, ii.

*Ulrich von Hutten* (2 vols.; Leipzig, 1857; the title page bears the date 1858); ET: *Ulrich von Hutten* (London, 1874).

1858 'L. Th. Spittler', *PJ*, 1 (1858); *KS*, III; *GS*, II.

'Zum Andenken an meine gute Mutter, für meine lieben Kinder', (for Georgine's Confirmation, 11 April 1858); *KS*, (1866) II; *GS*, I.

'Schwarzerd–Melanchthon', *KS*, x: 3; *GS*, II.

'Jugendgeschichte Klopstocks', First published in *KS* (1866), I; *GS*, x.

1859 'Klopstock und der Markgraf Karl Friedrich von Baden', first published in *KS*, II; *GS*, x.

Review: Böcking, *Ulrici Hutteni Opera*, Grenzboten Nrs. 20 and 46, 1859.

On Schiller's comedy 'Ich habe mich rasieren lassen', *AZ* (Beilage), 19 December 1859 and 17 January 1860 (Anonymous). The comedy, for which Strauss wrote a foreword and explanatory notes, was printed in 1862.

1860 'Lessing und Göze' (review of a book by Röpe entitled *Joh. M. Göze, eine Rettung*), Grenzboten, 16 March 1860.

*Gespräche von Ulrich von Hutten, übersetzt und erläutert* (Leipzig, 1860).

1861 Review: Vischer, *Kritische Gänge* (N.F.), Grenzboten, 22 February 1861.

'F. Chr. Baur und seine Bedeutung für die deutsche Theologie', *Die Zeit*, 21 March 1861, Beilage 3.

'Böckhs Rede zur Geburtstagsfeier des Königs von Preussen', *ibid.* 4 April; also printed by H. Künkler in *Zum Gedächtnis an D. Fr. Strauss* (Wiesbaden, 1898).

Strauss' articles on political topics in '*Die Zeit* (March 1861–May 1862) were published in the *Ludwigsburger Geschichtsblätter* (1911): 6.

Review: Hebler, *Lessingstudien*, Grenzboten, 11 October 1861.

'Worte der Erinnerung an Dr. Ph. F. Sicherer', *KS* (1866), v: 1; *GS*, I.

'Lessings Nathan der Weise'. The lecture given in December 1861 was first printed in *DJPL*, June 1863; also published as a book (Berlin, 1864) and in *GS*, II.

'Über Gervinus' Geschichte des 19. Jahrhunderts', *Die Zeit*, Nr. 219 (Beilage), 17 December 1861.

Review: Zeller, *Philosophie der Griechen*, *ibid.* Nr. 222 (Beilage), 20 December 1861.

'Barthold Heinrich Brockes und Hermann Samuel Reimarus', *KS*, I; *GS*, II.

*Hermann Samuel Reimarus und seine Schutzschrift für die vernünftigen Verehrer Gottes* (Leipzig, 1861; the title page bears the date 1862).

1862 *Kleine Schriften biographischen, literar- und kunstgeschichtlichen Inhalts* (Leipzig, 1862). It contains the following: I. B. H. Brockes und H. S. Reimarus. II. Klopstock und der Markgraf Karl Friedrich von Baden. III. L. T. Spittler. IV. A. W. Schlegel. V. Karl Immermann. VI. Ludwig Bauer. VII. 1. Freiherr K. F. E. von Uexküll und seine Gemäldesammlung; 2. Joseph Koch's Gedanken über ältere und neuere

Malerei. VIII. Zur Erinnerung an den Maler Eberhard Wächter. IX. Zur Lebensgeschichte des Malers Gottlieb Schick. X. Miscellen: 1. Der Bildhauer Isopi; 2. Die Asteroiden und die Philosophen; 3. Schwarzerd–Melanchthon; 4. Beethoven's neunte Symphonie und ihre Bewunderer. XI. Nachlese zu Frischlin. XII. Nachlese zu Schubart.

'Ein Schauspielerjubiläum' (Jakob Winter), *SMSK*, 23 February 1862; *KS* (1866), IX; *GS*, II.

'Der Hohenstaufen', *KS* (1866), VIII, 1; *GS*, I.

'Justinus Kerner' (Obituary), *SMSK*, 3–4 April 1862 (anonymous). *KS* (1866), IV; *GS*, I.

1863 'Worte des Andenkens an Fr. Wilhelm Strauss', *KS* (1866), V: 2; *GS*, I.

'Erinnerungen an Möhler, aufgezeichnet von einer Protestantin [Emilie Sigel] 1839', *DJPL* (1863), 8; *KS* (1866), VI; *GS*, II.

'Jesu Weheruf über Jerusalem'. 'Das Gleichnis von fruchtbringenden Acker'. 'Die Geschichte von dem Stater im Maule des Fisches', *Zeitschrift für wissenschaftliche Theologie*, 6 (1863), pp. 84–9; 209–14; 293–6. 'Schleiermacher und die Auferstehung Jesu', *ibid.* pp. 386–400.

1864 'Deutsche Gespräche' [concerning the Schleswig-Holstein question]. In the Deutsche Blätter of the Gartenlaube; reprinted in *KS* (1866), VII: 1–3.

*Das Leben Jesu für das deutsche Volk bearbeitet* (Leipzig, 1864); *GS*, III–IV. ET: A New Life of Jesus (2 vols.; London, 1865).

Review: Weber, *Carl Maria von Weber*, *SMSK*, 12 June 1864 (signed ♯).

'König Wilhelm von Württemberg', *DJPL* (1864); *KS* (1866), III; *GS*, I.

'Der Schenkelsche Handel in Baden', *National-Zeitung*, 24 September 1864; revised and printed as a supplement to the following essay, and also in *GS*, V.

1865 *Der Christus des Glaubens und der Jesus der Geschichte. Eine Kritik des Schleiermacher' schen Lebens Jesu* (Berlin, 1865); *GS*, V.

*Die Halben und die Ganzen. Eine Streitschrift gegen die HH. DD. Schenkel und Hengstenberg* (Berlin, 1865); *GS*, V.

'Ein Besuch bei der gefangenen Venus', *Kölnische Zeitung*, 1865; *KS* (1866), XII; *GS*, II.

'Die Todesstrafe', *KS* (1866), VIII: 3; *GS*, I.

'Der Kölner Dom', *KS* (1866), VIII: 2; *GS*, I.

'Jakob Winter' (Obituary), *SMSK*, 10 December 1865 (anonymous); *KS* (1866), IX; *GS*, II.

1866 *Kleine Schriften*, Neue Folge (Berlin, 1866). It contains: I. Klopstock's Jugendgeschichte. II. Zum Andenken an meine gute Mutter.

III. König Wilhelm von Württemberg. IV. Justinus Kerner. V. Zwei Leichenreden: 1. Dr. P. F. Sicherer; 2. Fr. Wilhelm Strauss. VI. Erinnerungen an Möhler. VII. Deutsche Gespräche. Politische, sechs: 1. Schleswig-Holstein und die deutschen Grossmächte; 2. Schleswig-Holstein und die deutschen Mittelstaaten; 3. Die Vormächte in Schleswig; 4. Der Krieg; 5. Was lernen wir daraus?; 6. Nach sieben Vierteljahren. VIII. Deutsche Gespräche. Unpolitische, drei: 1. Die Hohenstaufen; 2. Der Kölner Dom; 3. Die Todesstrafe. IX. Der alte Schauspieldirector. X. Barbara Streicherin von Aalen. XI. Der Papierreisende. XII. Die Göttin im Gefängnis.

1867 'Preussen und Schwaben; Ein Gespräch von Strauss', *PJ*, 19 (1867), pp. 186–99.

Review: Rosenkranz, *Diderots Leben und Werke*, *SMSK*, 17 February 1867 (signed #).

Review: Justi, *Winckelmann*, vol. 1, *SMSK*, 21 April 1867.

'Die unächten Erinnerungen an Möhler, oder: der Mythiker und der Benediktiner, eine Erwiderung', *PJ*, 19 (1867), pp. 580–3.

1870 *Voltaire. Sechs Vorträge* (Leipzig, 1870).

'Strassburg und ein württembergischer Dichter vor 300 Jahren' [Frischlin], *SMSK*, 13 October 1870 (signed D. F. St.).

'An Ernst Renan', *AZ* (Beilage), 18 August and 2 October. Then as a separate publication: *Krieg und Friede, zwei Briefe an Ernst Renan nebst dessen Antwort auf den ersten* (Leipzig, 1870); *GS*, 1. ET: 'D. F. Strauss to the People of France' in: *Letters on the War between Germany and France* (London, 1871).

'Zur Farben- und Titelfrage', *AZ* (Beilage), 25 October 1870.

Review: *Briefwechsel zwischen Lessing und seine Frau*, and *Zur Erinnerung an Lessing, Briefe und Aktenstücke*, *SMSK*, 18 December 1870 (signed 'St').

1871 *Ulrich von Hutten* (2nd revised edition; Leipzig, 1871).

Review: Adolf Fischer, *Hohenlohische Geschichte*, *SMSK*, 15 October 1871 (signed #).

1872 *Der alte und der neue Glaube. Ein Bekenntnis* (Leipzig, 1872); *GS*, VI. ET: *The Old Faith and the New* (London, 1873).

*Ein Nachwort als Vorwort zu der neuen Auflage meiner Schrift 'Der alte und der neue Glaube'*, ET: 'A Postscript as Foreword', in the third edition of *The Old Faith and the New*.

Louis Hetsch (Obituary), *SMSK*, 4 August 1872 (signed #).

1873 'Allerhand Aufzeichnungen. Von D. F. Strauss', *Die Gegenwart*, 1 February and 8 March 1873.

'Die nordamerikanische Präsidentenbotschaft und die Aussichten der Republik', *Deutsche Presse und Frankfurter Bösenhalle*, 9 March 1873.

'Zum Andenken an den Fürsten Pückler-Muskau', *Neue Freie Presse*, 16 March 1873, Morgenblatt.

'Ste. Beuve und die Prinzessin Mathilde', *ibid.* 1 and 2 May 1873. Morgenblatt.

'Schriftsteller und Verleger vor 100 Jahren', *Die Gegenwart*, 24 May 1873.

Two short essays 'Mozart und Beethoven' and 'Die Sinnlichkeit im Verhältnis der Geschlechter' were published posthumously in the *Schwabenspiegel*, 21 January 1908, pp. 117–20; they were probably written in the early 1850s.

## GESAMMELTE SCHRIFTEN

The *Gesammelte Schriften* (collected works), selected by Strauss before his death and edited by Eduard Zeller were published in 1876–8. The twelve volumes contain the following writings:

I–Literarische Denkwürdigkeiten. Zum Andenken an meine gute Mutter. Zwei Leichenreden: 1. auf Wilhelm Strauss; 2. auf Fr. Sicherer. Justinus Kerner, zwei Aufsätze. Der Romantiker auf dem Throne der Cäsaren. König Wilhelm von Württemberg. Sechs theologisch-politische Volksreden. Deutsche Gespräche: 1. der Hohenstaufen; 2. Der Kölner Dom; 3. Die Todesstrafe. Krieg und Friede (Briefe von und an Renan).

II–Brockes und Reimarus. Diderot. Lessings Nathan. L. T. Spittler. A. W. Schlegel. Karl Immermann. Ludwig Bauer. Erinnerungen an Möhler. Freiherr von Uexküll und seine Gemäldesammlung. Zur Erinnerung an den Maler Eberhard Wächter. Zur Lebensgeschichte des Malers Gottlieb Schick. Der Bildhauer Isopi. Die Asteroiden und die Philosophen. Schwarzerd–Melanchthon. Beethoven's Neunte Symphonie und ihre Bewunderer. Der alte Schauspieldirector. Barbara Streicherin von Aalen. Der Papierreisende. Die Göttin im Gefängniss. Zwei Vorreden.

III–IV–Das Leben Jesu für das deutsche Volk.

V–Der Christus des Glaubens und der Jesus der Geschichte. Der Schenkelsche Handel in Baden. Die Halben und die Ganzen. H. S. Reimarus.

VI–Der alte und der neue Glaube. Ein Nachwort als Vorwort.

VII–Ulrich von Hutten. Vorrede zu Huttens Gespräche.

VIII–IX–Chr. D. Fr. Schubarts Leben in seinen Briefen.

X–Christian Märklin. F. G. Klopstock.

XI–Voltaire.

XII–Poetisches Gedenkbuch.

## III   SELECTED BIBLIOGRAPHY

Backhaus, Gunther, *Kerygma und Mythos bei David Friedrich Strauss und Rudolf Bultmann* (Hamburg-Bergstedt, 1956).

Barnikol, Ernst, 'Das ideengeschichtliche Erbe Hegels bei und seit Strauss und Baur im 19. Jahrhundert', *Wissenschaftliche Zeitschrift der Martin-Luther-Universität Halle-Wittenberg*, Gesellschafts- und sprachwissenschaftliche Reihe, x, 1 (February 1961), pp. 281–328.

Barth, Karl, 'David Friedrich Strauss als Theologe', *Theologische Studien* 6 (Zollikon, 1939).
*Die protestantische Theologie im 19. Jahrhundert* (Zürich, 1947). ET: *From Rousseau to Ritschl* (London, 1959).
Bauer, Bruno, 'Das Leben Jesu kritisch bearbeitet von David Friedrich Strauss', *JWK*, 9 (1835), pp. 879–94; 896–911: 10 (1836), pp. 681–94; 696–703.
*Philo, Strauss und Renan* (Berlin, 1874).
Beard, J. R., *Voices of the Church in reply to D. F. Strauss* (London, 1845).
Beck, Carl, 'Kritische Anzeige von "Strauss, das Leben Jesu für das deutsche Volk bearbeitet"', *TSK*, 1865, pp. 71–126.
Benecke, Heinrich, *Wilhelm Vatke* (Berlin, 1883).
Biedermann, A. E., 'Strauss und seine Bedeutung für die Theologie', *Ausgewählte Vorträge und Aufsätze* (Berlin, 1885).
Brazill, W. J., *The Young Hegelians* (London, 1970).
Eck, Samuel, *David Friedrich Strauss* (Stuttgart, 1899).
Engelhardt, Moriz, *Schenkel und Strauss* (Erlangen, 1864).
Fischer, Kuno, 'Über David Friedrich Strauss', *Philosophische Schriften* 5 (Heidelberg, 1908).
Geisser, Hans, 'David Friedrich Strauss als verhinderter (Zürcher) Dogmatiker', *Zeitschrift für Theologie und Kirche*, 69: 2 (1972), pp. 214–58.
Gelzer, Heinrich, *Die Straussischen Zerwürfnisse in Zürich von 1839* (Hamburg und Gotha, 1843).
Handel, Leopold, *D. F. Strauss im literarischen Meinungsstreit von A. Knapp bis F. Nietzsche* (Phil. Diss. Tübingen, 1946).
Harräus, K., *David Friedrich Strauss* (Leipzig, 1901).
Hartlich, C. und Sachs, W., *Der Ursprung des Mythosbegriffes in der modernen Bibelwissenschaft* (Tübingen, 1952).
Hausrath, Adolf, *David Friedrich Strauss und die Theologie seiner Zeit* (Heidelberg, 1876–8).
'Über den religiösen Entwicklungsgang von David Friedrich Strauss', *Kleine Schriften religionsgeschichtlichen Inhalts* (Leipzig, 1883).
'Ziegler's Strauss-Biographie,' *Deutsche Rundschau* 134, pp. 467–72.
'Zur Lebensgeschichte von David Friedrich Strauss', *ibid.* 141, pp. 37–50.
Hengstenberg, E. W., 'Betrachtungen veranlasst durch den Aufsatz des Dr. Strauss: Über das Verhältnis der theologischen Kritik und Spekulation zur Kirche', *EKZ* (June, 1836) pp. 382–403.
'Die Zukunft unserer Theologie', *EKZ* (May 1836) pp. 281–91.
'Schenkels Charakterbild und Strauss' Leben Jesu', *EKZ* (1865) pp. 38ff.
'Vorwort', *EKZ* (1836) pp. 1–45.
Herrmann, Ernst, 'Erinnerungen an David Friedrich Strauss', *Deutsche Revue* 33 (1908) I, pp. 137–55
Hettingen, Franz, *David Friedrich Strauss* (Freiburg i. B., 1875).
Heusler, Irma, *Bilder aus dem Leben der Familien Strauss-Heusler* (Dillenburg, 1968).
Hirsch, Emanuel, *Geschichte der neuern evangelischen Theologie*, V (Gütersloh, 1954).
Honold, Wilhelm, *David Friedrich Strauss als Politiker* (Diss. Tübingen, 1922).

Huber, Martin, *Jesus Christus als Erlöser in der liberalen Theologie* (Winterthur, 1956).

Jäckh, E., 'Fr. Nietzsche und D. F. Strauss', *Schabenspiegel* 2 (1908/9), pp. 249–51; 258–61.

Kohut, A., *David Friedrich Strauss als Denker und Erzieher* (Leipzig, 1908).

Krauss, R., 'D. Fr. Strauss im Jahre 1848', *Württembergische Vierteljahrshefte für Landesgeschichte* 18 (1909), pp. 161–72.

Lang, Wilhelm, *David Friedrich Strauss* (Leipzig, 1874).
'Ferdinand Baur und David Friedrich Strauss', *PJ*, 160 (1915), pp. 474–504; 161 (1915), pp. 123–44.

Lange, F. A., *Geschichte des Materialismus und Kritik seiner Bedeutung in der Gegenwart* (3rd ed., Leipzig, 1866–7).

Levy, A., *David Frédéric Strauss. La vie et l'œuvre* (Paris, 1910).

Luthardt, C. E., *Die modernen Darstellungen des Lebens Jesu* (Leipzig, 1864).

Maier, Heinrich, *An der Grenze der Philosophie* (Tübingen, 1909).

Mehlhausen, J., *Dialektik, Selbstbewusstsein und Offenbarung. Die Grundlagen der spekulativen Orthodoxie Bruno Bauers in ihrem Zusammenhang mit der Geschichte der theologischen Hegelschule dargestellt* (Diss. Bonn, 1964).

Müller, Gotthold, *Identität und Immanenz* (Zürich, 1968).
'David Friedrich Strauss als Prediger und Katechet', *Monatschrift für Pastoraltheologie* 53 (1964), pp. 502–10; 54 (1965), pp. 33–9.

Nietzsche, Friedrich, 'David Friedrich Strauss als Bekenner und Schriftsteller', *Unzeitgemäße Betrachtungen*, I (Leipzig, 1873). ET: 'David Friedrich Strauss, the Confessor and Writer', *Thoughts out of Season*, I (Edinburgh and London, 1909).

Nippold, Friedrich, *Handbuch der neuesten Kirchengeschichte*, III (Berlin, 1901).

Rapp, Adolf, 'Baur und Strauss in ihrer Stellung zu einander und zum Christenthum', *BWKG* (3. F.) 52 (1952), pp. 95–149; 53 (1953), p. 157; 54 (1954), pp. 182–5.
'David Friedrich Strauss', *Schwäbische Lebensbilder* VI (Stuttgart, 1957), pp. 286–324.
'David Friedrich Strauss in einem bedeutsamen Abschnitt seines Lebens 1835 bis 1842', *ZWLG*, 12 (1953), pp. 147–68; 271–300.

Reuschle, C. G., *Philosophie und Naturwissenschaft. Zur Erinnerung an D. F. Strauss* (Bonn, 1874).

Sandberger, Jörg, *David Friedrich Strauss als theologischer Hegelianer* (Göttingen, 1972).

Schebest, Agnese, *Aus dem Leben einer Künstlerin* (Stuttgart, 1857).

Schenkel, Daniel, *Das Charakterbild Jesu* (Wiesbaden, 1864).
'Das Christenthum und die Humanitätsreligion des Herrn Dr. D. F. Strauss', *AKZ* (1865) pp. 225–36.

Schlawe, Fritz, *Friedrich Theodor Vischer* (Stuttgart, 1959).

Schlottmann, C., *Strauss als Romantiker des Heidenthums* (Halle, 1878).

Schwarz, Karl, *Zur Geschichte der neuesten Theologie* (4th ed., Leipzig, 1869).

Schweitzer, Albert, *Von Reimarus zu Wrede* (Tübingen, 1906). ET: *The Quest of the Historical Jesus* (London, 1910).

Schweizer, Alexander, *Biographische Aufzeichnungen* (Zurich, 1889).

Stephan, H. and Schmidt, M., *Geschichte der deutschen evangelischen Theologie seit dem deutschen Idealismus* (Berlin, 1960).

Steub, Ludwig, 'Erinnerungen an D. F. Strauss', *AZ*, 1877, (Beilage) Nrs. 159–61.

Traub, H., 'Die Stiftsakten über David Friedrich Strauss', *BWKG* (N.F. 27) pp. 48–64.

Vischer, Friedrich, 'Dr. Strauss und die Wirtemberger', *KG* (Tübingen, 1844) pp. 3–130.

'Der alte und der neue Glaube. Ein Bekenntnis von D. F. Strauss', *KG* (N.F.) 6, (1873) pp. 203–27.

Vogel, F., *Memorabilia Tigurina oder Chronik der Stadt und Landschaft Zürich* (Zürich, 1841).

Wandt, A., *D. F. Strauss' philosphischer Entwicklungsgang* (Diss. Münster, 1902).

Weinel, Heinrich, *Jesus im 19. Jahrhundert* (Tübingen und Leipzig, 1903).

Wolf, Ernst, 'Die Verlegenheit der Theologie. David Friedrich Strauss und die Bibelkritik', *Libertas Christiana* (Munich, 1957), pp. 219–39.

Zeller, Eduard, *David Friedrich Strauss in seinem Leben und seinen Schriften* (Bonn, 1874). ET: *David Friedrich Strauss in his Life and Writings* (London, 1874).

'Die Tübinger historische Schule', *HZ*, IV (1860), pp. 90–173.

Zeller, Johannes, *Stimmen der deutschen Kirche über das Leben Jesu von Doctor Strauss für Theologen und Nichttheologen* (Zürich, 1837).

Ziegler, Theobald, *David Friedrich Strauss* (Strassburg, 1908).

*Die geistigen und socialen Strömungen des neunzehnten Jahrhunderts* (Berlin, 1879).

# INDEX OF NAMES

Barnikol, E., 93n, 100n, 103n
Barth, Karl, 211n, 248n, 275
Bauer, Bruno, 80–1, 140, 167, 201, 247, 282
Bauer, G. L., 45, 262–4, 267, 270
Baur, F. C., ix–x, xi, 6, 17–18, 58, 70, 71, 83, 118, 133, 193, 197, 202f, 206, 259, 271, 274, 276, 278, 280, 281
    relations with and influence on S., 17, 85–116, 270
Bengel, E. G., 17
Biedermann, A. E., 238, 253
Binder, Gustav, xi, 7, 18, 36, 39, 82, 83, 117, 257
Bismarck, Otto von, 177, 213, 235–6
Blum, Robert, 170–4
Böhme, Jacob, 13–14
Bretschneider, K. G., 70n, 74, 118, 234
Bultmann, Rudolf, 272–3, 281

Darwin, Charles, 238, 242, 243, 248
Daub, Karl, 135
de Wette, W. M. L., 34, 53, 70n, 118, 213, 214, 264–5
Dorner, I. A., 99

Eichhorn, J. G., 45, 260–2, 270
Eliot, George, xii, 232–3
Eschenmayer, C. A., 10, 68n, 77, 86
Ewald, G. H. A., 201n, 202n, 215n

Feuerbach, Ludwig, 140, 141, 167, 183, 201, 242, 274, 282
Fischer, Kuno, xi, 183, 214, 215, 218, 219, 221–3, 228–9, 234, 245, 256
Flatt, K. C., 58, 63, 64
Friedrich Wilhelm IV of Prussia, 161, 163, 213
Frischlin, Nicodemus, 181, 183, 186

Gabler, J. P., 45, 260–2, 268, 270
Georgii, Louis, xi, 36, 93, 94, 148, 166
Goethe, J. W. von, 77–8, 120, 179, 191, 244, 248n
Greiling, J. C., 268

Grohmann, J. C. A., 266–7
Gunkel, H., 281, 281n

Haeckel, Ernst, 238, 242
Hartlich, C., 259n, 265, 270n
Hartmann, E. von, 238, 242
Hase, K. A. von, 70–1
Hausrath, A., x, xi, 29, 58, 152, 248n, 275
Hegel, G. W. F., 9, 18, 21, 26, 27–8, 53, 54, 69, 79–80, 242, 246, 247, 277
Heine, Heinrich, 78
Hengstenberg, E. W., 27, 74, 78–9, 81, 85, 90, 92–3, 118, 161, 221, 227, 228, 274
Henke, H. P. K., 266, 267, 270
Heyd, L. F., 86
Heyne, C. G., 45, 259–60, 262, 265
Hirzel, Bürgermeister, 127, 128, 129
Hitzig, Ferdinand, 117, 126, 127, 129
Hoffmann, Christoph, 163–5
Hoffmann, Wilhelm, 40, 68n, 69, 163
Horst, G. K., 268
Hug, J. L., 71
Hutten, Ulrich von, 108, 183, 187–8, 191–3

Jeremias, J., 279n

Kähler, M., 276, 279n
Kant, I., 10, 13, 38, 53, 190, 243, 277
Käsemann, E., 279n
Kauffmann, E. F., 151, 154, 155, 157, 158, 166, 179, 180, 182
Kauffmann, Marie, 150, 151, 155, 166, 179–80, 182
Keim, Theodor, 202, 225
Kern, Friedrich, 6, 17, 58, 68n, 83, 93, 96
Kerner, Justinus, 1, 14, 15–16, 154, 157, 198
Köstlin, Chr. Reinhold, 145, 146
Krug, Wilhelm, 267–8

Lang, Wilhelm, 85n, 86, 256
Lessing, G. E., 52, 66, 191, 248n

Locher, Marie, 230–2
Lücke, G. C. F., 95, 99
Luther, Martin, 32, 187–90

Marheineke, P. F., 19, 27, 29, 40, 53, 54, 80, 135
Marklin, Christian, xi, 7, 10, 18, 21f, 36, 82–3, 100, 103, 107, 151–2, 153, 154, 158, 166, 179, 180, 185–6
correspondence with S., 22, 29–31, 32, 95, 146, 150, 168
religious views of, 11, 21f, 83
resigns from ministry, 83
Menzel, Wolfgang, 77, 168, 177
Mohl, Robert von, 64
Mörike, Eduard, xi, 1, 9, 10, 13, 143, 156
Müller, Gotthold, 26n, 276n
Müller, Julius, 68n, 78, 81, 274

Neander, August, 27, 68, 85, 118, 201, 274
Neill, Stephen, 282
Nietzsche, Friedrich, 248n, 254–5, 282

Orelli, J. F., 126, 129
Oberbeck, F., 255, 282

Paulus, H. E. G., 31, 34, 35, 43–4, 49, 50, 70, 72, 76–7
Paulus, H. E. G., 31, 34, 35, 43–4, 49, 50, 70, 72, 76
Pfizer, Gustav, 7, 36
Princess Alice, 232, 233–4

Rapp, Adolf, 85n, 104, 143n
Rapp, Ernst, xi, 117, 134, 142, 146, 149, 151, 154, 190, 191, 192, 194, 236, 250–6 passim
Reimarius, H. S., 43, 196–7, 208, 260
Renan, Ernest, 200, 202, 212, 237
Ritschl, A., 276, 278, 279
Röhr, J. F., 70n, 81
Rosenkranz, Karl, 53, 54, 80–1

Sachs, W., 259n, 265, 270n
Sandberger, J., 265n, 271n
Schebest, Agnese, 143–59, 180–2, 231, 232
Schelling, F. W. J., 9, 10, 13, 18, 21, 27, 247, 248
Schenkel, Daniel, 213–29, 278
Scherr, Thomas, 124, 132

Schleiermacher, F. D. E., ix–x, 18, 21, 27, 31–5, 46, 52, 87, 107, 135, 139, 241, 266, 276, 278
coolness towards S., 28–9, 30
Schneckenburger, M., 18, 117
Schopenhauer, A., 238, 242, 248, 283
Schubart, C. F. D., 184–5, 187–8
Schwegler, A., xi, 96, 99n, 278
Schweickhardt, Minele, 36, 142, 146
Schweitzer, Albert, 47, 70, 72, 74, 212, 248n
Schweizer, Alexander, 125n, 126, 127, 128, 133
Sigel, Emile, 143, 145, 147, 150, 155, 159, 180, 182, 197–8
Spinoza, B., 137
Steub, Ludwig, 178–9
Steudel, J. C. F., 17, 37–8, 58, 69, 76, 96
Storr, G. C., 16
Strauss, Agnese (wife of S.),
    see Schebest
Strauss, David Friedrich,
    education, 3–8, 9–20, 26, 27–35
    pastoral work, 21–6
    tutor and lecturer at Tübingen, 36–8, 38–9, 56
    at Ludwigsburg, 64, 75, 250
    in Stuttgart, 75, 117, 142–54, 159
    post in Zürich, 123–33
    marriage, 147–58
    member of Württemberg Assembly, 159, 165–76
    failing eyesight, 195–6
    death, 255–8
    religious and philosophical views, 11–13, 19, 23, 30, 32–5, 41–3, 45–7, 52–7, 104–5, 110–15, 118–22, 130–1, 136–9, 188, 194, 203–12, 240–8, 265–73, 276–8, 283–4
    political views, 162–3, 169, 172–5, 176, 236–7
    influence, ix–x, 274–84
    works: biography of Luther, planned, 189, 191
        biography of Märklin, 107, 180, 185
        biography of Schubart, 185, 187–8
        Dogmatics, 97, 134–40, 191, 276
        Frischlin, 183, 186, 188
        The Halves and the Wholes, 221–2, 230, 233

Strauss, David Friedrich—*contd.*
  *Life of Jesus,* 41–57, 118–22, 134, 193
  New *Life of Jesus,* 198, 200–12
  *The Old Faith and the New,* 237–49
  *Streitschriften,* 75–81, 120, 135
  *The Transient and Permanent in Christianity,* 120, 138
  *Two peaceable Writings,* 134
  *Ulrich von Hutten,* 187–8
Strauss, Fritz (son of S.), 158, 180–2, 195, 230, 250, 255
Strauss, Georgine (daughter of S.), 157, 157–8, 180–2, 194–5, 230, 250
Strauss, Johann Friedrich (father of S.), 1–3, 75, 149
Strauss, Wilhelm (brother of S.), 3, 152, 153, 181, 197, 198

Teilhard de Chardin, 247n
Tholuck, F. A. G., 68, 274

Ullmann, K., 69, 78, 81, 274
Usteri, Leonard, 269–70

Vatke, Wilhelm, 29, 30, 35, 41, 80, 186n, 195, 230, 238, 274, 281
Victoria, Queen, 232–4
Vischer, Friedrich, 1, 3, 4, 36, 65, 83, 184, 227, 230, 245, 246, 256, 257
  at Blaubeuren, 6, 7, 10
  correspondence with S., xi, 19, 97, 127, 144, 176, 231, 235, 236
  quarrel with S., 36–7, 250–4
Voltaire, 41, 42, 233, 234, 237–9, 282

Wagner, Richard, 181, 246–7, 254
Weitzel, K. L., 109
Wellhausen, J., 281

Zeller, Eduard, x, 26, 36, 96, 99n, 107, 108, 109–15, 227–9, 245, 256, 257, 278
Ziegler, Theobald, x–xi, 29, 58, 83, 124, 133, 140, 153, 171, 178, 212, 237, 240, 250, 255
Zimmermann, Wilhelm, 7, 18
Zwingli, U., 187, 189